AF847085

The Impacts of Water Reforms in Rural and Urban China

Li Li

The Impacts of Water Reforms in Rural and Urban China

Evidence and Mechanisms

Springer

Li Li
School of Economics and Management
East China Normal University
Shanghai, China

ISBN 978-981-96-6901-1 ISBN 978-981-96-6902-8 (eBook)
https://doi.org/10.1007/978-981-96-6902-8

This work was supported by National Natural Science Foundation of China.

© The Editor(s) (if applicable) and The Author(s), under exclusive license to Springer Nature Singapore Pte Ltd. 2025

This work is subject to copyright. All rights are solely and exclusively licensed by the Publisher, whether the whole or part of the material is concerned, specifically the rights of translation, reprinting, reuse of illustrations, recitation, broadcasting, reproduction on microfilms or in any other physical way, and transmission or information storage and retrieval, electronic adaptation, computer software, or by similar or dissimilar methodology now known or hereafter developed.
The use of general descriptive names, registered names, trademarks, service marks, etc. in this publication does not imply, even in the absence of a specific statement, that such names are exempt from the relevant protective laws and regulations and therefore free for general use.
The publisher, the authors and the editors are safe to assume that the advice and information in this book are believed to be true and accurate at the date of publication. Neither the publisher nor the authors or the editors give a warranty, expressed or implied, with respect to the material contained herein or for any errors or omissions that may have been made. The publisher remains neutral with regard to jurisdictional claims in published maps and institutional affiliations.

This Springer imprint is published by the registered company Springer Nature Singapore Pte Ltd.
The registered company address is: 152 Beach Road, #21-01/04 Gateway East, Singapore 189721, Singapore

If disposing of this product, please recycle the paper.

To my mentors, collaborators, and loved ones—thank you for your guidance and support throughout this journey.

And to all those committed to improving water governance—may this work serve as a small contribution to that effort.

Preface

This monograph presents empirical evidence from four studies that examine the impacts of three key water reforms—the rural drinking water program, private sector participation in urban water supply, and the adoption of Increasing Block Tariffs (IBTs) in the urban domestic water sector—which have significantly shaped rural children's human capital development, urban water utilities' performance, and urban residents' water demand. Sophisticated microeconometric methods and rich micro-level data are employed for estimation.

The monograph is organized into six chapters. Chapter 1 provides an overview of the domestic water sector in China and the key water reforms implemented in the country, as well as the organization of the monograph. Chapter 2 examines the impact of *in utero* exposure to safe drinking water on childhood health in rural China. By exploiting the gradual rollout of the rural drinking water program across villages and utilizing data from the China Family Panel Studies, we demonstrate that *in utero* exposure to treated tap water increases children's height. Chapter 3 explores the relationship between early-life exposure to safe drinking water and cognitive skills, using the same program and survey data as in Chap. 2. We find that early-life exposure to treated tap water enhances cognitive test scores during adolescence. In Chap. 4, we investigate the impact of private investment on the performance of county-level water utilities. By leveraging changes in private sector participation and using utility-level panel data, we find that private investment significantly improves the performance of these utilities. Chapter 5 examines the water savings effect of adopting an unconventional IBT with an annually renewed budget. Relying on the 2015 water pricing reform in Hangzhou and combining household survey data with administrative water bills, we highlight a substantial water savings effect among high-use households. Finally, Chap. 6 concludes with a discussion of the policy implications of these findings and prospects for future water governance.

This monograph is intended for academic researchers, professionals, and policymakers working to ensure equitable access to safe drinking water while balancing economic efficiency and environmental sustainability. I hope the lessons from these water reforms will inspire solutions that advance equity, efficiency, and sustainability in water governance in China and beyond.

The studies presented in this monograph originated from a series of research projects I conducted while at the Institute of Water Policy (IWP) at the Lee Kuan Yew School of Public Policy, National University of Singapore (NUS). I joined IWP in 2013, after obtaining my Ph.D. in Economics from NUS. Trained as a labor economist with a focus on human capital, I found the transition to the field of water policy both slow and difficult. At the time, I could never have imagined that I would write a monograph on water policy. In 2018, I joined East China Normal University, where I successfully published these studies.

I am deeply grateful to Professor Wu Xun, then IWP's director, who formally introduced me to this field. Under his guidance, I developed my research interests in IBTs and private sector participation in the water sector. I extend my heartfelt thanks to Professor Marc Jeuland. During his visit to IWP, I was hesitant to embark on the challenging Hangzhou IBT project. His willingness to join the project gave me the confidence to pursue this project and made it possible. Additionally, I had the privilege of collaborating with Yvonne Chen Jie, then an Assistant Professor at LKYSPP, and her research assistant, Xiao Yun, to explore the link between water policy and human capital. Their support not only helped bridge my new research focus with my original field but also reignited my passion for economics research.

I am also indebted to Dennis Wichelns, Dale Whittington, Leong Ching, Lorenz Goette, Namrata Chindarkar, and Eduardo Araral for their understanding and support during my time at IWP. I am sincerely grateful to my Ph.D. thesis supervisor, Liu Haoming, and to my role models, Zhao Liqiu, Yi Junjian, Zhong Songfa, and Gong Jie, for their generous encouragement and guidance throughout my career.

Shanghai, China Li Li
March 2025

Acknowledgements Chapter 2 was modified from "Li, L., Xiao, Y., 2023. Beyond boiling: The effect of in utero exposure to treated tap water on childhood health. *Journal of Environmental Economics and Management* 119, 102814. https://doi.org/10.1016/j.jeem.2023.102814" The author acknowledges the contribution from Yun Xiao.

Chapter 3 was modified from "Chen, Y.J., Li, L., Xiao, Y., 2022. Early-Life Exposure to Tap Water and the Development of Cognitive Skills. *Journal of Human Resources* 57, 2113–2149. https://doi.org/10.3368/jhr.58.2.0917-9031R3" The author acknowledges the contributions from Yvonne Jie Chen and Yun Xiao.

Chapter 4 was modified from "Li, L., 2018. Private sector participation and performance of county water utilities in China. *China Economic Review* 52, 30–53. https://doi.org/10.1016/j.chieco.2018.06.001"

Chapter 5 was modified from "Li, L., Jeuland, M., 2023. Household water savings and response to dynamic incentives under nonlinear pricing. *Journal of Environmental Economics and Management* 119, 102811. https://doi.org/10.1016/j.jeem.2023.102811" The author acknowledges the contribution from Marc Jeuland.

Competing Interests This monograph was funded by the National Natural Science Foundation of China (72473044, 72103065).

The study in Chap. 2 was funded by the National Natural Science Foundation of China (72103065) and the Shanghai Pujiang Program (2019PJC032).

The study in Chap. 3 was funded by the National Natural Science Foundation of China (72103065, 72003129), the Shanghai Pujiang Program (2019PJC032), the Fundamental Research Funds for the Central Universities at East China Normal University (2019ECNU-HWFW025), the Academic Research Fund Scheme FY2017 at the Lee Kuan Yew School of Public Policy National University of Singapore (R-603-000-239-720), and the Thematic Research Grant at National University of Singapore (R-603-000-131-720).

The study in Chap. 4 was funded by the Staff Research Support Scheme (SRSS) FY2016 of Lee Kuan Yew School of Public Policy National University of Singapore.

The study in Chap. 5 was funded by the National Natural Science Foundation of China (72103065), the Institute of Water Policy Water Research Grant at the Lee Kuan Yew School of Public Policy National University of Singapore (R-603-000-215-490), and the Fundamental Research Funds for the Central Universities, China (2019ECNU-HWFW025).

The author has no conflicts of interest to declare that are relevant to the content of this monograph.

Ethics Approval The data used in Chaps. 2 and 3 are available online: Institute of Social Science Survey (ISSS), Peking University, 2015, "China Family Panel Studies (CFPS)," https://doi.org/10.18170/DVN/45LCSO, Peking University Open Research Data Platform, V37.

Access to the CFPS county-level restricted data was obtained by applying to the ISSS (https://www.isss.pku.edu.cn/cfps/en/data/restricted/index.htm).

The household survey in Chap. 5 was approved under the National University of Singapore IRB protocol A-15-258.

Contents

Chapter 1
Introduction

Abstract In this chapter, we introduce the institutional and empirical context of China's water sector reforms, with a focus on the rural-urban disparities in water access, human capital, and income. We highlight the health and developmental consequences of unsafe water in rural areas, despite the widespread practice of boiling water. We also discuss the challenges facing urban water systems amid rapid urbanization, including infrastructure constraints, resource scarcity, and the introduction of private sector participation and water pricing reforms. This chapter motivates our study of water policy as a driver of human capital development and water conservation in China. We outline the data sources, describe key policy interventions, and present the research framework that links water sector reforms to outcomes in health, education, utility performance, and household behavior, providing the foundation for the analyses in the following chapters.

1.1 Background of This Book

China has long been constrained by limited freshwater resources. Although it has the fifth largest amount of renewable water resources in the world, totaling 2,813 billion m^3 in 2021, its per capita water availability is only one-third of the world average and among the lowest for a major country. Moreover, along with China's unprecedented economic boom in recent decades, the water quality from industrial, domestic, and agricultural sources has deteriorated severely. Data from China's water monitoring system show that, in 2004, of all 745 monitored river sections, 28% were unsafe for any use (below the Grade V standard on a six-grade scale), and 32% were only safe for industrial and irrigation use (Grade IV–V standards) (Xie et al. 2009).

Treated water such as tap water is considered safe drinking water.[1] Figure 1.1 plots the nationwide county-level tap water coverage rates in 2000 and 2010, respectively, using the county-level assemblies of the 2000 and 2010 China Population Census. Over the ten years, tap water coverage expanded rapidly, with more counties achieving high coverage in 2010.

[1] Mineral water, purified water, and filtered water are also considered treated.

© The Author(s), under exclusive license to Springer Nature Singapore Pte Ltd. 2025
L. Li, *The Impacts of Water Reforms in Rural and Urban China*,
https://doi.org/10.1007/978-981-96-6902-8_1

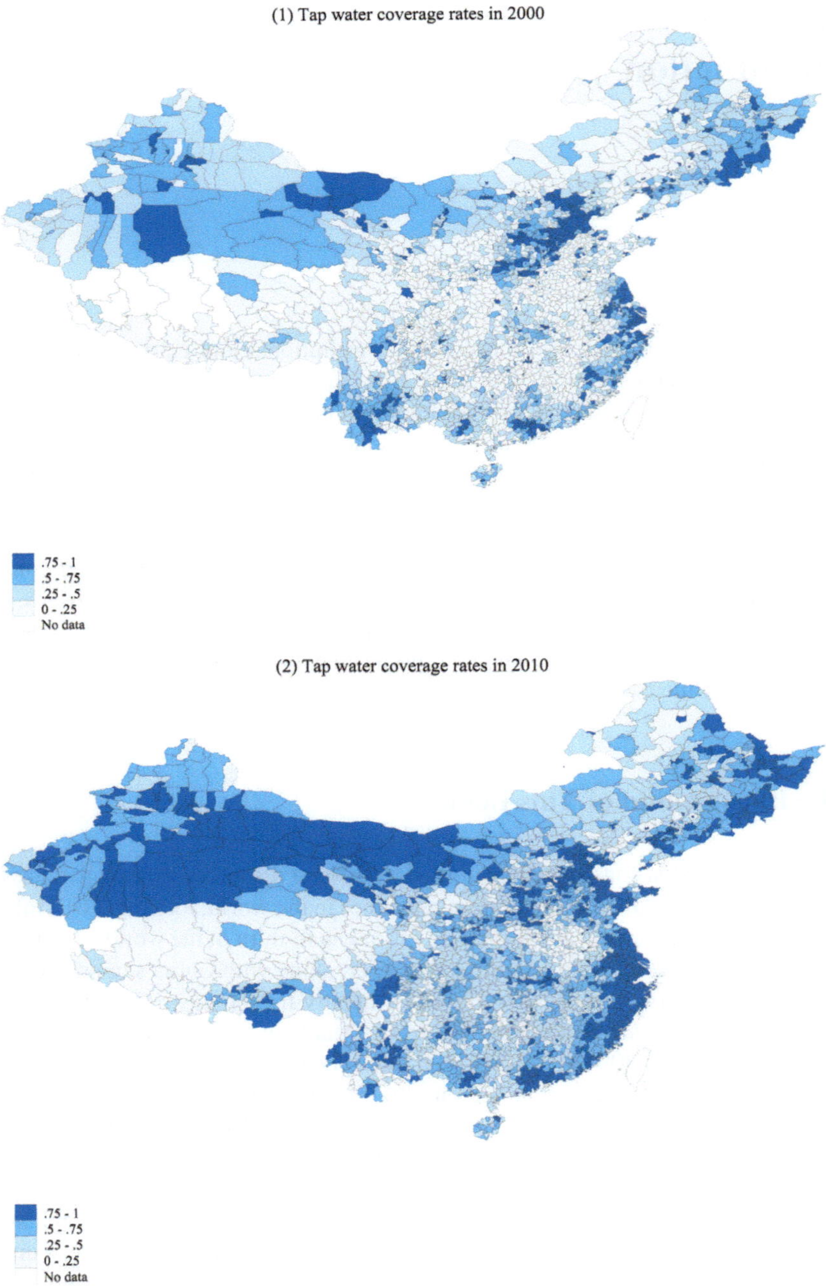

Fig. 1.1 County-level tap water coverage rates in 2000 and 2010. *Data sources* County-level assemblies of the 2000 and 2010 China Population Census

Public water supply in rural China lags substantially behind that of urban areas. According to the estimates of UNICEF and WHO (2015), in 1990, 92% of urban residents had access to on-premise treated water from water plants, while 88% of rural residents lacked on-premise tap water. Most rural residents without access to tap water relied on untreated water from wells, rivers, and lakes. According to our calculations—using the data from the 2010 wave of the China Family Panel Studies (CFPS)—more than 87% of rural households in villages without a tap water connection still relied on untreated water for cooking.

Drinking boiled water has been common in China since the central government launched the Patriotic Public Health Campaign (*Aiguo Weisheng Yundong* in Chinese) in 1951, which promoted this practice as a cost-efficient way to inactivate disease-causing microorganisms in water. Zhang et al. (2009) find that more than 85% of rural households in China boil water before drinking. Using Chinese Longitudinal Healthy Longevity Survey (CLHLS) data, a nationally representative survey of the elderly aged 65 and over in China, we also find that more than 90% of respondents reported drinking boiled water, regardless of the availability of tap water. According to the *WHO Technical Brief—Boil Water* (WHO 2015), the process of heating water to a rolling boil is sufficient to inactivate pathogenic bacteria, viruses, and protozoa. Such microorganisms are the primary drinking water contaminants in many developing countries. At least partly owing to the boiling practice, they have less adverse consequences in China (Zhang et al. 2009; Zhang and Xu 2016). Although diarrhea is the second leading cause of death in children under five years old in the world, it is not a common cause of child deaths in China (only accounting for 3% in 2008) (Rudan et al. 2010).[2]

While boiling water effectively inactivates microorganisms, it does not eliminate chemical contaminants, which pose another significant health risk. Mounting evidence has shown that the chemical impurities in drinking water can incur substantial health damage. For instance, high concentrations of fluoride and arsenic in drinking water are responsible for fluorosis and arsenicosis (Gordon et al. 2004). In New Jersey, chemicals in the water have more harmful effects on birth outcomes than exposure to fecal coliform does (Currie et al. 2013). The presence of nitrates in drinking water is linked to increased cancer rates (Morales-Suarez-Varela et al. 1995). Evidence from China reveals that poorer surface water quality is associated with a higher infant mortality rate (He and Perlof 2016) and a higher digestive cancer death rate (Ebenstein 2012), regardless of the common practice of drinking boiled water.

In addition to health outcomes, the time use of rural residents might be constrained by poor access to safe drinking water. For those who rely on surface water—such as rivers, lakes, and ponds—as their primary source of drinking water, considerable time and effort may be invested in fetching and treating the water. According to Meng et al. (2004)'s estimation, rural households without piped water spend an average of 20 to 60 minutes each day fetching water, and that time may increase significantly during dry seasons.

---

[2] There are many ways that waterborne diseases can continue to spread despite the boiling practice, such as recontamination in storage (Brown and Sobsey 2012) and use of unboiled water for washing vegetables or dishes.

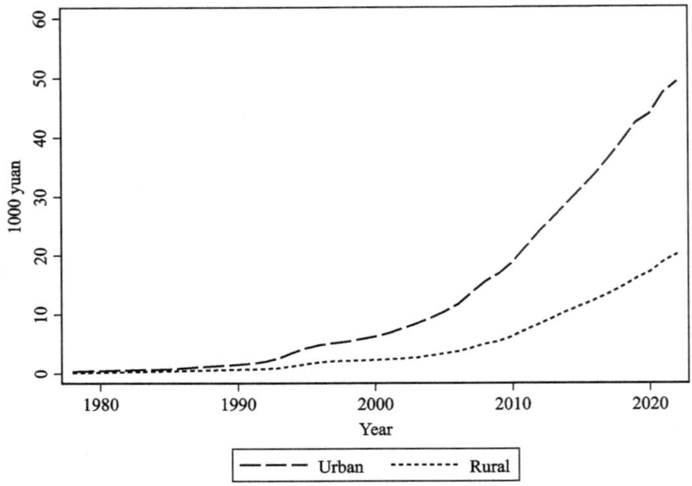

Fig. 1.2 Trends of income level in urban and rural China. *Data source* The 2023 China Statistical Yearbook

Beyond the urban-rural gap in access to safe drinking water, Fig. 1.2 shows that the urban-rural gap in per capita disposable income remains substantial and continues to enlarge in absolute terms since 1978, despite both urban and rural areas experiencing substantial increases. In 2022, per capita disposable income of urban households (49,283 yuan) was 2.4 times that of rural households (20,133 yuan).

Literature widely agrees that disparities in human capital drive income gaps between urban and rural China (Sicular et al. 2007; Chen, Binkai et al. 2010). We illustrate the disparity in human capital by comparing children's height and educational attainment between urban and rural populations. Height is generally considered as a good indicator of the long-run child health and nutritional status (Thomas et al. 1996). Figure 1.3 plots average children's height by age and gender. One month after birth, urban and rural infants have similar lengths (58 cm for boys and 57 cm for girls). However, the gap in height between urban and rural children accumulates to more than 0.6 cm by the age of one and persists into teenage. By age 17, urban children are, on average, over 2 cm taller than their rural counterparts for both genders. Figure 1.4 shows that the proportion of urban residents attaining at least a three-year college education increased more than sevenfold, from 9% in the 1960 birth cohort to 67% in the 2000 cohort; the corresponding proportion for rural residents rose from just 0.7% to 32%. However, for the youngest cohort, the gap in four-year college education remains significant, with only 11% of rural residents achieving this level compared to 37% in urban areas.

Improving rural residents' access to safe drinking water could boost their human capital accumulation, thereby narrowing the urban-rural gap in human capital and, consequently, reducing the urban-rural income gap. In the first two chapters of this book, we examine the impact of a rural drinking water program, launched by the Chi-

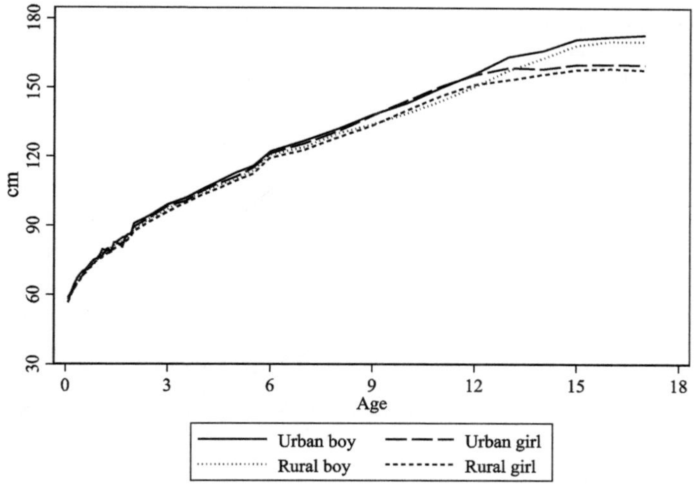

Fig. 1.3 Child height by age and gender in urban and rural China. *Data source* The 2023 China Health Statistical Yearbook

nese government in 1984, on rural residents' human capital formation. As part of the program, water treatment plants with water purification technology and equipment were constructed to remove microorganisms and chemical impurities. To improve accessibility and to avoid contamination during transport and storage, pipeline systems have also been installed to deliver treated water directly from water plants to households. We find strong evidence that exposure to tap water *in utero* increases childhood height and early-life (from one year before birth through the first five years of life) exposure to tap water increases adolescent cognitive test scores. These results underscore that ensuring access to safe drinking water plays a pivotal role in fostering human capital development among rural children.

In contrast to rural China, the water sector in urban China is challenged by an obsolete water supply system and general water shortages. During the economic boom, China experienced a rapid expansion of urban areas and large-scale rural-urban migration. As illustrated in Fig. 1.5, the population living in urban areas increased from 170 million (18% of the total population) in 1978 to 670 million (50%) in 2010 and further to 920 million (65%) in 2022. Such rapid urbanization has brought enormous pressure on the public services in urban areas, including transportation, water supply, wastewater treatment, and solid waste treatment.

In particular, the surge in urban population has placed a growing strain on the urban domestic water sector, exacerbating challenges in ensuring adequate supply, distribution efficiency, and quality control. Addressing these issues requires substantial investment in infrastructure and improvements in water management.

On the water supply side, the need to meet substantial financial demands for infrastructure investment and improve the economic performance of state-owned enterprises prompted the Chinese government to introduce private sector participa-

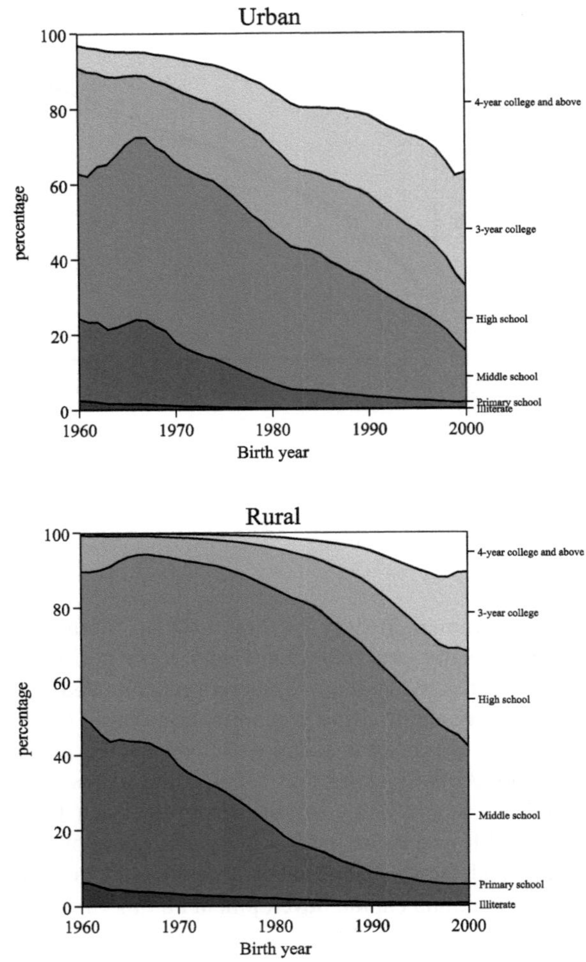

Fig. 1.4 Education level by cohort in urban and rural China. *Data source* The 2020 China Population Census Yearbook.

tion (PSP) in the early 1990s, drawing inspiration from reforms in other countries. In Chap. 4, we demonstrate that in Chinese counties—home to approximately 195 million urban residents in 2012—water utilities with private investment achieved significant gains in output, financial performance, profitability, and operational efficiency, and these improvements seldom translated into measurable changes in service outcomes. These findings underscore the potential value of private sector participation in China's urban water supply sector.

On the demand side, curbing excessive water consumption has been a policy priority. Since 1998, the Chinese government has implemented increasing block tariffs (IBT) for urban domestic water consumption, which accounts for 51% of the total urban public water supply nationwide (China Urban Construction Statistical Yearbook, 2022). Under this pricing scheme, consumers face higher marginal

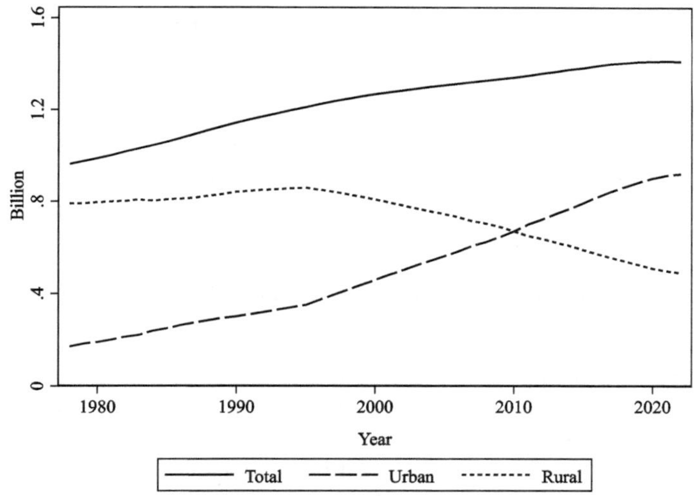

Fig. 1.5 Population growth in urban and rural China. *Data source* The 2023 China Statistical Yearbook

prices as their water consumption increases within a given budget period. Widely adopted across cities worldwide, IBT is considered an effective mechanism for promoting water conservation while safeguarding the welfare of disadvantaged groups. In Chap. 5, we examine the water savings effect of an unconventional IBT which sets prices based on annual cumulative consumption, by leveraging a water reform implemented in Hangzhou, a major city in China, in 2015. We detect a small effect of the IBT on low-use households but find large water savings among high-use households. This finding suggests that this unique IBT structure is an effective pricing tool for promoting water conservation in the urban domestic water sector.

1.2 Structure of This Book

We provide below individual synopses for each chapter of this book.

Chapter 2: Rural Drinking Water Program and Childhood Health

To improve rural residents' access to safe drinking water, the Chinese government initiated a rural drinking water program in the 1980s. As part of the program, water treatment plants with water purification technology and equipment were constructed to remove microorganisms and chemical impurities, and pipeline systems were installed to deliver treated water directly from water plants to households. Using data drawn from the China Family Panel Studies, we leverage the gradual rollout of this program across villages to examine the effect of *in utero* exposure to treated tap water on childhood health. We find that exposure to treated tap water *in utero* increases height at ages 1–11 by 0.3 standard deviations. We also document improvements in other health outcomes at different stages of childhood, as well as a reduction in the incidence of non-waterborne digestive diseases. Improving health by age one and inducing more health investments from parents are two possible channels. Results highlight the importance of removing chemical pollutants from drinking water to protect fetuses from environmental insults, in contexts where boiling water before drinking is a common practice.

Chapter 3: Rural Drinking Water Program and Adolescent Cognitive Skills

In this study, we exploit variations in the timing of village-level tap water connections under the rural drinking water program launched by the Chinese government in the 1980s. Using data drawn from the China Family Panel Studies, we find that one additional year of exposure to tap water in early life increases the cognitive test score at ages 10–15 by 0.132 standard deviations. The event study estimates confirm that the beneficial impacts of tap water exposure are concentrated in early life. The mechanism analysis reveals two key channels: improving childhood health and increasing maternal time for childcare. The findings suggest that improving access to tap water has considerable potential to increase rural children's cognitive skills, and eventually, to narrow the human capital disparity between rural and urban children in China.

Chapter 4: Private Sector Participation and Performance of County Water Utilities

In the early 1990s, China opened its urban water sector to private investors to secure the country's growing urban water demand. In Chinese counties, which accommodated around 195 million urban population in 2012, private sector participation (PSP) has progressed slowly but steadily among the county-level water utilities. Using a panel data set extracted from the annual surveys conducted by the National Bureau of Statistics of China (1998–2006), we exploit the changes in the PSP status of water utilities and apply a fixed-effects model to identify the causal effects of PSP on 12 performance indicators. We find that utilities with private investment enjoyed significant performance improvement in three areas: output, financial performance and profitability, and efficiency. Using supplementary data from population censuses and statistical yearbooks, we find that water quality is slightly lowered under PSP, while no significant effect is detected for the other service outcomes. The findings suggest that a greater role of PSP in the urban water supply sector of Chinese counties could be promoted.

Chapter 5: Increasing Block Tariffs and Household Water Savings

In 2015, Hangzhou, a major Chinese city, introduced a water pricing reform. This reform established an unconventional Increasing Block Tariff (IBT) featuring prices set according to annual cumulative consumption and a bimonthly billing cycle. Analyzing data from a household survey and administrative water bills, we detect a small effect on low-use households but find large water savings among high-use households. Moreover, we find strong evidence that high-use households respond to future price while current price remains fixed, and that the small share of households who appear myopic do not respond to dynamic incentives. These findings may inform future efforts to design price interventions in regions facing water scarcity.

In Chap. 6, we conclude by summarizing our findings and providing insights for policy makers and avenues for future research.

References

Brown J, Sobsey MD (2012) Boiling as household water treatment in Cambodia: a longitudinal study of boiling practice and microbiological effectiveness. Am J Trop Med Hygiene 87(3):394–398

Binkai Chen, Pengfei Zhang, Rudai Yang (2010) Government education investment, human capital investment, and urban-rural income gap in China. Manag World (Chinese) 1:36–43

Currie J, Graff Zivin J, Meckel K, Neidell M, Schlenker W (2013) Something in the water: contaminated drinking water and infant health. Can J Econ 46(3):791–810

Ebenstein A (2012) The consequences of industrialization: evidence from water pollution and digestive cancers in China. Rev Econ Stat 94(1):186–201

Gordon B, Mackay R, Rehfuess E (2004) Fluoride and arsenic in drinking water. In: Inheriting the world: the atlas of Children's health and the environment. Myriad Editions Limited, Brighton, UK

He G, Perlof JM (2016) Surface water quality and infant mortality in China. Econ Dev Cult Change 65(1):119–139

Meng S, Liu J, Tao Y (2004) Water supply and sanitation environment in rural China: promote service to the poor. Technical report, Poverty Reduction Conference (Chinese), Shanghai, China

Morales-Suarez-Varela MM, Llopis-Gonzalez A, Tejerizo-Perez ML (1995) Impact of nitrates in drinking water on cancer mortality in Valencia. Spain. Eur J Epidemiol 11(1):15–21

Rudan I, Chan KY, Zhang JS, Theodoratou E, Feng XL, Salomon JA, Lawn JE, Cousens S, Black RE, Guo Y, Campbell H (2010) Causes of deaths in children younger than 5 years in China in 2008. The Lancet 375(9720):1083–1089

Sicular T, Ximing Y, Gustafsson B, Shi L (2007) The urban-rural income gap and inequality in China. Rev Income Wealth 53(1):93–126

Thomas D, Lavy V, Strauss J (1996) Public policy and anthropometric outcomes in the Côte d'ivoire. J Public Econ 61(2):155–192

UNICEF and WHO (2015) Progress on sanitation and drinking water: 2015 update and MDG assessment. Technical report, United Nations Children's Fund and World Health Organization, New York

WHO (2015) Technical brief - Boil water. Technical report, World Health Organization, Geneva, Switzerland

Xie J, Liebenthal A, Warford JJ, Dixon JA, Wang M, Gao S, Wang S, Jiang Y, Ma Z (2009) Addressing China's water scarcity: recommendations for selected water resource management issues. World Bank, Washington, DC

Zhang J, Xu LC (2016) The long-run effects of treated water on education: the rural drinking water program in China. J Dev Econ 122:1–15

Zhang R, Li H, Wu X, Fan F, Sun B, Wang Z, Zhang Q, Tao Y (2009) Current situation analysis on China rural drinking water quality. J Environ Health (Chinese) 26(1):3–5

Part I
Rural Safe Drinking Water

Chapter 2
Rural Drinking Water Program and Childhood Health

Abstract We study the effect of *in utero* exposure to treated tap water on childhood health in rural China, where boiling water to inactivate disease-causing microorganisms before drinking is common. We exploit the gradual rollout of a rural drinking water program that supplies treated tap water to households. Besides microorganisms, the treatment removes chemical pollutants. We find that exposure to treated tap water *in utero* increases height at ages 1–11 by 0.3 standard deviations. We also document improvements in other health outcomes at different stages of childhood, as well as a reduction in the incidence of non-waterborne digestive diseases. Improving health by age one and inducing more health investments from parents are two possible channels. Results highlight the importance of removing chemical pollutants from drinking water to protect fetuses from environmental insults.

2.1 Background

Safe drinking water is one of the most important and basic environmental factors pertaining to fetal and child development. Medical evidence has shown that a mother's exposure to common chemical pollutants in drinking water that can pass through the placenta, such as arsenic, cadmium, and lead, is associated with the underdevelopment of the fetus (Rahman et al. 2009; Kippler et al. 2012; Renzetti et al. 2017). Moreover, disease-causing microorganisms in drinking water are linked to the transmission of diarrhea, a leading cause of death and malnutrition globally in children under five.[1] In this section, we first provide a brief overview of the state of drinking water in rural China. We then introduce the rural drinking water program, which was launched to improve rural residents' access to safe drinking water.

[1] Refer to the *World Health Organization Fact Sheets—Diarrhoeal disease*, https://www.who.int/news-room/fact-sheets/detail/diarrhoeal-disease, accessed on March 26, 2022.

© The Author(s), under exclusive license to Springer Nature Singapore Pte Ltd. 2025
L. Li, *The Impacts of Water Reforms in Rural and Urban China*,
https://doi.org/10.1007/978-981-96-6902-8_2

2.1.1 Drinking Water in Rural China

Along with China's unprecedented economic boom in recent decades, the water quality from industrial, domestic, and agricultural sources has deteriorated severely (Xie et al. 2009). For instance, data from China's water monitoring system show that in 2004, of all 745 monitored river sections, 28% were unsafe for any use, and 32% met the national safety standards for industrial and irrigation uses only (Xie et al. 2009).

Public water supply in rural China lags substantially behind that of urban areas. In 1990, 92% of urban residents had access to on-premise tap water from water plants, while 88% of rural residents had no access to on-premise tap water (UNICEF and WHO 2015). Rural residents without access to tap water mostly rely on untreated water from wells, rivers, and lakes. According to our calculation—using data from the 2010 wave of the China Family Panel Studies (CFPS)—more than 87% of rural households were still relying on untreated water for cooking in villages without a tap water connection.

At least partly owing to the common practice of boiling water before drinking, microorganisms—the primary drinking water contaminants in many developing countries— have less adverse consequences in China (Zhang et al. 2009; Zhang and Xu 2016). According to the *WHO Technical Brief - Boil Water* (WHO 2015), the process of heating water to a rolling boil is sufficient to inactivate pathogenic bacteria, viruses, and protozoa. Zhang et al. (2009) find that more than 85% of rural households in China boil water before drinking. Using Chinese Longitudinal Healthy Longevity Survey (CLHLS) data, a nationally representative survey of the elderly aged 65 and over in China, we also find that more than 90% of respondents reported drinking boiled water, regardless of the availability of tap water. As a result, although diarrhea is the second leading cause of death in children under five years old in the world, it is not a common cause of child deaths in China (only accounting for 3% in 2008) (Rudan et al. 2010).

Nevertheless, chemical pollutants in the water cannot be removed by boiling and can still incur significant health damage. For example, Currie et al. (2013) find that in New Jersey, chemicals in the water have more harmful effects on birth outcomes than exposure to fecal coliform does. Evidence from China reveals that poorer surface water quality is associated with a higher infant mortality rate (He and Perlof 2016) and a higher digestive cancer death rate (Ebenstein 2012), regardless of the common practice of drinking boiled water.

2.1.2 The Rural Drinking Water Program

To improve rural residents' access to safe drinking water, the Chinese government initiated a rural drinking water program in 1984. The program includes: (1) the construction of water treatment plants with water purification technology and equipment to remove microorganisms and chemical impurities; and (2) the construction of pipeline systems to deliver tap water directly from water plants to households, helping to improve accessibility and avoid contamination during transportation and storage. Under China's centralized political system and decentralized administrative and fiscal systems, the central government stipulated guidelines for the implementation of the program, including the *Interim Provision on Rural Drinking Water* (MWREP 1984) and the *Regulations on Construction of Rural Drinking Water Projects* (SPCMWR 2000). Local governments are responsible for the financing, planning, construction, and management of water infrastructure. In general, the central government, local government, rural residents, and other sponsors collectively bear the cost of the drinking water program, with their share of the contribution varying by region.

No explicit implementation rules have been documented due to the decentralized rollout of the program. In practice, areas in urgent need of safe drinking water are likely to have a higher chance of obtaining a tap water connection early. It is also likely that areas geographically close to a city center obtain a tap water connection earlier by taking advantage of the expansion of the urban water supply network. Using data from the 2010 wave of the CFPS, we employ a province fixed-effects model to show the correlation between community characteristics in 2010 and the probability and timing of community-level tap water connection. Factors that may have affected the probability and timing of tap water access include a community's location, population, area, level of economic development, and topographic characteristics. Population and area are proxies for the scale of a community. The level of economic development is indicated by average years of schooling. Topographic characteristics capture the difficulty of constructing the tap water infrastructure in the community.

Table 2.1 presents the regression results. We find that whether a community is a suburban village and the location of a community are among the most important determinants for both the placement of tap water connections and the timing of construction: a suburban village or a community closer to a town or city is more likely to have access to tap water in 2010 and would receive a tap water connection earlier than other villages located in the same province.[2] In estimating the effect of *in utero* exposure to tap water, we address the issue of the non-random program rollout with multiple empirical strategies (see Sect. 2.6).

Since the implementation of the program, rural residents' access to safe drinking water has greatly improved. Figure 2.1 plots the fraction of households using tap water as the main source of water for cooking in 2010 by the first year of a tap water connection at the community level, using data from the CFPS.[3] Water used for cooking indicates the type of water used for washing fruits and vegetables, cooking food, cleaning cooking vessels and cutlery. We show that among households residing in communities that had not obtained a tap water connection by 2010, less than 10% of them were using tap water for cooking in 2010. Among households residing in communities that newly received a tap water connection in 2009, around 50% of them reported using tap water for cooking in 2010, while, for communities that got

---

[2] Among the 404 villages, 90 are located in suburban areas, and the rest are located in rural areas.

[3] The data on first year of connection in or before 2010 is extracted from the CFPS 2010 community survey, and that after 2010 is extracted from the CFPS 2014 community survey.

Table 2.1 Determinants of tap water connection at the community level

Dep. var.:	Connected to tap water in 2010	Year first getting connection
	(1)	(2)
Suburban village	0.109*	–3.319***
	(0.064)	(1.105)
Log of distance to nearest town or city (hours)	–0.077**	1.732***
	(0.033)	(0.541)
Log of population	–0.023	–0.909
	(0.041)	(0.632)
Log of area (km^2)	0.007	–0.018
	(0.012)	(0.197)
Average years of schooling of 25–55-year-olds	0.018	–0.191
	(0.015)	(0.258)
Hills	–0.079	0.446
	(0.066)	(1.075)
Mountains	0.041	–0.478
	(0.097)	(1.460)
Plateaus	–0.054	–0.530
	(0.135)	(1.843)
Others	–0.012	–0.534
	(0.078)	(1.321)
Observations	404	404
R^2	0.198	
Province FE	Y	Y

Notes * means significant at 10%, ** significant at 5%, and *** significant at 1%. Column (1) reports OLS estimates. Column (2) reports the marginal effects of the Tobit model, conditional on community first getting tap water access no later than 2010. The villages are categorized into five types by topographic characteristics: hills, mountains, plateaus, plains, and others, and dummy variables are generated for each type. The type of plains is taken as the omitted group. Robust standard errors are in parentheses

a connection before 2009, the share of households using tap water for cooking falls in the range of 50% and 80%. This suggests that once tap water becomes available in the community, households take it up rapidly, and the penetration rate does not depend on the cumulative years of tap water availability at the community level.

In addition to being more accessible, tap water is expected to be of better quality than untreated water. While few regulations are imposed on untreated drinking water, strict regulations are imposed on tap water in terms of its source, process, distribution, and quality control. Water sources for tap water have to meet national standards.[4]

[4] For details, refer to the *Environmental Quality Standards for Surface Water* (GB 3838-2002) and the *Standard for Groundwater Quality* (GB/T 14848—9), available on the website of the Ministry of the Ecology and Environment of the People's Republic of China (https://www.mee.gov.cn).

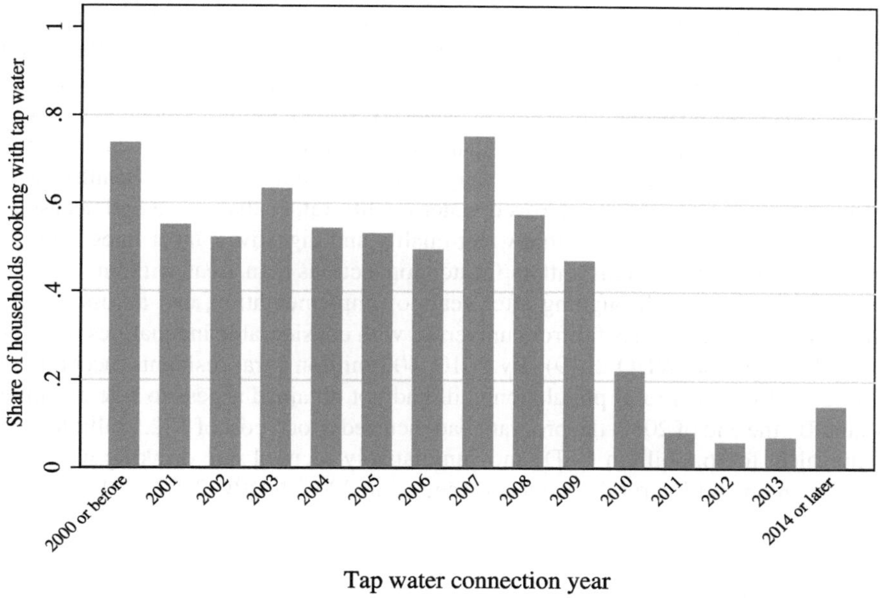

Fig. 2.1 Share of households using tap water for cooking in 2010, by the year of the first tap water connection in the village. *Notes* The figure plots the share of households reporting use of tap water for cooking in 2010 by the first tap water connection year for the 404 sampled villages in the 2010 CFPS. Information on the year of the first connection is from the 2010 CFPS data if the village received the tap water connection before 2010 and is from the 2014 CFPS data if the village received the connection between 2010 and 2013. If both waves recorded that the village had no tap water connection, then the tap water connection year is designated as "2014 or after."

Raw water should be treated with various technologies in four consecutive processes: coagulation, precipitation, filtration, and disinfection. Although the extent to which water treatment improves the quality of water depends on the nature of the raw water and the specific treatment technologies, the regular process of coagulation has proved to be efficient in removing heavy metals (Henneberry et al. 2011; WHO 2017). Before being delivered to households by pipelines as tap water, the treated water should meet a variety of standards, including general chemical, toxicological, bacteriological, and radiative indexes stipulated by the *Sanitary Standard for Drinking Water Quality* (MOH 1985, 2007). Moreover, the government authorities monitor the quality of tap water precisely and regularly.

Existing studies in China have generally shown that the water quality of tap water is better than that of untreated water. Zhang et al. (2009) collect 6,948 samples of drinking water from rural households and evaluate them using 14 indicators.[5] The authors find that, for each of the 14 indicators, the samples of tap water are more

[5] The 14 indicators are color, turbidity, pH value, total hardness, iron, manganese, chloride, sulfate, chemical oxygen demand (COD), fluoride, arsenic, nitrate nitrogen, bacteria, and coliform bacteria.

likely to meet at least the Level Two standard of the *Implementation Guidelines for the "Sanitary Standard for Drinking Water Quality" in Rural Areas* (PPHC and MOH 2000) than the samples of untreated water. The biggest difference between tap water and untreated water is in coliform bacteria (20.4%), followed by other forms of bacteria (17.36%), manganese (5.44%), and nitrate nitrogen (5.35%). Evaluating the same rural drinking water program, Zhang (2012) finds that the positive health effects of the program come from improved water quality rather than increased access to water. Ebenstein (2012) finds that water quality and digestive cancer rates is much less strongly linked in areas with tap water connections than areas without.

The program is still ongoing after years of implementation, and access to safe drinking water in China is far from universal, with considerable inequalities remaining (UNICEF and WHO 2019). By 2010, 400 million rural residents, accounting for 42% of the total rural population, still had not obtained access to safe drinking water. By the end of 2010, the program had incurred a total cost of 182.5 billion yuan (equivalent to 26.8 billion USD) and cumulatively secured safe drinking water for more than one billion rural residents (Meng et al. 2004; NDRC 2007, 2012).

2.2 Results Preview

In this study, we examine the relatively long-term effect of early-life exposure to safe drinking water on childhood health in the context of rural China. A unique feature of this setting is that drinking boiled water is a common practice (Zhang et al. 2009). As boiling can inactivate most microorganisms in water (WHO 2015), it protects Chinese children from being infected by disease-causing microorganisms in drinking water. Boiling, however, cannot remove the chemical pollutants from water, but water purification equipment can. We exploit the gradual rollout of the rural drinking water program in China that built water plants with water purification equipment and laid pipelines to supply treated tap water directly to rural households. Treated tap water has a lower concentration of active microorganisms and chemical pollutants than other sources of untreated water (Zhang et al. 2009). Our study provides suggestive evidence on whether the effect of treated tap water is attributable to the low concentration of chemical pollutants, as opposed to disease-causing microorganisms which are the main impurities in drinking water studied in previous research (e.g., Jalan and Ravallion 2003 on India and Bhalotra et al. 2021 on Mexico).

We utilize rich data at the village level and individual level from the China Family Panel Studies (CFPS). We start with an event study analysis to identify the dynamic effect of exposure to tap water. There is a growing consensus that environmental factors *in utero* and during the early years of life can have a persistent impact on health in later life (Almond et al. 2018). However, the critical window of exposure to safe drinking water for children's health is not yet clear. Combining the timing of the first tap water connection in villages and the birth dates of a sample of children from the CFPS data, we are able to determine a child's access to safe drinking water over time. We show that the beneficial impact of tap water on height-for-age, a marker of childhood health, comes from the *in utero* period and that there is a limited additional impact from postnatal exposure. We then use a difference-in-differences (DID) strategy, exploiting the variation in the timing of the first tap water connection across villages and comparing the children conceived before and after the connection within villages, to isolate the effect of *in utero* exposure to tap water on childhood health.

We find a sizable positive effect of *in utero* exposure to treated tap water on childhood height. Children with *in utero* exposure to tap water are 0.3 standard deviations taller at the ages of 1–11 than those of the same age and gender without the exposure. The estimate is very stable when we additionally control for province-specific cohort fixed effects, specific cohort effects for villages with similar characteristics, *in utero* exposure to health programs, and *in utero* exposure to other infrastructures (including electricity, roads, cable television, and landline phones). Moreover, the effect persists as the children grow up. For the same sample of children, the effect on height diminishes by one-third at the ages of 5–15, to 0.2 standard deviations, but is still of statistical and economic significance.

We also detect positive effects of *in utero* exposure to tap water on other health outcomes measured at birth and during childhood, such as the incidence of sickness and doctor visits. Examining children's most severe diseases since birth by cause, we find that *in utero* exposure to tap water significantly reduces the incidence of non-waterborne digestive diseases, whereas the incidence of other disease types, including waterborne diseases, is not affected. These findings are consistent with the existing evidence that an improvement in water quality significantly reduces morbidity and mortality related to the digestive system (Ebenstein 2012; Alsan and Goldin 2019). They also lend support to our argument that the effect of *in utero* exposure to treated tap water on health is most likely driven by the low concentration of chemical pollutants rather than disease-causing microorganisms.

We further explore the mechanisms mediating the effect of *in utero* tap water exposure on childhood health. We probe two channels implied by the model of life-cycle human capital formation in Cunha and Heckman (2007) and Heckman (2007): (1) the direct channel, operating through the immediate effect of *in utero* exposure on health before age one; and (2) the behavioral channel, emphasizing parental investments in response to the exposure. We test both channels by exploring the heterogeneity by maternal education. We find that when the village has no tap water connection, low-educated mothers are less likely than high-educated mothers to use safe water for cooking, and having a tap water connection in the village reduces the difference. Consequently, the positive effect of *in utero* exposure to publicly provided tap water on height is greater for children of low-educated mothers than that for children of high-educated mothers. We then show that only for children of low-educated mothers does *in utero* tap water exposure improve health outcomes at birth and in infancy and induce postnatal health investments by parents. Therefore, our findings support both channels and are consistent with the argument that behavioral responses magnify the baseline effects of early-life conditions (Adhvaryu and Nyshadham 2016).

2.3 Literature Review

In this section, we first review the existing evidence from public health, epidemiological, and economic literature on the link between chemical pollutants and fetal development. We then discuss our study's contributions to the economic literature.

2.3.1 *Chemical Pollutants in Water and Fetal Development*

In general, exposure to environmental chemicals during pregnancy is found to threaten fetal growth. Environmental chemicals and other xenobiotics can cross the placenta and enter the fetal bloodstream (Myllynen et al. 2005). Concentrations of nicotine and its major metabolite, illicit drugs, prescription pharmaceuticals, alcohol, and environmental chemicals such as pesticides have been detected in cord blood, amniotic fluid, or meconium (see the summary by Barr et al. (2007)). In particular, arsenic and fluoride, two common environmental contaminants in drinking water, can also cross the placenta and transfer to the fetus (Concha et al. 1998; Agency for Toxic Substances and Disease Registry (ATSDR) 2003). Due to immature organ systems and underdeveloped detoxification enzymes or enzymatic processes, when exposures occur, fetuses are extremely vulnerable to these environmental insults. For instance, prenatal exposure to perfluoroalkyl and polyfluoroalkyl substances can result in several adverse effects on fetal growth and development, including reduced head circumference and low birth weight (Apelberg et al. 2007; Chen et al. 2012; Callan et al. 2016). Prenatal exposure to diverse environmental chemicals can dysregulate the fetal epigenome, with potential consequences for later life (see the review by Perera and Herbstman (2011)).

It is well documented that *in utero* exposure to contaminated drinking water can lead to health damage in early life. The epidemiological literature has revealed the connections between water pollution and diseases such as leukemia for children (DEEOH and NJDHSS 2003). The economic literature has documented a strong link between chemicals in drinking water and infant and child mortality. Cutler and Miller (2005) argue that the adoption of clean water technologies such as filtration and chlorination was responsible for the decline in the infant mortality rate in early 20th-century America. Brainerd and Menon (2014) find that an increase in the concentration of fertilizer chemicals in water in the first trimester of pregnancy increased infant and neonatal mortality in rural India. They also find that *in utero* exposure to fertilizer chemicals in water reduces the height and weight of children under age five. He and Perlof (2016) find that a modest level of deterioration in surface water quality in China, graded on the basis of chemical pollutant indicators, leads to higher infant mortality.

Evidence also suggests that chemical pollutants are important sources of drinking water contamination that leads to damaged fetal development. Epidemiological evidence suggests an association between organic chemical contaminants in drinking water and worse birth outcomes (Bove et al. 1995). Currie et al. (2013) probe into the causal relationship between water quality and fetal health. They find that in New Jersey, *in utero* exposure to contaminated drinking water has large and statistically significant effects on birth weight and the gestation of infants born to less-educated mothers. In addition, they show that chemicals in the water have more harmful effects than exposure to fecal coliform.

2.3.2 Contributions to the Economic Literature

A vast economics literature has examined the causal link between early-life exposure to safe drinking water and child health, but with a focus on the short-term effect. Early-life exposure to unsafe drinking water results in poor birth outcomes and infant health (Currie et al. 2013; Rocha and Soares 2015; Hill and Ma 2022). In contrast, improving access to safe drinking water is found to have positive short-term effects on the well-being of infants, children, and adults.[6] Zhang (2012), the study most related to ours, explores the same rural drinking water program in China and shows that the introduction of treated tap water in villages has a strong immediate effect on the health status of both adults and children. However, the effect becomes much smaller and insignificant when village fixed effects are controlled for. Our study finds a strong and persistent effect of *in utero* tap water exposure when village fixed effects are controlled for. The difference between our study and Zhang (2012) could be attributed to differences in the data sets, the construction of the treatment variable, and the stage of the life cycle when the exposure occurs. Using data from the China Health and Nutrition Survey, Zhang (2012) constructs the treatment variable as the presence of a water plant in the village, based on the share of households reporting using water from a water plant. She then estimates the instantaneous effect of village-level access to a water plant on adults' and children's health. Our study combines individual- and village-level data from the China Family Panel Studies and constructs the treatment variable reflecting a child's *in utero* exposure to the tap water connection at the village level. We are particularly interested in the relatively long-term effect of prenatal exposure to tap water on childhood health. However, to the extent that we detect a negligible impact of postnatal exposure to tap water on childhood health in the event study, it echoes the finding of Zhang (2012) that the instantaneous effect of treated water on childhood health becomes small and insignificant when village fixed effects are controlled for.

To the best of our knowledge, only two studies, which also explore the same rural drinking water program in China, assess the long-term effects of early-life exposure to tap water. Zhang and Xu (2016) find that individuals exposed to the program from age 0 to 2 had attained, on average, 1.68 additional years of education by early

[6] See, for example, Jalan and Ravallion (2003); Galiani et al. (2005); Mangyo (2008); Gamper-Rabindran et al. (2010); Devoto et al. (2012); Zhang (2012); Kosec (2014); Meeks (2017); Zhang and Xu (2016); Alsan and Goldin (2019); Bhalotra et al. (2021).

adulthood. Chen et al. (2022) find that exposure to tap water between conception and age five significantly enhances cognitive development at ages 10–15. Quantifying the long-term effect on childhood health is important for at least three reasons. First, it enriches knowledge about the first-order effect of safe drinking water on health outcomes. Second, it helps us understand to what extent improving childhood health underlies the effects of early-life conditions on non-health outcomes in later life. Third, it sheds light on the actual return of investments in improving access to safe drinking water.

In the past two decades, the fetal origins literature has blossomed. Early-life exposure to extreme negative shocks such as disease outbreaks (Almond and Mazumder 2005; Almond 2006), air pollution (Currie et al. 2014), radioactive fallout (Almond et al. 2009; Black et al. 2019), natural disasters (Karbownik and Wray 2019), and famines (Chen and Zhou 2007; Meng and Qian 2009), or to mild shocks like fasting during Ramadan (Almond et al. 2015) have been causally linked to adult outcomes observed decades later. Knowledge is expanding rapidly on the long-term effects of *in utero* conditions, but much less is known about the middle years between early life and adulthood (Almond et al. 2018). Our study fills some gaps in the missing evidence by focusing on the effects of early-life conditions on childhood outcomes. Moreover, our study enriches the knowledge on the interplay of public interventions in early life and household disadvantages. We find that exposure to treated water under the rural drinking water program has a much larger effect on the height of children of low-educated mothers, which supports the mitigating role of publicly provided treated water on household disadvantages. Finally, our study enhances the understanding of parents' behavioral responses to early-life events. Whether parental responses undermine or magnify the immediate effect of early-life events is a long-standing debate, and the existing evidence is mixed (Almond and Mazumder 2013). We show that parents increase health investments in response to their children's exposure to tap water *in utero*, which magnifies the baseline effect of the exposure.

2.4 A Simple Model of Human Capital Formation

Following Cunha and Heckman (2007) and Heckman (2007), the technology of human capital formation for a child in period t can be constructed as

$$\theta_{t+1} = f_t(\theta_t, h_t, I_t), \ \ t \in \{-1, 0, 1, 2, 3, ..., T\}, \tag{2.1}$$

where θ denotes the vector of human capital, normally containing health, education, and cognitive and non-cognitive skills. For simplicity, here, we assume that health is the only form of human capital, such that θ_t denotes fetal or child health stocks in period t. h_t denotes parents' human capital in period t, such as parental education and height. I_t represents all health investments in period t made by parents and the government. The technology in period t, $f_t(.)$, is assumed to be weakly increasing in I_t and twice continuously differentiable in all of its arguments.

For the purpose of this study, $t = -1$ is the period *in utero*, $t = 0$ corresponds to the time of birth, and $t = 1$ to T denotes the year of age 1 to the year of age T, respectively. Therefore, h_{-1} indicates parental human capital stocks while the child is *in utero*, I_{-1} represents parental and public health investments in the child while the child is *in utero*, and θ_0 represents children's health endowment at birth, which is jointly determined by h_{-1} and I_{-1}. We are particularly interested in the effect of improved access to tap water *in utero* I_{-1} on human capital stocks after birth θ_t: $\frac{\partial \theta_t}{\partial I_{-1}}$, $t \in \{0, 1, 2, 3, ..., T\}$. The model implies two potential channels through which the public investment *in utero* could affect the health stocks after birth: a direct channel and a behavioral channel.

The direct channel

One key insight of the dynamic model of human capital accumulation is the self-productivity of human capital (Heckman 2007). Such self-productivity implies that higher levels of human capital in one period create higher levels of human capital in future periods. Therefore, if tap water exposure *in utero* improves health at birth θ_0,

$$\frac{\partial \theta_0}{\partial I_{-1}} > 0, \tag{2.2}$$

the improved health at birth creates better health in future periods θ_t,

$$\frac{\partial \theta_t}{\partial I_{-1}} > 0, \ t \in \{1, 2, 3, ..., T\}. \tag{2.3}$$

We consider this mechanism to be a direct channel via which tap water exposure *in utero* affects health in childhood. If we are able to find evidence that exposure to tap water *in utero* consistently improves health at birth, in infancy, and in childhood, it would suggest that self-productivity of health stocks is at play.

The behavioral channel

Improved access to publicly provided tap water *in utero* I_{-1} could affect child health after birth θ_{t+1} by inducing more health investments in children I_t, $t \in \{0, 1, 2, 3, ..., T\}$. Such behavioral responses may arise from multiple sources. If improved access to tap water *in utero* increases parents' human capital (e.g., maternal health) and household resources, parents might be able to invest more in children at later stages of child development. Furthermore, the model implies that parents may increase later investments in the presence of dynamic complementarity in investments in the production of health stocks. Formally, the dynamic complementarity in human capital investments can be expressed as

$$\frac{\partial^2 \theta_{t+1}}{\partial I_{-1} \partial I_t} > 0, \ t \in \{0, 1, 2, 3, ..., T\}. \tag{2.4}$$

The complementarity arises when the following two conditions are both met:

(a) *In utero* investments I_{-1} increase health stocks after birth θ_t, $t \in \{0, 1, 2, 3, ..., T\}$, that is, conditions (2.2) and (2.3) hold;

(b) Health stocks and investments after birth are static complements, that is, health stocks θ_t make health investments I_t more productive:

$$\frac{\partial^2 \theta_{t+1}}{\partial \theta_t \partial I_t} > 0, \ t \in \{0, 1, 2, 3, ..., T\}. \tag{2.5}$$

In our context, dynamic complementarity indicates that *in utero* investments—improved access to tap water—may increase the marginal return to later investments, so that the improved access to tap water *in utero* could induce more parental health investments at later stages of child development.

In Sect. 2.9, we provide ample evidence in support of both the direct channel and the behavioral channel. We also discuss the possible reasons that receiving exposure to tap water *in utero* leads to more parental health investments in children's later life.

2.5 Data

2.5.1 Data Source

We use data provided by the China Family Panel Studies (CFPS), which was launched in 2010 by the Institute of Social Science Survey of Peking University, China (Xie 2012). The CFPS is a longitudinal study of a nationally representative sample of Chinese communities, families, and individuals. The target sample of the CFPS consists of 16,000 households in 25 regions in China, excluding Hong Kong, Macao, Taiwan, Xinjiang, Tibet, Qinghai, Inner Mongolia, Ningxia, and Hainan. A total of 14,798 households and 42,590 individuals from 645 communities were interviewed in the 2010 baseline survey. Follow-up surveys were conducted every other year.[7] All surveys provide detailed information at the community, household, and individual levels, which is essential for our analysis. As we are interested in the expansion of tap water systems under the rural drinking water program, we focus on the villages (rural communities) sampled by the CFPS and exclude urban communities.

[7] A community is the lowest-level administrative region in China, above which there is a province, a prefecture, a county, and a township. A community can be either urban or rural. A rural community is also called a village. Villages are governed by village committees, which usually consist of three to seven local residents, as well as several members of the Communist Party in the village. The village committees are responsible for implementing policies from higher-level governments, such as enforcing the one-child policy, collecting taxes and grain levies, distributing subsidies to poor households, and constructing basic infrastructures. As the land is collectively owned in rural China, the village committees are also responsible for overseeing land leasing, rotation, and disputes.

2.5.2 Treatment Variable

The treatment variable in this study is *in utero* exposure to tap water at the village level. The treatment status takes the value one if a tap water connection was available in the child's birth village in the year of conception and zero otherwise. The year of conception for each child is deduced from information on the birth date and the length of gestation. The information on the availability of a tap water connection over time is extracted from the CFPS community survey data collected in 2010. The village questionnaire was administered to an individual in each village who knows the village well and has access to the village's statistical material. Usually, the person is the director or the accountant of the village committee or the secretary of the village committee of the Communist Party of China (Xie 2012). The village questionnaire asks whether the village has a tap water connection. If the answer is yes, the survey further asks in which year the connection first became available in the village. We take the answer to this question as the year the village received the first connection. As tap water connections, once built, are unlikely to be turned off, we assume that treated tap water has always been available in a village since the year of the first connection. Figure 2.2 plots the number of villages newly connected to tap water systems each year and the cumulative distribution of the village-level tap water rollout between 1980 and 2010 among 404 villages from the 2010 CFPS. The tap water connections have been rolled out rapidly across villages since the 1980s. In 1980, less than 5% of the villages had a tap water connection. By 2010, over 55% of the villages had received a connection.

One may be concerned with the credibility of the reported data on the year when tap water was first introduced into the village. We argue that the reported data are credible for three reasons. First, receiving tap water connections is a salient and socially desirable event for rural residents. Hence, the year of the first tap water connection is likely to be accurately reported even many years later (Beckett et al. 2001). In addition, the construction of a public water system is standard information provided in village statistical materials (such as village chronicles of events), which the respondents could easily refer to. In Sect. 2.8.1, we show that our results are robust to accounting for the possible issue of reporting error.

Our data reveal that a higher share of households used tap water in a village with a tap water connection than in a village without a connection and that the pattern of household tap water take-up is consistent with the reported year of the first connection. In Figure 2.1 we show the share of households reporting the use of tap water for cooking in 2010 for villages differing in the reported year of the first connection. In villages that got the first connection before 2010, around 50%–75% of the households reported using tap water for cooking in 2010, whereas the take-up rate is about 10% in villages that had not been connected by 2010. The sharp contrast in the take-up rate in 2010 between villages receiving the first connection before and after 2010 lends support to the credibility of the reported year of the first connection. It also provides suggestive evidence that receiving a tap water connection in the village increased the share of households using tap water by around 40 to 65 percentage points.

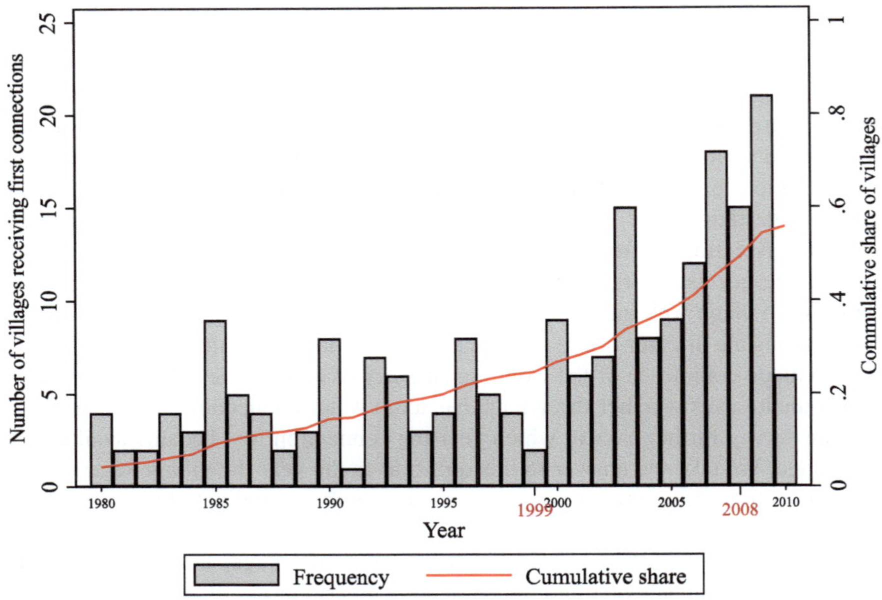

Fig. 2.2 Phase-in of tap water connections in CFPS sampled villages. *Notes* The figure plots the phase-in of tap water connections under the rural drinking water program in 404 sampled villages in the 2010 CFPS between 1980 and 2010. The bar displays the number of villages that obtained the first tap water connection in a given year. The curve shows the cumulative share of villages with a tap water connection over time. In this study, the variation in exposure to tap water *in utero* comes from the villages that received the first tap water connection between 1999 and 2008

The treatment variable reflects *in utero* exposure to the tap water connection at the village level. As shown in Figure 2.1, the household take-up rate of tap water is not 100% in villages with a tap water connection. What we obtain is thus an intention-to-treat (ITT) estimate of the treatment effect of *in utero* exposure to tap water. It is also policy relevant to explore the effect of *in utero* exposure to the tap water connection at the household level (the local average treatment effect, LATE). However, there is no retrospective information in the CFPS data on the household usage of tap water when the child was conceived. In Sect. 2.10, we discuss in detail the first stage using data on household take-up rates and provide a possible range of the estimate for the LATE.

Due to a lack of information on the exact date a village received the first tap water connection, we use the availability of a tap water connection in the village of birth in the conception year as a proxy for *in utero* exposure to tap water. However, the proxy may be subject to measurement error when the conception year coincides or is one year before the year of the first connection. For example, in a village that received the first connection in December 2005, a child conceived in January 2005 had no tap water exposure *in utero*, but the proxy equals one. Another example is that, in a village that was connected in January 2005, a child conceived in December 2004 had nine months of exposure *in utero*, but the proxy equals zero. At most 155 of the sampled children (4.8%) would suffer from this type of measurement error. This measurement error would attenuate the estimated impact of *in utero* exposure to tap water. As we detect a positive effect of *in utero* exposure to tap water on childhood health, dealing with the measurement error would strengthen our results. In Sect. 2.8.2, we construct an alternative measure of exposure, the number of months *in utero* with tap water exposure, under four different assumptions on the distribution of the month of the first village-level tap water connection. The simulation results show that the estimates under all four assumptions are close to the main results.

2.5.3 Sample

Our sample consists of 3,252 rural children aged between 13 and 132 months (between 1 and 11 years) in 2010, and thus conceived between 1998 and 2008.[8] We restrict our sample to children born in the surveyed villages, to ensure a precise measure of tap water exposure *in utero*. As the CFPS did not provide information on the exact geographic location of individuals' birthplaces, we use two dummy variables to impose sample restrictions: (1) whether the village of *hukou* (Chinese household registration) is located in the county of residence in 2010; (2) whether the village of birth and the village of *hukou* correspond. Thus, the main sample consists of children whose village of *hukou* is located in the county of residence in 2010 and corresponds to the village of birth. The main analysis excludes 906 children (21.8%) who fail the sample restrictions, as we are unable to determine their *in utero* tap water exposure.[9] Under these restrictions, our analysis may still be subject to the issue of sample selection. If sample selection correlates with both the *in utero* exposure to tap water and children's outcomes, our estimates may be biased. In Sect. 2.8.3, we show that two types of sample selection—fertility selection and migration—are unlikely to alter our main results.

The sampled children were conceived between 1998 and 2008. During this period, the share of villages with a tap water connection increased by almost 30 percentage points (see Fig. 2.2), suggesting a substantial variation in the treatment variable. Panel A of Table 2.2 presents the summary statistics of the treatment variable. Among the 3,252 children in our final sample, 949 were conceived when the villages had a tap water connection, accounting for 29% of the final sample.

---

[8] We focus on this age range because ages 1–11 are a crucial period in the life cycle for human capital accumulation (Cunha et al. 2010). Moreover, little attention has been paid to children in this age range in the existing research despite extensive discussion on the impact of early-life conditions on infancy and adulthood outcomes.

[9] We thank an anonymous referee for pointing out that these sample restrictions do not rule out the possibility of after-birth within-county migration to a surveyed village. We show in Sect. 2.8.3 that this type of migration would lead to an underestimation of the treatment effect of *in utero* exposure to tap water. Since we detect a positive treatment effect on childhood health in the analysis, accounting for this type of migration would strengthen our findings. We also show that estimation without imposing sample restrictions yields an estimate of the treatment effect that is smaller in magnitude than the main estimate but remains statistically and economically significant.

Table 2.2 Summary statistics

	Full sample	Exposed children	Unexposed children	Difference[a]
	(1)	(2)	(3)	(4)
Panel A. Treatment variable				
Tap water IU[d]	0.292	1	0	
Panel B. Outcome variables				
Height-for-age z-score	0.054	0.170	0.006	0.263***
Height (cm)	103.832	101.167	104.921	2.950**
Panel C. Individual and household controls				
Boy[d]	0.539	0.529	0.543	0.011
Mother's age at birth	26.547	26.323	26.639	0.250
Birth order	1.688	1.580	1.733	0.063
Father's years of schooling	7.298	7.754	7.111	–0.128
Mother's years of schooling	5.917	6.554	5.653	–0.462
NCMS IU[d]	0.300	0.382	0.266	0.018
Health facility IU[d]	0.488	0.583	0.448	0.023
Electricity IU[d]	0.886	0.974	0.849	0.025
Road IU[d]	0.683	0.849	0.614	0.020
Cable IU[d]	0.415	0.627	0.331	0.056
Landline phone IU[d]	0.753	0.883	0.702	0.033
Panel D. Village characteristics				
Suburban village[d]	0.179	0.318	0.121	
Plain[d]	0.317	0.311	0.320	
Hill[d]	0.311	0.282	0.322	
Mountain[d]	0.187	0.181	0.190	
Plateau[d]	0.043	0.041	0.044	
Other[d]	0.142	0.184	0.124	
Traveling time to nearest town or city (hour)	1.180	0.924	1.285	
Average years of schooling of 25–55-year-olds	5.944	6.349	5.777	
Area (km^2)	46.422	50.363	44.744	
Observations	3252	949	2303	

Notes *, **, and *** indicate significance at 10%, 5%, and 1%, respectively. The table shows summary statistics for a sample of 3,252 children conceived between 1998 and 2008 and aged 13–132 months in 2010. Other sample restrictions are detailed in Sect. 2.5.3. Exposed children are those with tap water exposure *in utero*. Column (4) reported the difference between exposed and unexposed children adjusted for village and conception year fixed effects. "[Facility/program] IU" is an indicator for *in utero* exposure to a specific public facility or program, which equals one if the public facility or program is available in the child's birth village in the year of conception and zero otherwise; "NCMS" is the abbreviation for the New Cooperative Medical Scheme in rural China. Missing data in variables other than the treatment variable are ignored in producing this table

[a] Adjusted for village and conception year fixed effects

[d] Denotes dummy variables

2.5.4 *Outcome Variables and Other Controls*

Our primary outcome of interest is the standardized height adjusted for age and gender (height-for-age z-score) observed in 2010 and 2014. The sampled children were aged between 1–11 in 2010 and 5–15 in 2014. Height-for-age is generally accepted as an indicator of long-run nutritional status and physical development for children at these ages (Thomas et al. 1996). Common causes of low height-for-age include poor *in utero* conditions, recurrent infections, and chronic diseases during childhood that lead to inadequate nutrient intake, absorption, or utilization (Fernandez et al. 2002; WHO 2010). Childhood height is also an important intermediary outcome that predicts labor market outcomes (Persico et al. 2004; Case and Paxson 2008b; Lundborg et al. 2014) as well as health and cognitive ability in old age (Case and Paxson 2008a).

We obtain the height-for-age z-scores by subtracting the mean and dividing by the standard deviation of the comparison group. The comparison group consists of children who are of the same gender and age range (by six months), who lived in villages with no tap water connection in 2010.[10] By construction, all children in the comparison group had no tap water exposure during the *in utero* period. We report the sample means of height (in cm) and the height-for-age z-score in Panel B of Table 2.2 for the whole sample and for exposed and unexposed children separately.

In addition to the height-for-age z-score, we explore the impact of *in utero* tap water exposure on other health measures covering different stages of childhood, including birth and infancy outcomes, other childhood outcomes, and cause-specific morbidity from birth to current age.

Panel C presents the sample means of the individual and household characteristics for the whole sample and by treatment status. The exposed and unexposed children are different in many dimensions; however, these differences become small and statistically insignificant once we control for village and conception year fixed effects, as shown in Panel C, column (4). In contrast, column (4) of Panel B shows that the difference in the height-for-age z-score between exposed and unexposed children remains significant even when we control for village and conception year fixed effects. The sample means of the village characteristics are reported in Panel D.

2.6 Empirical Strategy

This section first presents an event study analysis, then formalizes the DID strategy, and finally provides more supporting evidence for the identification assumption.

[10] For example, for a girl aged 15 months, the comparison group is composed of girls aged 13–18 months and living in villages without a tap water connection in 2010.

2.6.1 Event Study Analysis

The fetal origins literature has expanded to include both *in utero* conditions and early-childhood environment. This study focuses on the influence of tap water exposure during the prenatal period, which is inspired by the event study estimation below showing that the prenatal period is the critical time window during which tap water exposure improves childhood health.

We define an event time as the difference between the year a village received the first tap water connection and the year of conception. A negative event time implies that exposure to tap water starts before the year of conception. For children with an event time of 0, the exposure to tap water starts in the year of conception. A positive event time implies that the exposure to tap water starts after conception. For example, in a village that received its first tap water connection in 2002, a child conceived in 2001 would have an event time of 1. The child would not have been exposed to tap water *in utero* but would have been exposed to it from birth.

We define a cohort t consisting of children conceived in year t.[11] The event study estimation is based on the following equation:

$$Y_{ict} = \sum_{j=-4}^{5} \alpha_j D_{ij} + \gamma_c + \eta_t + \epsilon_{ict}, \tag{2.6}$$

where Y_{ict} indicates the height of child i belonging to cohort t and born in village c, D_{ij}s denote event time indicators, η_t represents cohort fixed effects, and γ_c represents village fixed effects. For $j = -3, ..., 4$, D_{ij} takes the value one if an individual has an event time of j and zero otherwise. To reduce the collinearity between event time and conception year, two end points -4 and 5 are defined as open brackets: $D_{i,-4}$ equals one for those individuals with event times less than or equal to -4, and $D_{i,5}$ equals one for those individuals with event times greater than or equal to 5.

The coefficients of interest are α_js, which capture the differences in height-for-age z-scores across event times and hence, the timing of initial exposure to a tap water connection, conditional on village fixed effects and cohort fixed effects. We focus on the α_js for the event times from -3 to 4. Notice that each individual has one and only one D_{ij} that equals one. Hence, the D_{ij}s and the village fixed effects are perfectly collinear. To address this issue, we take the children conceived two years before the first connection (an event time of 2) as the base group and restrict α_2 to zero.

Figure 2.3 plots the estimates of α_js and the 90% confidence intervals from estimating Equation (2.6) for the height-for-age z-score. There is a clear mean shift in the height-for-age z-score from negative to positive event times, at a size of about 0.25. Children exposed to tap water *in utero* (non-positive event times) are, on average, 0.25 standard deviations taller than children with no exposure *in utero* (positive event times).

---

[11] Our results hold if we define cohorts by the year of birth instead of the year of conception.

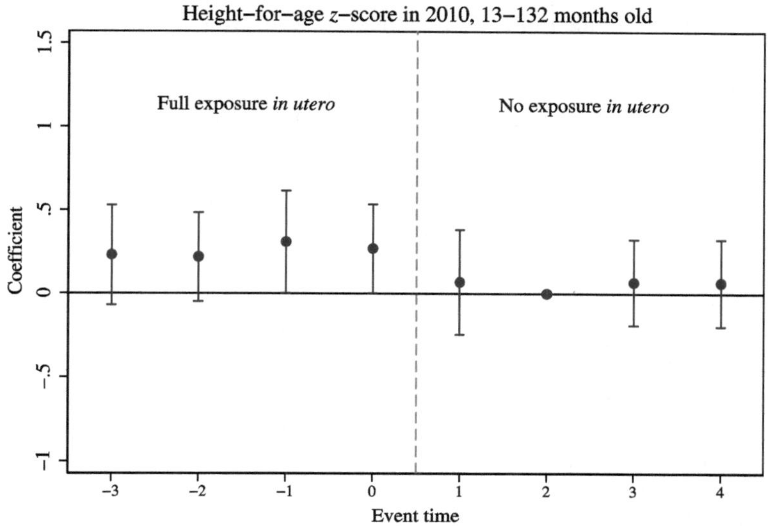

Fig. 2.3 Event study estimates of tap water exposure on children's height-for-age. *Notes* The figure shows the coefficients and 90% confidence intervals (based on standard errors clustered at the village level) from the event study analysis. The main sample is used for analysis. Event time is defined as the difference between the year when a tap water connection first becomes available in a child's birth village and the year of conception. The regression includes event time dummies, village fixed effects, and conception year fixed effects. The event time of 2 is taken as the base group. Left of the dashed line are the groups that had been exposed to tap water at least since the year of conception. Right of the dashed line are the groups that were exposed to tap water only after the year of conception

The change in the height-for-age is most salient from the event time of 0 to the event time of 1 (full exposure *in utero* to no exposure *in utero*). This finding points to the additional benefits of tap water exposure *in utero* relative to exposure from birth; on average, children first exposed to tap water one year after conception are 0.25 standard deviations shorter than children whose exposure starts, at the latest, in the year of conception. The estimates for positive event times are all close to zero, suggesting there is little additional benefit from exposure beginning at birth or ages 1, 2, or 3. Therefore, the results from the event study analysis suggest that the prenatal period is the critical time window for tap water to improve childhood health, and that postnatal exposure has a negligible impact.[12]

It is reasonable to assume that exposure before conception has a limited impact on childhood health. Under this assumption, we should observe similar estimates among the non-positive event times in the absence of heterogeneous cohort trends across

[12] Our study represents the first attempt to identify the critical window of exposure to safe drinking water for children's health. Existing studies have explored the critical window of exposure for other outcomes. Zhang and Xu (2016) find that the period from age zero to two is the critical window for educational attainment. Chen et al. (2022) show that the period spanning from one year before birth to the first five years of life is the critical window for cognitive development.

villages that differ in the timing of treatment. Indeed, we find similar estimates for non-positive event times. This pattern suggests that there are no differential cohort trends among children who were exposed to tap water *in utero* across villages. This finding provides suggestive evidence of the common trends assumption of our DID strategy, which we elaborate on in the next subsection.

The above event study analysis comes with two caveats. First, the event times from -3 to 4 are unbalanced in the sample. For instance, children conceived in 2008 can never have an event time of 3 or 4, while children conceived between 1998 and 2005 can have any event time in the range from -3 to 4. In Sect. 2.8.7, we provide a detailed discussion on the issue of unbalanced event times and conduct an event study analysis using a sample of children with balanced event times. The pattern observed in Fig. 2.3 remains. Note that the DID framework in our main analysis does not suffer from this issue. The second is the measurement error in the event times due to a lack of information on the exact date of the first tap water connection. Children with an event time of 0 may actually be exposed to tap water *in utero*, and children with an event time of 1 may actually have no exposure *in utero*. As discussed in Sect. 2.5.2, this caveat also applies to the treatment variable in the DID framework, where we use the availability of a tap water connection in the village of birth in the conception year as a proxy for *in utero* exposure to tap water. We argue that controlling for the measurement error would strengthen our results. Moreover, in Sect. 2.8.2, we show that our main results are robust to using an alternative exposure measure that does not suffer from this caveat.

2.6.2 Main Econometric Specification

The event study confirms the period *in utero* as the critical time window for exposure to tap water to improve childhood health. Now, we turn to the formal econometric specification to identify the causal effect of *in utero* exposure to tap water. Using a DID strategy, we exploit the different timing of the first tap water connection across villages and compare health outcomes for cohorts conceived before and after a village's first connection. We estimate the following equation:

$$Y_{ict} = \delta \text{TapwaterIU}_{ct} + X_{ict}\beta + \gamma_c + \theta_{pt} + \phi_t Z_c + \text{OtherexposureIU}_{ct}\tau + \epsilon_{ict}, \quad (2.7)$$

where Y_{ict} indicates the health outcome of a child i conceived in year t and born in village c. TapwaterIU_{ct} is an indicator measuring whether the child is exposed to tap water *in utero*. It equals one if a tap water connection is available in the year of conception in the village of birth and zero otherwise. The parameter of interest is δ, which can be interpreted as the causal effect of *in utero* exposure to tap water on the health outcome. Since not all households use tap water when a tap water connection is available in the village, δ is an ITT estimate. In Sect. 2.10, we discuss the possible range of the estimate for the LATE inferred from the estimation.

X_{ict} is a vector of exogenous individual and household characteristics observed in 2010, including age in months, gender, mother's age at birth, birth order, and both parents' years of schooling.[13] Village fixed effects γ_c are included to control for any time-invariant village-level characteristics that may be associated with both the timing of the first tap water connection and changes in childhood health outcomes.

We include province-specific cohort fixed effects θ_{pt} to control for any time trends in children's health outcomes that are common to all villages in a given province. This would also prevent any province-level policy changes from confounding the estimate of δ. To allow for potentially different trends across villages, we follow Gentzkow and Shapiro (2008) and Hoynes et al. (2016) and include a set of village characteristics Z_c that interact with a cohort-specific coefficient vector ϕ_t. These village controls include an indicator for a suburban village, traveling time to nearest town or city in hours, area in square kilometers, average years of schooling of 25–55-year-olds, and topographic characteristics. With all the fixed effects and control variables, the DID estimator δ may still be biased if the treatment variable varies with other interventions that affect childhood health. For example, exposure to other infrastructures might have driven the effect instead of the exposure to tap water. Hence, we additionally control for *in utero* exposure to health programs (i.e., health facilities and the New Cooperative Medical Scheme, NCMS) and other infrastructures (i.e., electricity, roads, cable television, and landline phones), denoted by $\text{OtherexposureIU}_{ct}$.

We deal with missing data by imputing the mean value of the sample and include a dummy variable for the imputed responses in the regressions. To account for any serial correlation across different cohorts within the same village, we cluster the standard errors at the village level (Bertrand et al. 2004). Moreover, to address the concern about multiple hypothesis testing, we compute the false discovery rate (FDR) q-value that allows inference when conducting a large number of tests, following Benjamini and Hochberg (1995) and using the code provided by Anderson (2008). The FDR q-value indicates the proportion of rejections that are "false discoveries".

2.6.3 Supports for the Common Trends Assumption

The validity of our identification strategy relies on the common trends assumption that in the absence of a tap water connection, the outcome would follow the same cohort trend in villages of similar characteristics within a given province. We provide evidence in support of the assumption from the event study analysis in Sect. 2.6.1. To further assess the assumption, we apply the same event study framework to four pre-determined variables including paternal and maternal years of schooling and height. Since children's exposure to tap water *in utero* should not affect pre-determined parental outcomes, we expect to observe similar estimates for event times ranging from −3 to 4.

---

[13] In Sect. 2.8.4, we show that our results are robust to controlling for current household income and a dummy for agricultural households.

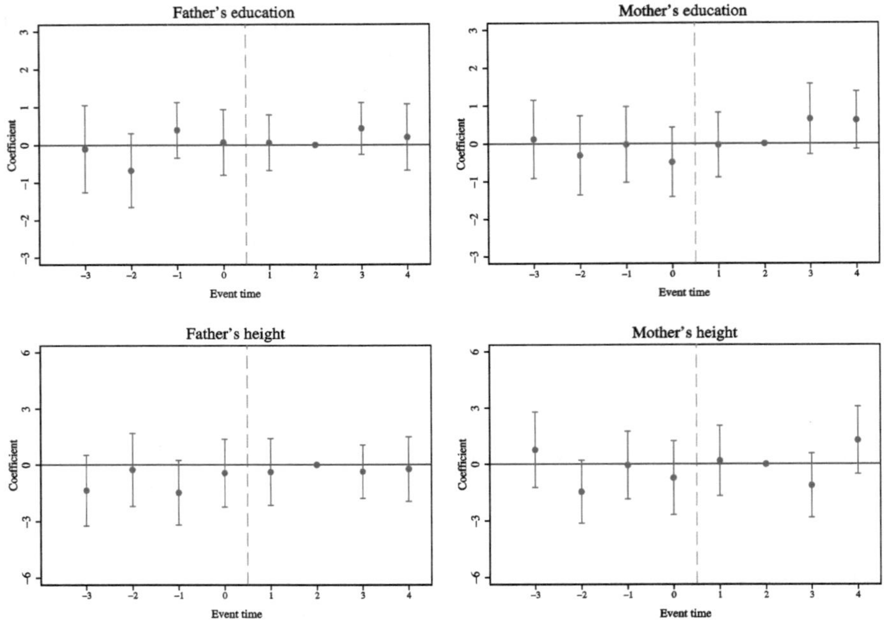

Fig. 2.4 Event study for education and height of the parents. *Notes* The figure shows the coefficients and 90% confidence intervals (based on standard errors clustered at the village level) from the event study analysis. The main sample is used for analysis. Event time is defined as the difference between the year when a tap water connection first becomes available in a child's birth village and the year of conception. The regression includes event time dummies, village fixed effects, and conception year fixed effects. The event time of 2 is taken as the base group. Left of the dashed line are the groups that had been exposed to tap water at least since the year of conception. Right of the dashed line are the groups that were exposed to tap water only after the year of conception

We plot the estimates for each pre-determined variable in Fig. 2.4. The children with an event time of 2 are taken as the base group, and the estimate for the event time of 2 is restricted to zero. Most of the estimates for other event times are close to zero, suggesting no differential pre- and post-intervention trends. The only exception is that children with an event time of 3 or 4 tend to have a better-educated mother. However, the higher maternal education level for children with positive event times is unlikely to challenge our main finding of a positive effect of *in utero* exposure to tap water on childhood health. First, we control for both maternal and paternal education in all regressions. Second, both the estimates for the event times of 3 and 4 (relative to the event time of 2) are statistically insignificant. Third, as maternal education is usually positively correlated with childhood health, we would underestimate the positive effect of *in utero* exposure to tap water if we do not control for maternal education. Overall, the event study estimates for parental height and education provide another piece of evidence in support of the common trends assumption.

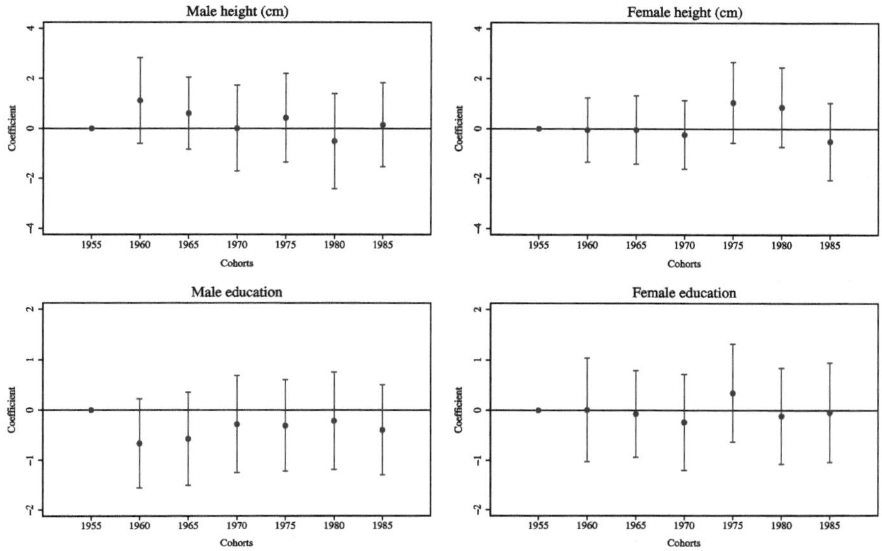

Fig. 2.5 Cohort trends in height and education between early and late treated villages. *Notes* The figure plots the differences in pre-intervention characteristics between villages that received a tap water connection from 1998 to 2008 (early treated) and villages that had not received a tap water connection by 2008 (late treated or untreated). We calculate the average characteristics for every five-year age group from the sample of individuals born between 1955 and 1989 in the 2010 data of the CFPS. Height is measured in cm and education level is measured in years. Each subfigure is from a separate regression. The dots represent the estimated coefficients on the interactions between five-year-age-group dummies and a binary variable indicating early treated. The solid vertical lines represent the 95% confidence intervals. The group of people born between 1955 and 1959 is taken as the base group. In addition to the above-mentioned interactions, the model controls for village fixed effects, age-group fixed effects, and interactions between village characteristics and age-group dummies, where village characteristics include an indicator for a suburban village, log of traveling time to nearest town or city (hours), log of area (km^2), and topographic characteristics (hills, mountains, plateaus, plains, and others)

An alternative way to examine pre-treatment trends is to look at the trends in observables of older cohorts born in treated and untreated villages. While the villages differ in their treatment timing, the older cohorts are never treated because they were born before the introduction of tap water. As a result, we should not observe different cohort trends in these villages. Figure 2.5 plots the differences in individual characteristics (i.e., male height, female height, male education, and female education) for the cohorts of 1955 to 1989 by five-year age groups between villages that received the first connection between 1998 and 2008 and villages that received the first connection after 2008. These plots reveal pre-treatment trends, because even the members of the youngest cohort, who were born in 1989, were not exposed to tap water *in utero*. For all dimensions, we observe similar trends between the two types of villages.

In Sect. 2.8, we conduct additional analyses to rule out other identification issues, such as potential confounding factors, sample selection, reporting error in the data, and measurement error in the treatment variable. In particular, in Sect. 2.8.5, we show that the interpretation of our DID estimate is not challenged by the issue of negative weights accompanied by treatment effect heterogeneity in two-way fixed effects models (de Chaisemartin and D'Haultfœuille 2020).

2.7 Effects of *in Utero* Exposure to Tap Water

In this section, we present the main results on height-for-age, then show the results for other health outcomes, and finally discuss the possible mechanisms mediating the persistent health effects of *in utero* exposure.

2.7.1 *Main Results on Height-for-Age*

Columns (1)–(4) of Table 2.3 report the main results for height-for-age z-scores of children aged 1–11 in 2010. We find a positive and highly significant (p-value < 0.01) effect of *in utero* exposure to tap water in all four specifications.[14] Although the FDR q-values are larger than the unadjusted p-values, the coefficients remain statistically significant. Assuming common cohort trends nationwide in column (1), we estimate that exposure to tap water *in utero* increases children's average height-for-age z-scores by 0.27. In column (2), we allow the cohort trends to vary across provinces and across villages with different characteristics. The point estimate changes to 0.3, reflecting the existence of different latent trends in child height across provinces and villages with different characteristics. Column (3) reports estimates from the specification controlling for *in utero* exposure to health facilities and the NCMS. The estimated coefficient on the treatment variable hardly changes. In our preferred specification in column (4), we further control for *in utero* exposure to electricity, roads, cable television, and landline phones, and the point estimate remains the same. Thus, we show that the effect of *in utero* exposure to tap water is not driven by other concurrent public programs. In summary, we find that on average, a child with *in utero* exposure to tap water is 0.3 standard deviations taller than his or her counterparts of the same age and gender without exposure.

To get a sense of the effect magnitude and to check the robustness of our z-score measure, column (5) of Table 2.3 reports the estimated effect on height measured in centimeters instead of z-scores. Holding everything else constant, exposure to tap water *in utero* increases a child's height by 4 cm. As one standard deviation of

---

[14] Following Adukia et al. (2020), in Sect. 2.8.6 we conduct a permutation test to show that the p-value in the main analysis is estimated correctly.

Table 2.3 The effect of *in utero* exposure to tap water on height of children aged 1–11 in 2010

Dep. var.:	Height-for-age z-score				Height in cm
	(1)	(2)	(3)	(4)	(5)
Tap water IU	0.270***	0.305***	0.304***	0.304***	4.045***
	(0.083)	(0.098)	(0.099)	(0.102)	(1.432)
	[0.020]	[0.020]	[0.020]	[0.021]	[0.025]
Observations	2982	2982	2982	2982	2982
R^2	0.330	0.406	0.407	0.408	0.799
Number of clusters	385	385	385	385	385
$\overline{Y}$ of the comparison group	–0.003	–0.003	–0.003	–0.003	102.6
Individual and household controls, village FE	Y	Y	Y	Y	Y
Cohort FE	Y	N	N	N	N
Province-cohort FE, village controls × FE	N	Y	Y	Y	Y
Health programs IU	N	N	Y	Y	Y
Other infrastructures IU	N	N	N	Y	Y

Notes *, **, and *** indicate significance at 10%, 5%, and 1%, respectively. The main sample consists of children aged between 13 and 132 months from the 2010 CFPS. Other sample restrictions are detailed in Sect. 2.5.3. Each column represents a separate regression. "Tap water IU" refers to *in utero* exposure to tap water, which equals one if a tap water connection is available in the village of birth in the year of conception and zero otherwise. The individual and household characteristics include gender, mother's age at birth, birth order, and both parents' years of schooling. The village characteristics used to construct interactions with cohort fixed effects include an indicator for a suburban village, log of traveling time to nearest town or city (hours), log of area (km^2), average years of schooling of 25–55-year-olds, and topographic characteristics (hill, mountain, plateau, plain, and other). Health programs IU refers to *in utero* exposure to health facilities and exposure to the New Cooperative Medical Scheme. Other infrastructures IU refers to a series of dummy variables measuring *in utero* exposure to electricity, roads, cable television, and landline phones. $\overline{Y}$ of the comparison group is the mean outcome of children who live in villages without a tap water connection in 2010. Standard errors in parentheses are clustered at the village level. FDR q-values are computed over all regressions in Tables 2.3 to 2.13 and are shown in brackets

the height distribution for a given gender-specific age group is around 14 cm, the point estimate for height in cm is consistent with the estimate for the height-for-age z-score.

We next check whether this substantial effect on height observed at ages 1–11 persists in later childhood. If the effect fades, then it reflects the existence of catch-up growth, that is, rapid physical growth compensating for past health insults (Currie and Vogl 2013). We explore the presence of catch-up growth by comparing the effect of *in utero* exposure on height in 2010 with that in 2014 for the same sample of children. We restrict the sample of analysis to children whose height data are available in both the 2010 and 2014 CFPS. These children were 1–11 years old in 2010, and 5–15 years old in 2014. The results in column (1) of Table 2.4 show that *in utero* exposure to tap water raises height-for-age z-scores in 2014 by 0.2. The effect remains significant, but the size drops by one-third compared to the 0.32 increase in height-for-age z-scores in 2010 using the same sample of children (column (3)). In columns (2) and (4), we compare the effects on height in cm. The effect on height in 2014 (2.6 cm) is about two-thirds the height gain in 2010 (4.3 cm). Overall, the comparison of the effects in 2010 and 2014 reveals the existence of catch-up growth.[15] Nevertheless, the effect on height after four years of catch-up growth in our study is still substantial. The effect size is similar in absolute value to the effect of *in utero* exposure to air pollution due to forest fires or severe famine.[16]

Given the significant costs incurred under the rural drinking water program, it is essential to know whether the benefits from expanding tap water connections are worth the cost. We conduct a cost–benefit analysis in Sect. 2.11 based on our estimated effect on height at ages 5–15, which would translate into an increase in future income (Persico et al. 2004). We find that *in utero* exposure to tap water has an internal rate of return beyond 11%, which is large enough to pass the cost–benefit test at reasonable discount rates.

2.7.2 Effects on Other Health Outcomes

We use height as a marker of childhood health throughout this study. To confirm that our estimated effect on the height-for-age z-score reflects improvements in childhood health, we estimate the effects of *in utero* exposure to tap water on other health outcomes measured at different stages of childhood for the sampled children aged 1–11 in 2010. The sample means of these outcome variables are reported in Table 2.5. In Table 2.6, we report the estimation results for birth and infancy outcomes, other childhood outcomes, and cause-specific morbidity since birth.

Birth and infancy outcomes — Column (1) of Table 2.6 Panel A reports the estimated effect on the incidence of low birth weight (less than 2,500 grams). Treated children are 1.7 percentage points less likely to have low birth weight, although the effect is not precisely estimated. Columns (2) and (3) of Panel A show that exposure to tap water significantly lowers the probability of experiencing illnesses and the

[15] We also explore the CFPS data collected in 2016 for the same group of children. We find that *in utero* exposure to tap water raises height-for-age z-scores (height) at ages 7–17 by 0.1 (2 cm), and the estimates are not significantly different from zero. The results suggest that the catch-up growth persists. However, the estimation is subject to the issues of sample attrition and low power. As migration becomes more common after age 15, when the compulsory schooling concludes, the sample size drops by one-third from 2010 to 2016. Therefore, the results using the 2016 data should be interpreted with caution.

[16] For example, Rosales-Rueda and Triyana (2019) show that *in utero* exposure to air pollution reduces height at age three by 0.35 standard deviations, which translates to a 1.5 cm reduction in height 10 and 17 years after the exposure. Chen and Zhou (2007) find a 3.03 cm decrease in height for those born or conceived during the Great Chinese Famine between 1959 and 1961, and Meng and Qian (2009) find that early childhood exposure to the same famine decreases height by 2.8 cm.

Table 2.4 Catch-up growth: Comparing the effects in 2010 and 2014

	Outcomes in 2014		Outcomes in 2010	
	Height-for-age z-score	Height in cm	Height-for-age z-score	Height in cm
	(1)	(2)	(3)	(4)
Tap water IU	0.201*	2.638*	0.319**	4.252**
	(0.104)	(1.579)	(0.136)	(1.924)
	[0.106]	[0.137]	[0.064]	[0.073]
Observations	2436	2436	2436	2436
R^2	0.399	0.785	0.412	0.809
Number of clusters	375	375	375	375
$\overline{Y}$ of the comparison group	0.018	131.691	0.032	103.007

Notes *, **, and *** indicate significance at 10%, 5%, and 1%, respectively. The sample consists of 2,437 children who are included in the main sample and have information on height available in both the 2010 and 2014 waves of the CFPS. Each column represents a separate regression of the outcome variable on Tap water IU (availability of a tap water connection in the village of birth in the year of conception). All regressions control for individual and household characteristics, village fixed effects, province-specific cohort fixed effects, and village controls interacted with cohort fixed effects, health programs IU, and other infrastructures IU. $\overline{Y}$ of the comparison group is the mean outcome of children who live in villages without a tap water connection in 2010. Standard errors in parentheses are clustered at the village level. FDR q-values are computed over all regressions in Tables 2.3 to 2.13 and are shown in brackets

probability of visiting doctors in the first year of life by 14 and 13 percentage points, respectively. The impacts are large, probably because infants are more frequently ill and the outcome variables are annual measures.

Other childhood outcomes — Panel B of Table 2.6 reports the estimated effects of *in utero* exposure on other childhood health outcomes. The estimated effect on weight adjusted for gender and age (weight-for-age) is close to zero. A possible explanation for the discrepancy between the effect on height and the effect on weight is that weight-for-age hinges more on recent rather than *in utero* conditions. The existing literature has shown that weight is more sensitive than height to contemporaneous nutritional deficiencies and morbidity, but less so to previous health insults (Thomas et al. 1996; de Onis 2000). A lack of access to safe drinking water during pregnancy could result in poor maternal health, underdevelopment of the fetus, and frequent illness episodes of the child after birth. These poor health outcomes would later manifest as lower height-for-age, but not necessarily lower weight-for-age during childhood.

Columns (2)–(5) report the estimates for other childhood health outcomes including experiencing illnesses the previous month, visiting doctors, being hospitalized, and having top 25% health expenditure the previous year. Although only the estimate for health expenditure is statistically significant, all estimates point toward the same conclusion—*in utero* exposure to tap water improves childhood health. When we average the outcomes in columns (2)–(5) into a health index, we find that the effect of tap water exposure *in utero* is statistically significant with a p-value of 0.06 and

Table 2.5 Summary statistics of other outcome variables

	Full sample	Exposed children	Unexposed children
	(1)	(2)	(3)
Panel A. Birth and infancy outcomes			
Low birth weight (< 2500 grams)[d]	0.069	0.054	0.075
Any illness in 1st year of life[d]	0.680	0.664	0.688
Any doctor visit in 1st year of life[d]	0.589	0.569	0.597
Panel B. Other childhood outcomes in 2010			
Weight-for-age z-score	–0.013	0.014	–0.024
Any illness the previous month[d]	0.335	0.339	0.333
Any doctor visit the previous year[d]	0.559	0.575	0.552
Total health expenditure the previous year (CNY)	459.991	479.865	451.695
Hospitalization the previous year[d]	0.088	0.095	0.085
Panel C. Cause-specific morbidity			
Any severe disease since birth[d]	0.619	0.642	0.610
Digestive[d]	0.072	0.070	0.072
Respiratory[d]	0.412	0.442	0.400
Waterborne infectious or parasitic[d]	0.031	0.036	0.030
Other infectious or parasitic[d]	0.016	0.011	0.017
Other[d]	0.089	0.083	0.091
Observations	3252	949	2303

Notes The table shows summary statistics of other outcome variables for a sample of 3,252 children conceived between 1998 and 2008 and aged 13–132 months in 2010. Exposed children are those with tap water exposure *in utero*. Other sample restrictions are detailed in Sect. 2.5.3.
[d] denotes dummy variables

an FDR q-value of 0.12. Overall, these results show that our estimated effect on the height-for-age z-score reflects improvements in the general health in childhood.

Cause-specific diseases — Table 2.6 Panel C reports the estimated effects of *in utero* exposure on cause-specific morbidity since birth. The CFPS recorded children's most severe morbidity from birth to date from a list of 153 types of diseases. The reported diseases are categorized into five mutually exclusive types: non-waterborne digestive diseases, respiratory diseases, waterborne infectious or parasitic diseases, other infectious or parasitic diseases, and other diseases.[17] We find that *in utero*

[17] Non-waterborne digestive diseases include diseases of the gastrointestinal tract, excluding waterborne infectious or parasitic diseases related to the gastrointestinal tract. Respiratory diseases include diseases of the respiratory system. Waterborne infectious or parasitic diseases include typhoid fever, bacterial food poisoning, dysentery, hepatitis A and other infectious gastrointestinal diseases, and schistosomiasis. The most common respiratory diseases in our sample include influenza (14%), common cold (9.7%), pneumonia (5.4%), and acute upper respiratory tract infection (5.4%). The most common non-waterborne digestive disease is acute or chronic gastroenteritis (2.6%). The most common waterborne disease is typhoid fever or paratyphoid fever (2%). These are also the six most

exposure to tap water lowers the probability of getting any severe diseases after birth by five percentage points. By disease type, our analysis shows that non-waterborne digestive diseases are the only type whose probability is lowered significantly by tap water exposure *in utero*, and the reduction is the most among all five types. For the other four types of diseases, including waterborne infectious or parasitic diseases, the estimates are relatively small in magnitude, and none are statistically significant.

These findings are consistent with the evidence in the existing literature on the strong causal link between water quality and the incidence of digestive diseases. Ebenstein (2012), for instance, detects a causal relationship between water contamination and the prevalence of digestive cancers, but not other types of cancers, in China. Alsan and Goldin (2019) find that improved water and sewage systems in the United States lower child mortality caused by digestive diseases, but do not affect deaths from etiologies with a different pathological basis. Therefore, our results suggest that the positive effect of exposure to tap water *in utero* on childhood health is likely due to the better quality of tap water compared to untreated water.

In particular, the finding of little effect on the incidence of waterborne diseases echoes the facts discussed in Sect. 1.1 that disease-causing microorganisms in drinking water have less adverse consequences in China. Although worldwide diarrhea is a leading cause of malnutrition in children under five years old, the common practice of boiling water before drinking in China protects children from getting infected by microorganisms in polluted water. As a result, exposure to treated tap water has limited effect in reducing diarrhea episodes for children.

However, boiling cannot remove chemical pollutants in the water. Thus, the positive effect of tap water exposure on childhood health may stem from the low concentration of chemical pollutants in treated tap water.[18] In Sect. 2.3.1, we review the existing evidence from the public health, epidemiological, and economic literature on the pathway from chemical contamination in water to the impaired development of fetuses and infants. Together with the existing evidence, our results suggest that exposure to chemical pollutants in water during pregnancy may impair the development of the fetus and lead to poor health outcomes even after birth.[19]

---

common diseases in our sample. Refer to *The CFPS Disease Code*, https://www.isss.pku.edu.cn/cfps/wdzx/sjwd/1357972.htm, accessed on October 14, 2018.

[18] Recontamination of stored boiled water could reduce the effectiveness of boiling practice in improving drinking water quality. Interpreting the removal of chemical pollutants as the driving force in the effect of tap water exposure relies on the assumption that improved access to safe drinking water does not trigger a change in the households' behavior of storing boiled water. Our finding that tap water exposure does not affect the incidence of waterborne diseases provides suggestive evidence for this assumption. Moreover, the incidence of diarrhea is low among Chinese children, suggesting that recontamination is a relatively minor issue in our setting.

[19] It is worth noting that the pathway from *in utero* exposure to chemical contamination to non-waterborne digestive diseases in early childhood is not well established in the literature. While our study provides suggestive evidence that the removal of chemical pollutants from water leads to a reduction in the incidence of non-waterborne digestive diseases, direct evidence on the causal link awaits future research with better data on water quality and child morbidity.

Table 2.6 Effects of *in utero* exposure to tap water on other health outcomes

	(1)	(2)	(3)	(4)	(5)	(6)
Panel A. Birth and infancy outcomes						
	Low birth weight (< 2,500 g)	Any illness by age one	Any doctor visit by age one			
Tap water IU	–0.017	–0.141***	–0.132**			
	(0.032)	(0.049)	(0.054)			
	[0.447]	[0.025]	[0.057]			
Observations	2670	2828	2819			
R^2	0.286	0.423	0.432			
Number of clusters	382	380	380			
$\overline{Y}$ of the comparison group	0.079	0.668	0.580			
Panel B. Other childhood outcomes in 2010						
	Weight-for-age z-score	Any illness the previous month	Any doctor visit the previous year	Hospitalized the previous year	Top 25% health exp. the previous year	Health index (2)–(5)
Tap water IU	–0.016	–0.033	–0.059	–0.040	–0.106**	–0.060*
	(0.111)	(0.058)	(0.053)	(0.035)	(0.047)	(0.032)
	[0.687]	[0.447]	[0.267]	[0.267]	[0.071]	[0.120]
Observations	3075	3234	3125	3125	3252	3120
R^2	0.357	0.330	0.454	0.278	0.352	0.417
Number of clusters	386	386	385	385	386	385
$\overline{Y}$ of the comparison group	–0.010	0.343	0.546	0.094	0.218	0.296
Panel C. Cause-specific morbidity						
		The type of most severe disease since birth				
	Any severe disease since birth	1. Digestive	2. Respiratory	3. Waterborne infectious or parasitic	4. Other infectious or parasitic	5. Other
Tap water IU	–0.050	–0.055**	–0.032	0.016	–0.007	0.027
	(0.048)	(0.026)	(0.056)	(0.019)	(0.008)	(0.031)
	[0.285]	[0.090]	[0.447]	[0.367]	[0.367]	[0.367]
Observations	3083	3083	3083	3083	3083	3083
R^2	0.606	0.265	0.480	0.409	0.334	0.294
Number of clusters	383	383	383	383	383	383
$\overline{Y}$ of the comparison group	0.625	0.070	0.413	0.032	0.018	0.091

Notes *, **, and *** indicate significance at 10%, 5%, and 1%, respectively. The main sample is used for analysis. Each column of each panel represents a separate regression of the outcome variable (shown as the column name) on Tap water IU (availability of a tap water connection in the village of birth in the year of conception). All regressions control for individual and household characteristics, village fixed effects, province-specific cohort fixed effects, and village controls interacted with cohort fixed effects, health programs IU, and other infrastructures IU. In Panel C, digestive diseases include diseases of the gastrointestinal tract, excluding waterborne infectious or parasitic diseases related to the gastrointestinal tract; respiratory diseases include diseases of the respiratory system; waterborne infectious or parasitic diseases include typhoid fever, bacterial food poisoning, dysentery, hepatitis A and other infectious gastrointestinal diseases, and schistosomiasis. $\overline{Y}$ of the comparison group is the mean outcome of children who live in villages without a tap water connection in 2010. Standard errors in parentheses are clustered at the village level. FDR q-values are computed over all regressions in Tables 2.3 to 2.13 and are shown in brackets

2.8 Robustness Checks

2.8.1 Dealing with the Reporting Error in the Year of First Connection

As mentioned in Sect. 2.5.2, in each village, a knowledgeable individual who had access to village statistical materials was invited to answer the village questionnaire of the CFPS survey. As part of the survey, they were asked to provide information on the year when a tap water connection first became available in the village. We use the answer to this question to construct the treatment variable. The reported data should be reliable, given that obtaining the first tap water connection is a salient and socially desirable event, and the information is available in village statistical materials, such as village chronicles of events. However, reporting error in the year of the first connection, if it exists and is correlated with outcome-determining (un)observables, may bias our estimates.

We address the issue of reporting error in two ways. Beckett et al. (2001) suggest that data quality likely deteriorates with the length of the recall period. Hence, we exclude villages whose reported year of the first connection is more than 16 years, 12 years, and 8 years ago—that is, if the reported year of the first connection is before 1994, 1998, or 2002. Columns (1)–(3) of Table 2.7 show that excluding observations from long-term recalls generates similar estimates to the main results.

Second, there is likely to be a correlation between interviewers' impressions of the quality of respondents' answers and the quality of the reported data. After completing each community questionnaire, the interviewers evaluated the reliability of each respondent's answers on a scale of 1 to 7, with 1 being very unreliable and 7 very reliable. We restrict our analysis to the sampled villages that received a score of at least 6. Column (4) of Table 2.7 shows that the estimate from this sample is larger than our main estimate. One possible explanation is that the reporting error, if present, may have attenuated the estimated effect of *in utero* exposure to tap water.

2.8.2 Dealing with the Measurement Error in the Treatment Variable

The CFPS did not collect the village-level exact date of the first tap water connection. In the main analysis we use the availability of a tap water connection at the village level in the conception year, TapwaterIU_{ct}, as a proxy for *in utero* exposure to tap water, without imposing any assumption on the timing of a village's first connection to tap water within a year. The proxy equals one if the conception year is equal to or greater than the year of the first tap water connection at the village level, and zero otherwise. It can precisely capture a child's *in utero* exposure to tap water if the conception year is after the year of the first connection (having full exposure *in utero* and $\text{TapwaterIU}_{ct} = 1$), or two years before the year of the first connection

Table 2.7 Robustness check: Reporting errors

	Dep. var.: Height-for-age z-score			
	Year of the first tap water connection			
	≥1994	≥1998	≥2002	Reliable village answers
	(1)	(2)	(3)	(4)
Tap water IU	0.300***	0.317***	0.329***	0.388***
	(0.111)	(0.117)	(0.118)	(0.132)
Observations	2592	2425	2303	1802
R^2	0.411	0.413	0.406	0.461
Number of clusters	315	295	275	243
$\overline{Y}$ of the comparison group	–0.003	–0.003	–0.003	0.037

Notes *, **, and *** indicate significance at 10%, 5%, and 1%, respectively. Each column represents a separate regression of Height-for-age z-score on Tap water IU (availability of a tap water connection in the village of birth in the year of conception) with the sample restriction (shown as the column name) imposed on the main sample. All regressions control for individual and household characteristics, village fixed effects, province-specific cohort fixed effects, and village controls interacted with cohort fixed effects, health programs IU, and other infrastructures IU. $\overline{Y}$ of the comparison group is the mean outcome of children who live in villages without a tap water connection in 2010. Standard errors in parentheses are clustered at the village level

(no exposure *in utero* and $\text{TapwaterIU}_{ct} = 0$). However, the proxy may be subject to the issue of measurement error if the conception year coincides the year of the first connection, or the conception year is one year before the first connection. For example, in a village that received the first connection in December 2005, a child conceived in January 2005 had no tap water exposure *in utero*, but the proxy equals one. In a village that got connected in January 2005, a child conceived in December 2004 had nine months of exposure *in utero*, but the proxy equals zero. At most 155 of the sampled children (4.8%) would suffer from this type of measurement error. This measurement error would bias the estimated treatment effect toward zero. This measurement error would attenuate the estimated impact of *in utero* exposure to tap water. As we detect a positive effect of *in utero* exposure to tap water on childhood health, controlling for the measurement error would strengthen our results. Indeed, dropping these children increases the estimated effect on the height-for-age from 0.304 to 0.389 standard deviations.

In this section, we investigate the issue of measurement error in the treatment variable by considering an alternative measure, the number of months *in utero* with tap water exposure. We first make four different assumptions on the timing of a village's first connection to tap water in a given connection year. Under each assumption, we assign the exact month of the first connection to the 404 sampled villages accordingly.

Assumption 1 The first connection takes place in any month from January to December with an equal probability.

Under this assumption, we randomly assign the 12 months from January to December to the 404 villages, so that the villages' first connection month is uniformly distributed after assignment.

Assumption 2 The first connection takes place with an equal probability in any non-busy month.

Busy months refer to three months: May, June, and October, the period in a year when the farm work is usually intensive. Under this assumption, we randomly assign the nine non-busy months to the 404 villages so that after the assignment the villages' first connection month is uniformly distributed, and no village receives the first connection in the three busy months.

Assumption 3 The month of the first tap water connection for a village is drawn from a discrete uniform distribution with 12 possible values indicating 12 months.

We first sample a month from the uniform distribution with replacement, and then assign the month to one village as the village's month of the first tap water connection. We do the same sampling for all 404 villages.

Assumption 4 The month of the first tap water connection for a village is drawn from a discrete uniform distribution with nine values indicating nine non-busy months.

The same sampling and assignment procedures as those in Assumption 3 are applied, except that the possible values of the uniform distribution include only nine non-busy months.

We are able to construct a sampled child's number of months *in utero* being exposed to tap water using the assigned month of the village's first tap water connection, the reported year of the first connection, and the child's birth date. Applying the preferred specification (column (4) of Table 2.3) for estimation with TapwaterIU_{ct} replaced by the alternative measure generates an estimate capturing the effect of one additional month of exposure *in utero* on children's height-for-age. Under each assumption, we do the random assignment 2,000 times and end up with 2,000 estimates.

We plot the distribution of the simulation results in Fig. 2.6. For ease of comparison with the main results, we add to each plotting a dash line which falls on 0.033, the value calculated from the main estimate. We learn from the main analysis that having exposure to tap water *in utero* increases children's height-for-age by 0.304 standard deviations. The mean gestation length is 9.27 months for sampled children. Assuming a linear effect of gestation length on height, the main estimate suggests a 0.033 standard deviation increase in height-for-age for one additional month of tap water exposure *in utero*. For all four assumptions, the mean and the median of the estimated effect of one additional month of *in utero* exposure is around 0.031. Under each of the four assumptions, we cannot reject the null hypothesis that the mean (or median) of the simulated estimates is equal to the main estimate (p-values greater than 0.5).

To summarize, we deal with the measurement error in tap water exposure *in utero* by making assumptions on the timing of the first tap water connection in the village

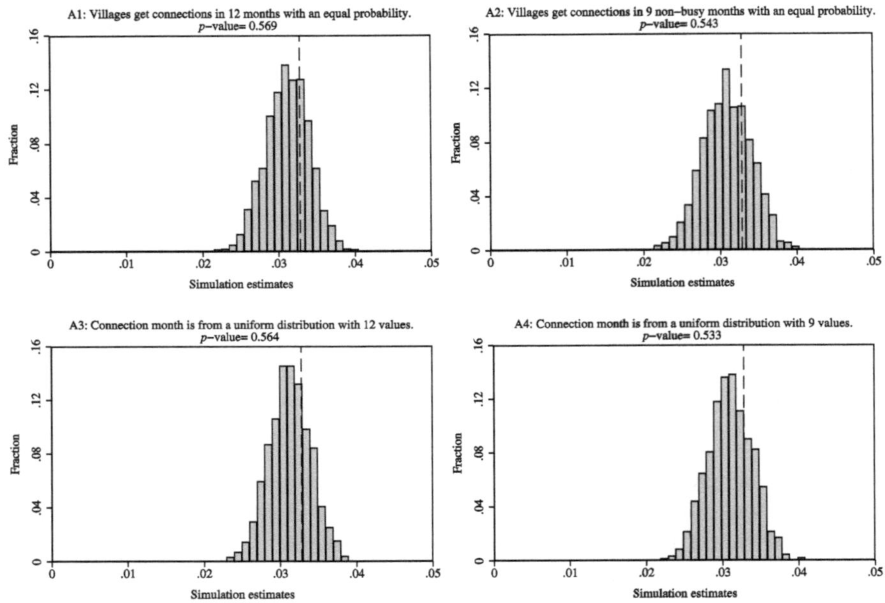

Fig. 2.6 Simulation results from using the number of months *in utero* with exposure. *Notes* Each histogram displays the distribution of the simulation results from regressions using the number of months *in utero* with tap water exposure as a measure of *in utero* exposure to tap water under the assumption shown as the histogram title. The dashed line falls on 0.033, which indicates the increase in the height-for-age z-score for one additional month of tap water exposure *in utero* calculated from the main estimate (column (4) of Table 2.3). See Sect. 2.8.2 for details of the simulation

within a year and constructing a measure which captures the length of exposure *in utero*. The simulation results show that the estimates under all four assumptions are close to the main results. Because the proxy for *in utero* exposure to tap water in the main analysis, the availability of a tap water connection at the village level in the conception year, does not rely on any assumption on the timing of the village-level tap water connection, we prefer to employ the availability measure in our main analysis.

2.8.3 Selection

Our estimated effect would be biased if the sample of children used for analysis is not randomly selected. Three types of sample selection are potentially the most problematic: fertility selection, mortality selection, and migration. Due to a lack of accurate death data, we cannot test for the mortality selection directly in this study. However, mortality selection, if any, would not overturn our main findings. First, the child mortality rate is low in China. According to the WHO, China's under-five mortality rate (probability of dying by age five per 1,000 live births) in 2010 was 15.76, while the global average was 51.[20] Moreover, if exposure to tap water *in utero* lowers child mortality as shown in existing studies (He and Perlof 2016; Alsan and Goldin 2019), our results may reflect a lower bound of the real effect of *in utero* exposure to tap water. This is because survivors of the positive event tend to be negatively selected (Almond and Currie 2011). Below, we show that sample selection is unlikely to be a serious concern in our study. In particular, in the discussion of fertility selection we implicitly address the issue of mortality selection and detect no evidence of biases.

Fertility selection

If tap water availability tends to affect women's fertility outcomes, both the population of children who were born and the timing of the birth would be different from what they would otherwise have been. For example, if parents care more about the child's *in utero* conditions, they may decide to give birth to a child in response to the availability of tap water. Then, parents' decision to have a child is correlated with both *in utero* exposure to tap water and the child's outcome. As a result, the estimation based on the sample of children born could generate biased results. To address this concern, we follow La Ferrara et al. (2012) and estimate the probability that a woman gives birth in a given year between 1998 and 2009 as a function of tap water accessibility at the village level, and other individual and village controls.[21] We construct a data set with the retrospective history of women's fertility outcomes between ages 15 and 49. We estimate the following linear probability model:

$$F_{ict} = \psi \text{Tapwater}_{c,t-1} + X_{ict}\beta + \text{Otherprograms}_{c,t-1}\rho + \gamma_c + \theta_{pt} + \phi_t Z_c + \epsilon_{ict}, \tag{2.8}$$

where F_{ict} is the fertility outcome of a woman i living in village c in year t. It equals one if the woman gives birth to a living child in year t and zero otherwise.[22] The treatment variable, $\text{Tapwater}_{c,t-1}$, is an indicator for the availability of a tap water connection in village c. It equals one if a tap water connection is available in year $t-1$ to account for the length of gestation and zero otherwise. The parameter of interest ψ captures the effect of having a tap water connection at the village level on the likelihood of giving birth in the following year. X_{ict} is a vector of individual controls, including age, number of living children in year t, years of education, and the quadratic terms of the above-mentioned variables. $\text{Otherprograms}_{c,t-1}$ is a vector of dummy variables capturing the availability of health facilities, NCMS, electricity,

---

20 Data are from the Global Health Observatory of the WHO at https://www.who.int/data/gho/data/indicators/indicator-details/GHO/under-five-mortality-rate-(probability-of-dying-by-age-5-per-1000-live-births), accessed on 22 November 2020.

21 We choose the period that consists of the birth years of the children in the main sample.

22 We notice that among the 6,917 fertility outcomes with F_{ict} equal to one, only 2 did not survive to 2010. Considering that the under-five mortality rate was 15.76 per 1,000 live births in China in 2010, we cannot rule out the possibility that some women did not report the births of children who had died by 2010. Then the fertility outcome may actually capture mortality, that is, F_{ict} equals one if the woman gives birth to a living child in year t and the child is still alive in 2010, and zero otherwise. Therefore, the analysis for the fertility selection may also pertain to the mortality selection. However, in the absence of more evidence, we should refrain from over-interpreting the results from the analysis of fertility selection.

Table 2.8 Robustness check: Fertility selection

Dep. var.:	Whether giving birth in year t			
Sample:	Full sample	Age 15–19	Age 20–34	Age 35–49
	(1)	(2)	(3)	(4)
Tap water$_{t-1}$	–0.002	0.004	–0.008	0.001
	(0.004)	(0.006)	(0.008)	(0.003)
Observations	94575	15004	38390	41181
R^2	0.065	0.070	0.078	0.043
Number of clusters	343	343	343	343
$\overline{Y}$ of the comparison group	0.046	0.012	0.103	0.008

Notes *, **, and *** indicate significance at 10%, 5%, and 1%, respectively. The sample consists of the retrospective history of 15–49-year-old women's fertility outcomes between 1998 and 2009. Each column of each panel represents a separate regression of whether giving birth in year t on Tap water$_{t-1}$ (an indicator for the availability of a tap water connection in the village of living in year $t-1$) with the sample restriction (shown as the column name) imposed. All regressions control for individual characteristics in year t, village health programs and other infrastructures in year $t-1$, and fixed effects for village, province-specific year, and village controls interacted with year. See Sect. 2.8.3 for details. Standard errors in parentheses are clustered at the village level

roads, cable television, and landline phones in the village of living in year $t-1$. γ_c represents village fixed effects. To account for different pre-existing trends in fertility rates across villages, we include the province-specific year fixed effects θ_{pt} and the interactions between a set of village controls and year dummies, denoted by $\phi_t Z_c$. The set of village controls contains an indicator for a suburban village, traveling time to nearest town or city in hours, area in square kilometers, average years of schooling of 25–55-year-olds, and topographic characteristics.

In Table 2.8, we report the results from the full sample of women aged 15–49 and the subsamples by age brackets (15–19, 20–34, and 35–49). The estimates are close to zero, providing no evidence that fertility selection is biasing the estimates.

Migration

Other sources of sample selection are household or individual migration. Below, we discuss the possible selection issues of three types of migration: (1) migration before a child's birth, (2) migration into a surveyed village after a child's birth, and (3) migration out of a surveyed village after a child's birth.

(1) Migration before a child's birth

Among the sampled children, some may be from households that migrated into the surveyed villages before the children were born. It is of concern if a household's migration decision is correlated with the destination's tap water accessibility and the children's outcomes. For example, a household may move to a village before a child's birth to take advantage of tap water availability, and children born in such households may have better health outcomes regardless of tap water exposure. We address this concern by identifying these households.

The CFPS asks households when they moved into the current residential unit. We use this information to construct an indicator of "mover," which equals one if a household moved into the current residential unit after a tap water connection first became available in the village but before the child's birth, and zero otherwise. Among 2,794 children whose "mover" status is available, about 10% are "movers." However, we cannot distinguish whether a household moved into the current residential unit from a different residential unit in the same village (moves within village) or from another village (moves across villages). The former case is common and would not bias our estimates. The latter case is rare owing to China's strict household registration system (*hukou*), but would lead to biased estimates if "movers" are different from other households.

We first conduct a balancing test to compare children whose households are considered to be "movers" with other children. We detect no significant difference between these two groups of children for all observed individual and household characteristics (detailed regression results are reported in Table 2.9). Next, to account for the potential confounding effect of migration before a child's birth on our main estimate, we include the indicator of "mover" in our preferred specification (column (4) of Table 2.3) for the estimation. The results reported in Panel A of Table 2.10 show that the estimated effect of *in utero* exposure to tap water is very stable before and after controlling for the indicator of "mover." Put together, these findings suggest that our main estimate is not biased by household migration before a child's birth.

(2) Migration into a surveyed village after a child's birth

Some children who were surveyed in 2010 might have moved into a surveyed village after birth. The sample restrictions imposed in the main analysis rule out the possibility of after-birth across-county migration into a surveyed village but do not rule out after-birth within-county migration. To check whether our main estimate is sensitive to the sample restrictions, we assume that all children in the 2010 CFPS were interviewed in their villages of birth and run regressions with the children who fail the sample restrictions included. The new estimate is reported in Panel B of Table 2.10. The estimated effect of *in utero* exposure to tap water on the height-for-age z-score is now 0.204 standard deviations, which is still significant at the 5% level but smaller in magnitude than our main estimate shown in Table 2.3.

We argue that the estimate of a 0.2 standard deviation increase in height-for-age is a lower-bound of the treatment effect of *in utero* tap water exposure. We consider two possible cases. First, households relocate after the child's birth without tap water accessibility at the village level in mind. Then the assumption of classical errors-in-variables holds, that is, the measurement error in *in utero* exposure is uncorrelated with the unobserved real exposure. Under this assumption, the estimated effect of tap water exposure is attenuated to zero. Second, households relocate with tap water accessibility at the village level in mind. Although the relocation behavior is not random, it is more likely that households sort themselves into villages with better facilities. For example, households from villages without a tap water connection might be attracted by the tap water connection of the surveyed villages and move in to take advantage of the good accessibility. In this case, some of the excluded children

Table 2.9 Balancing test: Migration before a child's birth

Dep. var.:	Boy	Age in months	Mother's age at birth	Birth order	Father's years of schooling	Mother's years of schooling
	(1)	(2)	(3)	(4)	(5)	(6)
Moved for tap	0.057	0.414	0.199	–0.015	–0.371	0.072
	(0.045)	(0.296)	(0.541)	(0.070)	(0.359)	(0.375)
Observations	3042	3042	3018	2862	3010	3009
R^2	0.142	0.991	0.184	0.293	0.379	0.478
Number of clusters	382	382	382	382	382	382
$\overline{Y}$ of the comparison group	0.552	72.256	26.687	1.755	7.260	5.821
Dep. var.:	NCMS IU	Health facility IU	Electricity IU	Road IU	Cable IU	Landline phone IU
	(7)	(8)	(9)	(10)	(11)	(12)
Moved for tap	–0.003	0.007	0.011	–0.014	0.006	–0.021
	(0.027)	(0.010)	(0.013)	(0.017)	(0.024)	(0.014)
Observations	2993	3016	2959	2994	2962	2958
R^2	0.743	0.956	0.945	0.839	0.805	0.856
Number of clusters	373	375	372	374	371	366
$\overline{Y}$ of the comparison group	0.303	0.428	0.822	0.620	0.320	0.680

Notes *, **, and *** indicate significance at 10%, 5%, and 1%, respectively. The main sample is used for analysis. Each column represents a separate regression of the outcome variable (shown as the column name) on Moved for tap (an indicator for households that moved into the current residential unit after a tap water connection becomes available in the village but before the child's birth). All regressions control for fixed effects for village and conception year. $\overline{Y}$ of the comparison group is the mean outcome of children who live in villages without a tap water connection in 2010. Standard errors in parentheses are clustered at the village level

who are considered to be treated are in fact untreated. Then the estimated effect is also biased toward zero. Therefore, we conclude that in either case, including the moved children in the analysis yields a lower bound of the treatment effect.

The same argument applies to after-birth within-county migration to a surveyed village. Since we detect a positive treatment effect of *in utero* exposure to tap water in the main analysis, addressing the possible issue of this within-county migration would strengthen our findings.

(3) Migration out of a surveyed village after a child's birth

Our main sample does not contain children who were born in the surveyed villages but had left the village of birth by the survey time, due to a lack of information on health outcomes. It is of concern if the migration decision is correlated with the treatment variable and the outcome. For example, if *in utero* exposure to tap water leads to better health outcomes, and healthier children are more likely to leave home at a younger age, then the effect on childhood health could be underestimated. Here, we consider sample selection issues resulting from this type of migration.

We examine whether *in utero* exposure to tap water affects the likelihood of children's absence from the survey data when their households are surveyed. Among 3,640 children who were from the surveyed households and were 13–132 months old in 2010, 388 are not included in the final sample because they were not present during the survey. For these unsurveyed children, we can determine whether they were exposed to tap water *in utero* by using information on the birth date reported by their parents or other household members. We assume the length of gestation to be nine months to deduce the year of conception. Using our preferred specification (column (4) of Table 2.3) for the estimation, we detect no effect of tap water exposure *in utero* on the probability of not being surveyed (column (1) in Panel C of Table 2.10).

We further check whether *in utero* exposure to tap water affects a child or a household's decision to leave the child's village of birth by the age of 132 months. Due to a lack of information on households that had moved to other villages by 2010, we use a sample of children aged 0–84 months in 2010 who were not yet 132 months old in 2014. The outcome variable is an indicator of being absent in the 2014 CFPS. Again, we apply our preferred specification for the estimation. Column (2) in Panel C of Table 2.10 shows that *in utero* exposure to tap water has a small and insignificant effect on the likelihood of absence in the 2014 CFPS. Therefore, we conclude that our estimates are unlikely to be biased by the sample selection due to migration after a child's birth.

2.8.4 Potential Confounders

Our main analysis shows the robustness of our results to confounding factors, such as *in utero* exposure to health facilities, health insurance programs, and other types of public infrastructures including electricity, roads, cable television, and landline phones. In this subsection, we discuss the potential confounding effect of household income and household agricultural work status.

The CFPS data do not contain any information on household income before the conception of the children in our sample. As the household income measured in 2010 is not pre-determined, we do not include it in our empirical model. As a robustness check, in Table 2.11, we show the results from regressions controlling for current household income and a dummy for agricultural households. Our estimates do not change.

2.8.5 Heterogeneous Treatment Effects and Negative Weights

Recently, de Chaisemartin and D'Haultfœuille (2020) raise concerns about the interpretation of DID estimates. According to their study, our DID estimate is the weighted sum of the average treatment effects (ATE) for each treated cell (a cohort in a village with *in utero* exposure to tap water). The weights associated with the ATEs can be

Table 2.10 Robustness check: Migration

	(1)	(2)
Panel A. Migration before birth		
	Dep. var.: Height-for-age z-score	
Tap water IU	0.331*** (0.113)	0.337*** (0.114)
Moved in for tap		–0.155 (0.109)
Observations	2794	2794
R^2	0.414	0.415
Number of clusters	381	381
$\overline{Y}$ of the comparison group	0.021	0.021
Panel B. Migration into a surveyed village after birth		
	Dep. var.: Height-for-age z-score	
Tap water IU	0.204** (0.085)	
Observations	3804	
R^2	0.370	
Number of clusters	396	
$\overline{Y}$ of the comparison group	0.002	
Panel C. Migration out of a surveyed village after birth (Dep. var. shown as column name)		
	Children not in the main sample	Children not surveyed in 2014
Tap water IU	–0.009 (0.030)	0.022 (0.047)
Observations	3640	2289
R^2	0.397	0.359
Number of clusters	396	377
$\overline{Y}$ of the comparison group	0.078	0.142

Notes *, **, and *** indicate significance at 10%, 5%, and 1%, respectively. Each column of each panel represents a separate regression of the outcome variable on Tap water IU (availability of a tap water connection in the village of birth in the year of conception). All regressions control for individual and household characteristics, village fixed effects, province-specific cohort fixed effects, and village controls interacted with cohort fixed effects, health programs IU, and other infrastructures IU. The regressions in Panel A additionally control for "Moved in for tap" (an indicator for household moving into the current residential unit after the first connection of tap water in the village but before the child's birth). Only children in the main sample with moving information available are included. In Panel B, we add to the main sample those children whose village of birth does not match with the village of living at the survey time. In column (1) of Panel C, among 3,640 children aged 13–132 months in 2010 whose households were surveyed, 388 children have not finished the individual survey and hence are not included in the main sample. In column (2) of Panel C, among 2,289 children aged 0–84 months in 2010, 326 are not found in the 2014 CFPS data. Standard errors in parentheses are clustered at the village level

Table 2.11 Robustness check: Controlling for current household income and farming status

	(1)	(2)	(3)	(4)	(5)	(6)
Panel A. Height and birth and infancy outcomes						
	Height-for-age z-score	Height in cm	Low birth weight (<2,500 g)	Any illness by age one	Any doctor visit by age one	
Tap water IU	0.303***	4.030***	−0.017	−0.142***	−0.133**	
	(0.102)	(1.431)	(0.032)	(0.050)	(0.055)	
Observations	2982	2982	2670	2828	2819	
R^2	0.409	0.799	0.287	0.424	0.434	
Number of clusters	385	385	382	380	380	
$\overline{Y}$ of the comparison group	−0.003	102.611	0.079	0.668	0.580	
Panel B. Other childhood outcomes in 2010						
	Weight-for-age z-score	Any illness the previous month	Any doctor visit the previous year	Hospitalized the previous year	Top 25% health exp. the previous year	Health index (2)–(5)
Tap water IU	−0.014	−0.033	−0.059	−0.039	−0.104**	−0.059*
	(0.111)	(0.058)	(0.054)	(0.035)	(0.046)	(0.032)
Observations	3075	3234	3125	3125	3252	3120
R^2	0.359	0.333	0.454	0.278	0.353	0.418
Number of clusters	386	386	385	385	386	385
$\overline{Y}$ of the comparison group	−0.010	0.343	0.546	0.094	0.218	0.296
Panel C. Cause-specific morbidity						
		The type of most severe disease since birth				
	Any severe disease since birth	1. Digestive	2. Respiratory	3. Waterborne infectious or parasitic	4. Other infectious or parasitic	5. Other
Tap water IU	−0.051	−0.055**	−0.033	0.017	−0.007	0.027
	(0.048)	(0.026)	(0.056)	(0.019)	(0.009)	(0.031)
Observations	3083	3083	3083	3083	3083	3083
R^2	0.606	0.266	0.480	0.411	0.334	0.296
Number of clusters	383	383	383	383	383	383
$\overline{Y}$ of the comparison group	0.625	0.070	0.413	0.032	0.018	0.091

Notes *, **, and *** indicate significance at 10%, 5%, and 1%, respectively. The main sample is used for analysis. Each column of each panel represents a separate regression of the outcome variable (shown as the column name) on Tap water IU (availability of a tap water connection in the village of birth in the year of conception). All regressions control for individual and household characteristics, village fixed effects, province-specific cohort fixed effects, and village controls interacted with cohort fixed effects, health programs IU, and other infrastructures IU. In Panel C, digestive diseases include diseases of the gastrointestinal tract, excluding waterborne infectious or parasitic diseases related to the gastrointestinal tract; respiratory diseases include diseases of the respiratory system; waterborne infectious or parasitic diseases include typhoid fever, bacterial food poisoning, dysentery, hepatitis A and other infectious gastrointestinal diseases, and schistosomiasis. $\overline{Y}$ of the comparison group is the mean outcome of children who live in villages without a tap water connection in 2010. Standard errors in parentheses are clustered at the village level

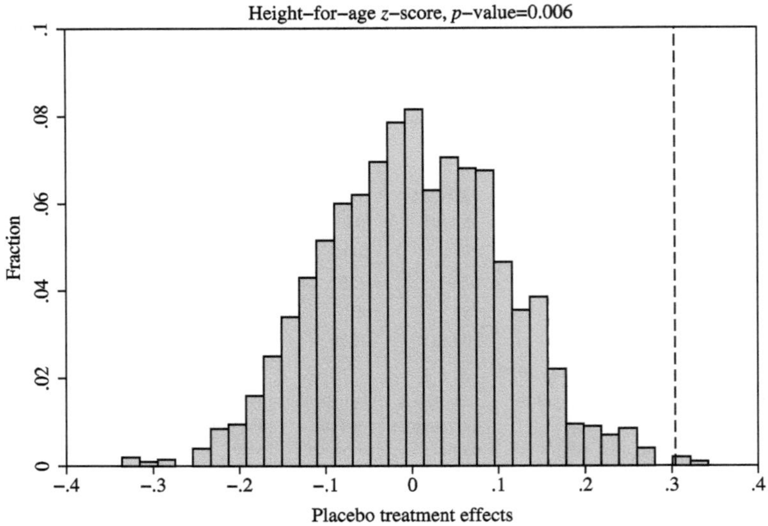

Fig. 2.7 Estimated coefficients from the permutation placebo test. *Notes* The histogram displays the distribution of placebo treatment effect of *in utero* exposure to tap water on height-for-age *z*-scores from 2,000 random assignments of the year a village first received a tap water connection. The dashed line falls on the main estimate of 0.304 taken from column (4) of Table 2.3. The *p*-value of 0.006 is the proportion of placebo estimates that are equal to or larger in absolute value than the main estimate of 0.304. See Sect. 2.8.6 for the details of the permutation test

negative, which could be an issue when the ATEs are heterogeneous across villages or cohorts. In an extreme case, when negative weights are large and correlated with the heterogeneous treatment effects, the DID estimate can have a different sign from all ATEs. We address this concern by applying the method of de Chaisemartin and D'Haultfœuille (2020) to calculate negative weights in our main analysis. We find that using the full sample, 33% of the weights are negative with a sum of −0.189. Once we drop villages where even the oldest children were treated, that is, villages receiving a tap water connection before 1998, only 13% of the weights are negative with a sum of −0.022. These results imply that most of the negative weights are assigned to ATEs for villages where children who differ in the conception year are all treated *in utero*. Moreover, we find that excluding villages that received the first tap water connection before 1998 yields an estimate very close to the main estimate, suggesting no evidence of heterogeneous treatment effects.[23] To conclude, we believe that the interpretation of our DID estimate is not challenged by the issue of negative weights accompanied by treatment effect heterogeneity.

[23] Our DID estimates are very stable when we exclude villages receiving the first tap water connection before 1994, 1998, and 2002. See Table 2.7.

2.8.6 Permutation Test

Following Adukia et al. (2020), we verify whether the p-value in our main analysis is correctly estimated. We conduct 2,000 random assignments. In each one, we generate a placebo year of the first connection for each village by randomly dividing the 404 villages into 13 groups with different timing of the first tap water connection: one before 1998, one after 2008, and 11 between 1998 and 2008 (one group for each year). The number of villages in each group is consistent with that in the actual data, so that each randomization can produce a histogram the same as that in Fig. 2.2. We then estimate Equation (2.7) as if the placebo year were the actual year of the first connection.

Figure 2.7 shows the distribution of the placebo estimated effect of *in utero* exposure to tap water on height-for-age. All placebo estimates are centered around zero, and only 0.6% of the placebo estimates in absolute value are equal to or larger than the main estimate of 0.304. This test suggests that the p-value in the main analysis is estimated correctly.

2.8.7 Event Study Analysis Using a Sample with Balanced Event Times

In the event study analysis in Sect. 2.6.1, the event times are unbalanced for the range from −3 to 4 that we are interested in. Specifically, children conceived in 2006 can never have an event time of 5, children conceived in 2007 can never have an event time of 4 or 5, and children conceived in 2008 can never have an event time of 3, 4, or 5. In contrast, children conceived between 1998 and 2005 can have any event time falling in the range from −3 to 4. Consequently, children with an event time of greater than or equal to 3 tend to be older than those with an event time less than 3, leading to the concern that the children sampled are not comparable across event times.

To address this concern, we conduct the event study analysis again using a sample with balanced event times. We only keep children who were conceived before the year of 2006 and were aged at least 48 months old in 2010. In this sample, all the event times between −3 and 4 can map to children conceived in the same year range from 1998 to 2005. Figure 2.8 plots the estimates for this sample. The estimates of negative event times are similar to, if not larger than, those in Figure 2.3. The estimates of nonnegative event times remain very close to zero. Hence, using the sample with balanced event times does not change the conclusion from the event study analysis in Sect. 2.6.1.

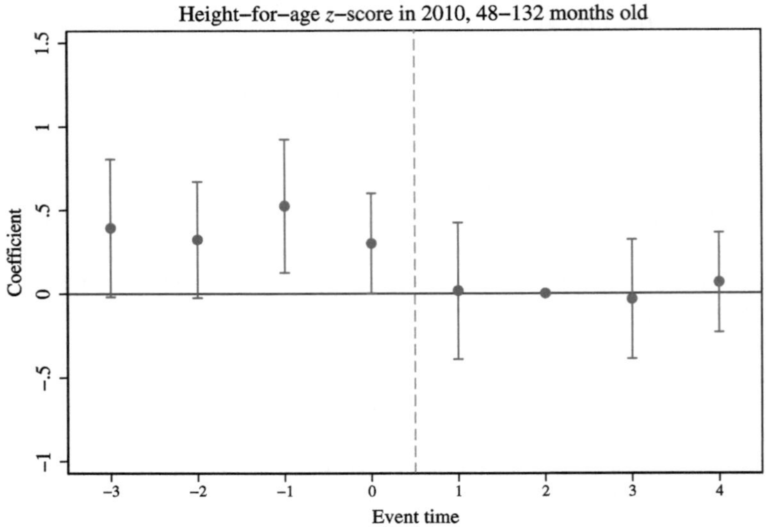

Fig. 2.8 Event study estimates of tap water exposure on older children's height-for-age. *Notes* The figure shows the coefficients and 90% confidence intervals (based on standard errors clustered at the village level) from the event study analysis. The sample consists of children conceived between 1998 and 2005 and aged 48–132 months in 2010. Event time is defined as the difference between the year when a tap water connection first becomes available in a child's birth village and the year of conception. The regression includes event time dummies, village fixed effects, and conception year fixed effects. The event time of 2 is taken as the base group. Left of the dashed line are the groups that had been exposed to tap water at least since the year of conception. Right of the dashed line are the groups that were exposed to tap water only after the year of conception

2.9 Potential Channels

In this section, we explore the mechanisms underlying the persistent effects of *in utero* tap water exposure on height-for-age. We discuss two potential channels implied by a simple model of human capital formation adapted from Cunha and Heckman (2007) and Heckman (2007) (outlined in Sect. 2.4). The first is a direct channel, operating through the direct effect of exposure to tap water *in utero* as a form of health investment that improves health before age one. Because human capital, including health, is *self-productive*, better health before age one would lead to better health at later ages. The second is a behavioral channel, based on the idea that the improvement in *in utero* conditions and health before age one may induce more health investments by parents, which improves children's health at later ages.

We test these two channels by discussing the heterogeneity in the impact of *in utero* tap water exposure by maternal education.[24] Our choice of maternal education in the heterogeneity analysis is motivated by existing literature documenting considerable

[24] A mother's educational level is considered "low" if her schooling is less than nine years and "high" otherwise. We then divide the sampled children by mother's educational level and run regressions

heterogeneities in the effects of *in utero* conditions by maternal education (Almond et al. 2018). In most cases, children born to low-educated mothers are more exposed and sensitive to worse *in utero* conditions (e.g., Currie 2011). In particular, when we consider safe drinking water, low-educated mothers are less likely to take preventive measures (such as purchasing bottled water and using private water treatment tools) to protect themselves and their children from contaminated drinking water than high-educated mothers. For example, Currie et al. (2013) find that drinking water contamination has larger consequences on the health of infants born to low-educated mothers.

The CFPS data allow us to check whether household choices of drinking water differ by maternal education and by the availability of a tap water connection in the village.[25] Table 2.12 reports our findings. In villages that have no tap water connection, households with low-educated mothers are less likely to use safe water for cooking than those with high-educated mothers. On the other hand, in villages with a tap water connection, no significant difference is detected in the choice of water used for cooking between households with low- and high-educated mothers. As households tend to use the same type of water for drinking and cooking, we expect that children of low-educated mothers would benefit more from *in utero* exposure to publicly provided tap water.

Column (1) of Table 2.13 confirms that children of low-educated mothers gain more height from *in utero* exposure to tap water than those of high-educated mothers, and the difference is statistically significant. This finding echoes the existing evidence that *in utero* exposure to contaminated water has the most detrimental effect on the infants of low-educated mothers (e.g., Currie et al. 2013). Next, we discuss the two potential channels by estimating the heterogeneous treatment effects on health before age one and postnatal health investments from parents.

2.9.1 The Direct Channel

Columns (2) to (4) of Table 2.13 show the effects on birth and infancy health outcomes by maternal education. We find that *in utero* exposure to tap water lowers the probability of low birth weight and the incidence of illnesses and doctor visits in the

---

separately in the two subsamples. Hausman tests are implemented to check whether the differences in the estimated treatment effects are statistically significant between the subsamples.

[25] Another possibility is that low-educated mothers boil water less diligently than high-educated ones in the absence of tap water. We use a sample of rural women aged 65 and over from the 2008–2009 wave of the CLHLS to explore this possibility. The survey collects information on individuals' choice of drinking water and whether they routinely boil water before drinking. Unfortunately, we lack details on the frequency and extent of boiled water consumption and the methods of storing boiled water. We find that more than 90% of the rural women reported drinking boiled water, no matter tap water was their main source of drinking water or not. Moreover, for those who reported not drinking tap water, there is no correlation between years of schooling and the probability of drinking boiled water. This finding suggests that the heterogeneity in the treatment effect could not be explained by the difference in the boiling practice. We thank an anonymous referee for this point.

Table 2.12 Household choices of water for cooking

Dep. var.:	Household using safe water for cooking	
Sample:	No tap water in village	Having tap water in village
	(1)	(2)
Low-educated mother	–0.042*	–0.008
	(0.024)	(0.051)
Observations	694	718
R^2	0.581	0.595
Number of clusters	81	103
$\overline{Y}$	0.135	0.616

Notes *, **, and *** indicate significance at 10%, 5%, and 1%, respectively. Households that had at least one child aged 0–60 months in the 2010 CFPS are divided into two groups by the availability of a tap water connection in the village in 2010: no tap water in village (column (1)) and having tap water in village (column (2)). Each column represents a separate regression of household using safe water for cooking (an indicator for household using tap water, mineral water, purified water, or filtered water for cooking in 2010) on low-educated mother (an indicator for schooling less than nine years). All regressions control for village fixed effects, mother's age in 2010, number of children under age five, number of household members, and whether having any child aged 0–12 months at the survey time. $\overline{Y}$ is the mean outcome of the households in the respective group. Standard errors in parentheses are clustered at the county level

first year of life, but only for children of low-educated mothers. Although the effects on both subsamples are not precisely estimated for low birth weight, the difference between subsamples is statistically significant. Hence, for children of low-educated mothers, *in utero* exposure to tap water improves their birth and infancy outcomes more than those of high-educated mothers. The heterogeneity in the effects on these outcomes is in line with the heterogeneity in the effect on height-for-age, suggesting that the direct effect on health before age one could be one of the channels through which *in utero* tap water exposure improves childhood health.

2.9.2 *The Behavioral Channel*

Besides the direct effect of *in utero* exposure to tap water on health at birth and in infancy, we would like to know whether parents change health investments as a response to the exposure. We use duration of breastfeeding, health-seeking behavior, and take-up of private health insurance to measure health investments from parents.[26] The last three columns of Table 2.13 report the estimated effects on parental

[26] Existing studies have used duration of breastfeeding (Adhvaryu and Nyshadham 2016; Adhvaryu et al. 2019) and health-seeking behavior (Rossi and Villar 2020) as parental investment outcomes. Here, duration of breastfeeding is measured in months. The indicator of health-seeking behavior takes the value one if the parents state that they would seek formal healthcare when the child is sick and zero otherwise. The indicator of private health insurance take-up takes the value one if the parents have purchased private health insurance for the child and zero otherwise.

Table 2.13 Heterogeneous effects of *in utero* exposure to tap water on height-for-age and intermediary outcomes by maternal education

		The direct channel			The behavioral channel		
		Birth and infancy outcomes			Parental health investment		
	Height-for-age z-score	Low birth weight	Any sickness in 1st year of life	Any doctor visit in 1st year of life	Breast-feeding duration (month)	Health-seeking behavior	Private health insurance
	(1)	(2)	(3)	(4)	(5)	(6)	(7)
Panel A. Low-educated mothers							
Tap water IU	0.443***	–0.114	–0.189***	–0.172**	2.190*	0.115*	0.095*
	(0.141)	(0.084)	(0.068)	(0.086)	(1.276)	(0.063)	(0.054)
	[0.020]	[0.186]	[0.026]	[0.098]	[0.137]	[0.120]	[0.120]
Observations	1705	1408	1628	1625	1872	1872	1874
R^2	0.507	0.463	0.526	0.530	0.458	0.548	0.562
Number of clusters	334	329	321	321	335	335	334
$\overline{Y}$ of the comparison group	–0.135	0.092	0.659	0.575	13.962	0.777	0.130
Panel B. High-educated mothers							
Tap water IU	0.109	0.008	–0.094	0.032	0.471	–0.041	–0.062
	(0.218)	(0.047)	(0.117)	(0.141)	(1.218)	(0.078)	(0.076)
	[0.447]	[0.733]	[0.372]	[0.637]	[0.509]	[0.447]	[0.380]
Observations	1243	1237	1171	1166	1322	1325	1322
R^2	0.583	0.515	0.644	0.643	0.647	0.634	0.608
Number of clusters	332	329	320	320	337	338	337
$\overline{Y}$ of the comparison group	0.194	0.060	0.683	0.590	11.308	0.713	0.153
p-value	0.072	0.085	0.313	0.085	0.203	0.045	0.023

Notes *, **, and *** indicate significance at 10%, 5%, and 1%, respectively. The main sample of children is divided into two groups by mother's educational level. A mother is "low-educated" if her schooling is less than nine years, and "high-educated" if greater than or equal to nine years. Each column of each panel represents a separate regression of the outcome variable (shown as the column name) on Tap water IU (availability of a tap water connection in the village of birth in the year of conception). All regressions control for individual and household characteristics, village fixed effects, province-specific cohort fixed effects, and village controls interacted with cohort fixed effects, health programs IU, and other infrastructures IU. $\overline{Y}$ of the comparison group is the mean outcome of children who live in villages without a tap water connection in 2010. The bottom row reports p-values from the seemingly unrelated estimations, which test whether the estimated coefficients on "Tap water IU" in Panel A and Panel B of the same column are equal using a generalized Hausman specification test. Standard errors in parentheses are clustered at the village level. FDR q-values are computed over all regressions in Tables 2.3 to 2.13 and are shown in brackets

health investments by maternal education. For all three measures of parental health investments, we detect positive effects of *in utero* exposure to tap water, but only for children of low-educated mothers who have already benefited more from the exposure in terms of health before age one. By contrast, for children of high-educated mothers, the estimated effects are small and insignificant. This finding suggests how the behavioral channel operates: subsequent parental investments in health may play a role in mediating the persistent effects of *in utero* exposure to tap water on children's health outcomes.[27]

There are many possible reasons that tap water exposure *in utero* could induce more health investments from parents. We are able to test and rule out two of them. First, tap water exposure *in utero* may improve maternal health, which makes later investments more productive. If mothers gain better postnatal health due to tap water exposure during pregnancy, they may be able to breastfeed their children for a longer period or spend more time in childcare, which would consequently improve children's health. In addition, improved maternal health owing to tap water exposure could also directly enhance the development of the fetus and thus lead to better postnatal health of the child.

Ideally, we should examine the effect of exposure to tap water during pregnancy on maternal health for the mothers of the sampled children. However, the CFPS did not collect historical maternal health outcomes for the mothers. Nor did it record women's pregnancy status at the survey time in 2010. Therefore, we are not able to check the contemporaneous effect of exposure during pregnancy on expectant mothers' health outcomes. Instead, we choose ever-married women at ages 20–45 from the 2010 CFPS. We compare the difference in health outcomes of women with and without a newborn child (under six months old) between villages with and without a tap water connection. To exclude women whose exposure during the last pregnancy is unable to be determined, we include only villages that had no tap water connection before 2004 and women in those villages who have a newborn, whose youngest child is over 60 months old, or who have no children.

We employ the following DID strategy:

$$Y_{ic}^{W} = \psi Newborn_{ic} + \eta Newborn_{ic} \times Tapwater_c + X_{ic}\beta + \gamma_c + \epsilon_{ic}, \quad (2.9)$$

where Y_{ic}^{W} denotes the outcome of a woman i living in village c, including body mass index (BMI), self-rated health status (on a five-point scale with a higher score indicating better health), and incidence of severe discomfort in the past two weeks. The indicator $Newborn_{ic}$ takes the value one if the woman had a newborn in the 2010 CFPS, and the interaction $Newborn_{ic} \times Tapwater_c$ equals one if the woman had a newborn and was living in a village with a tap water connection in 2010. X_{ic} includes the following characteristics of the woman: number of siblings, height, number of children ever born, *hukou* status, years of schooling fixed effects, and age fixed effects. γ_c denotes village fixed effects. The coefficient of interest, η, captures

---

[27] We thank an anonymous referee for pointing out investments in sanitation as a potential channel. The literature has shown a significant complementary relationship between access to tap water and improved sanitation (e.g., Alsan and Goldin 2019). We find that a child's *in utero* exposure to tap water does not affect a household's access to different types of toilets in 2010, regardless of maternal education. However, we cannot rule out parental investments in sanitation as a potential channel, as our measure of access to sanitation is not retrospective and does not consider other sanitation improvements (e.g., access to sewage systems). A full analysis of parental investments in sanitation awaits future research.

the effect of having a tap water connection during pregnancy on the woman's health status after giving birth.

Table 2.14 reports the estimation results. For both low- and high-educated women, we find no evidence that having a tap water connection in the village during pregnancy affects BMI, self-rated health, and the incidence of severe discomfort. In other words, we find no evidence that having a tap water connection during pregnancy improves postnatal maternal health. This finding suggests that maternal health is not a channel through which *in utero* exposure to tap water improves parents' postnatal investments, nor a channel through which the exposure affects the development of the fetus and the health of the child after birth.

Second, *in utero* exposure to publicly provided tap water may foster the accumulation of household resources, which empowers parents to invest more in children's health. We use whether a household engages in agricultural production and household income as indicators of household resources. For children of either low- or high-educated mothers, we detect no significant effect on these two resource indicators, and we observe no significant difference in the estimated effect between the two groups of children (columns (1) and (2) of Table 2.15). If some unobserved household resources increase due to tap water, in addition to health investments we would expect parents to increase investments in other dimensions, such as educational investments. However, for both groups of children, we find no evidence of increased educational investments, measured by whether a child had ever attended kindergarten and whether the household had any educational savings (columns (3) and (4) of Table 2.15). Moreover, we find no difference between the two groups of children in the estimated effects on educational investments. Thus, it is implausible that *in utero* tap water exposure causes an increase in health investments by facilitating the accumulation of household resources.

Another plausible explanation for the behavioral channel is the dynamic complementarity in human capital investments, which is a central assumption of the multi-stage model of human capital formation developed by Cunha and Heckman (2007) and Heckman (2007) (outlined in Sect. 2.4). The dynamic complementarity in human capital investments implies that early investments increase the marginal return to later investments. Hence, parents would invest more at later stages of child development in response to increased early investments. The dynamic complementarity can arise when two conditions are met: (a) early investments increase initial human capital; and (b) initial human capital and subsequent human capital investments are complements. Recent evidence has been largely consistent with the assumption of dynamic complementarity. For example, Adhvaryu and Nyshadham (2016) find that children with higher *in utero* exposure to a large-scale iodine supplementation program in Tanzania were breastfed longer and received more necessary vaccines after birth. Attanasio et al. (2020) estimate production functions for cognition and health for children aged 1–12 in India and find evidence supporting complementarity between initial health and subsequent health investments. Rossi and Villar (2020) show that an anti-malaria public intervention in Senegal increased parental health-seeking behavior against other diseases like diarrhea. In our study, we hypothesize that after observing the improvement in children's health at birth and in early child-

Table 2.14 Effects of tap water connections on mothers' health

Dep. var.:	Body Mass Index	Self-rated health	Severe health condition
	(1)	(2)	(3)
Panel A. Low-educated women			
Newborn	–0.460	–0.161	0.004
	(0.514)	(0.179)	(0.056)
Newborn × Tap	–1.180	–0.050	0.041
	(1.014)	(0.209)	(0.068)
Observations	1425	1443	1442
R^2	0.327	0.277	0.286
Number of clusters	247	249	249
$\overline{Y}$ of the comparison group	21.029	1.385	0.038
Panel B. High-educated women			
Newborn	2.302***	–0.178	–0.028
	(0.804)	(0.230)	(0.052)
Newborn × Tap	–0.563	–0.011	–0.051
	(1.021)	(0.259)	(0.050)
Observations	734	739	739
R^2	0.381	0.416	0.452
Number of clusters	213	213	213
$\overline{Y}$ of the comparison group	22.013	1.396	0.019

Notes *, **, and *** indicate significance at 10%, 5%, and 1%, respectively. The sample consists of ever-married women aged 20–45 meeting two criteria: (1) from villages that had no tap water connection before 2004; (2) have no child, have a newborn, or have children but youngest child is over 60 months old. The sample is divided into two groups by mother's educational level. A mother is "low-educated" if her schooling is less than nine years, and "high-educated" if greater than or equal to nine years. Each column of each panel represents a separate regression of the outcome variable (shown as the column name) on Newborn and the interaction of Newborn and Tap. Newborn indicates whether a woman had given birth within the past six months when surveyed by the 2010 CFPS. Tap indicates the availability of a tap water connection in the village in 2010. Self-rated health is measured on a five-point scale with a higher score indicating better health. Severe health condition is a dummy variable which equals one if there has been any incidence of severe discomfort in the past two weeks and zero otherwise. All regressions control for number of siblings, height, number of children ever born, *hukou* status, and fixed effects for years of schooling, age, and village. $\overline{Y}$ of the comparison group is the mean outcome of women with a newborn and living in a village without a tap water connection in 2010. Standard errors in parentheses are clustered at the village level

hood as a result of tap water exposure *in utero*, parents perceive a higher marginal return to health investments and consequently, increase health investments in their children. While this hypothesis cannot be explicitly tested in our setting due to data limitations, we consider it to be a plausible explanation for the increased health investments and worthy of further investigation.

2.9.3 Robustness Checks for Potential Channels

In the previous subsections, we test the direct channel and behavioral channel by discussing the heterogeneity in the impact of *in utero* tap water exposure by maternal education. As a robustness check, we explore the heterogeneous effects by two additional measures of household socioeconomic (SES) status: paternal education and net household income. A father is "low-educated" if his schooling is less than nine years, and "high-educated" if greater than or equal to nine years. A household is "low-income" if the net household income is below sample median and "high-income" if otherwise. We present the results in Table 2.16 and Table 2.17. In general, these results reveal a pattern similar to the heterogeneity analysis by maternal education: children from low-SES households benefit more from exposure to tap water *in utero*. However, the heterogeneity is not as salient as that by maternal education.

2.10 From Intention to Treat to Average Treatment Effects

In this study, we are interested in the effect of *in utero* exposure to tap water at the village level. However, having a tap water connection in a village in the conception year does not mean that a child was exposed to tap water *in utero* at the household level. It is possible that it may take some time before a household individually receives a tap water connection. It is also possible that a household may never be connected. Therefore, what we are estimating is thus an intention-to-treat estimate (ITT).

To get a sense of the effect of *in utero* exposure to tap water at the household level (the local average treatment effect, LATE), we need first-stage results such as whether households use tap water when it is available at the village level, and whether households quickly opt in to tap water once a tap water connection becomes available at the village level. Figure 2.1 provides some detailed information. We detect a sharp contrast in the tap water take-up rate of households in 2010 between villages that received the first tap water connection before and after 2010. For villages that received a connection before 2010, the take-up rate falls in the range of 50% and 75%, whereas the take-up rate is about 10% in villages that were not yet connected by 2010. In particular, in villages that received the first connection in 2009, almost 50% of the households already reported using tap water for cooking the following year in 2010.

Further, we learn from Fig. 2.1 that once tap water becomes available in the village, households opt in quickly. In villages that were connected in 2009, almost 50% of the households already reported using tap water for cooking the following year in 2010. It is thus possible for children conceived in the year of the first village-level tap water connection to be exposed to treated tap water immediately. Moreover, the household take-up rate does not depend on the cumulative years of having a tap water connection at the village level.

Table 2.15 Effects of *in utero* exposure to tap water on household resources and educational investments

Dep. var.:	Household in non-agricultural sector	Log of household income	Ever attended kindergarten	Any educational savings
	(1)	(2)	(3)	(4)
Panel A. Low-educated mothers				
Tap water IU	–0.015	0.128	0.040	–0.039
	(0.037)	(0.116)	(0.080)	(0.053)
Observations	1883	1821	1512	1884
R^2	0.615	0.570	0.725	0.487
Number of clusters	335	332	324	335
$\overline{Y}$ of the comparison group	0.133	9.675	0.372	0.172
Panel B. High-educated mothers				
Tap water IU	0.070	–0.044	–0.095	0.023
	(0.086)	(0.219)	(0.196)	(0.096)
Observations	1322	1242	810	1325
R^2	0.668	0.672	0.871	0.582
Number of clusters	338	330	301	338
$\overline{Y}$ of the comparison group	0.168	10.045	0.540	0.208
p-value	0.228	0.355	0.312	0.453

Notes *, **, and *** indicate significance at 10%, 5%, and 1%, respectively. The main sample of children is divided into two groups by mother's educational level. A mother is "low-educated" if her schooling is less than nine years, and "high-educated" if greater than or equal to nine years. Each column of each panel represents a separate regression of the outcome variable (shown as the column name) on Tap water IU (availability of a tap water connection in the village of birth in the year of conception). All regressions control for individual and household characteristics, village fixed effects, province-specific cohort fixed effects, and village controls interacted with cohort fixed effects, health programs IU, and other infrastructures IU. $\overline{Y}$ of the comparison group is the mean outcome of children who live in villages without a tap water connection in 2010. The bottom row reports p-values from the seemingly unrelated estimations, which test whether the estimated coefficients on "Tap water IU" in Panel A and Panel B of the same column are equal using a generalized Hausman specification test. Standard errors in parentheses are clustered at the village level

Figure 2.1 suggests that if a village has a tap water connection, the fraction of households using tap water increases by about 40 to 65 percentage points. Therefore, we could obtain an estimate for the effect of *in utero* exposure to the household-level tap water connection by multiplying the main ITT estimate by a factor in the range of 1.5 to 2.5. Considering the main ITT estimate of 0.304 on height-for-age, the estimate for the LATE would be in the range of 0.456 to 0.76.

Table 2.16 Heterogeneous effects of *in utero* exposure to tap water by paternal education

		The direct channel			The behavioral channel		
		Birth and infancy outcomes			Parental health investment		
	Height-for-age z-score	Low birth weight	Any sickness in 1st year of life	Any doctor visit in 1st year of life	Breast-feeding duration (month)	Health-seeking behavior	Private health insurance
	(1)	(2)	(3)	(4)	(5)	(6)	(7)
Panel A. Low-educated fathers							
Tap water IU	0.272	−0.034	−0.285***	−0.270**	2.337	0.034	0.060
	(0.177)	(0.116)	(0.094)	(0.116)	(1.597)	(0.080)	(0.058)
Observations	1315	1097	1277	1274	1451	1455	1463
R^2	0.548	0.503	0.585	0.591	0.520	0.588	0.538
Number of clusters	307	301	299	299	314	313	314
$\overline{Y}$ of the comparison group	−0.128	0.111	0.637	0.549	13.738	0.754	0.125
Panel B. High-educated fathers							
Tap water IU	0.174	−0.014	−0.071	−0.031	0.680	0.011	−0.014
	(0.155)	(0.045)	(0.089)	(0.100)	(0.880)	(0.056)	(0.071)
Observations	1633	1548	1522	1517	1743	1742	1749
R^2	0.527	0.415	0.543	0.545	0.569	0.588	0.537
Number of clusters	350	345	342	342	356	357	357
$\overline{Y}$ of the comparison group	0.099	0.053	0.696	0.608	12.241	0.750	0.156
p-value	0.570	0.813	0.036	0.040	0.237	0.778	0.265

Notes *, **, and *** indicate significance at 10%, 5%, and 1%, respectively. The main sample of children is divided into two groups by father's educational level. A father is "low-educated" if his schooling is less than nine years, and "high-educated" if greater than or equal to nine years. Each column of each panel represents a separate regression of the outcome variable (shown as the column name) on Tap water IU (availability of a tap water connection in the village of birth in the year of conception). All regressions control for individual and household characteristics, village fixed effects, province-specific cohort fixed effects, and village controls interacted with cohort fixed effects, health programs IU, and other infrastructures IU. $\overline{Y}$ of the comparison group is the mean outcome of children who live in villages without a tap water connection in 2010. The bottom row reports p-values from the seemingly unrelated estimations, which test whether the estimated coefficients on "Tap water IU" in Panel A and Panel B of the same column are equal using a generalized Hausman specification test. Standard errors in parentheses are clustered at the village level

2.11 Cost–Benefit Analysis

Given the strong evidence of the effectiveness of tap water connections in improving childhood health, it is natural to ask whether the benefits from expanding tap water connections outweigh the costs. In this section, we conduct a cost–benefit analysis based on the estimated effect on height at ages 5–15.[28]

[28] Case and Paxson (2008b) show that height in childhood is highly correlated with height in adulthood.

Table 2.17 Heterogeneous effects of *in utero* exposure to tap water by household income level

		The direct channel			The behavioral channel		
		Birth and infancy outcomes			Parental health investment		
	Height-for-age *z*-score	Low birth weight	Any sickness in 1st year of life	Any doctor visit in 1st year of life	Breast-feeding duration (month)	Health-seeking behavior	Private health insurance
	(1)	(2)	(3)	(4)	(5)	(6)	(7)
Panel A. Low-income households							
Tap water IU	0.330**	–0.022	–0.101	–0.086	1.727	0.045	0.067
	(0.150)	(0.084)	(0.082)	(0.100)	(1.546)	(0.062)	(0.068)
Observations	1393	1173	1353	1349	1537	1539	1545
R^2	0.530	0.480	0.562	0.559	0.493	0.564	0.491
Number of clusters	307	301	298	297	312	313	313
$\overline{Y}$ of the comparison group	–0.068	0.095	0.635	0.536	13.968	0.711	0.127
Panel B. High-income households							
Tap water IU	0.203	–0.046	–0.165*	–0.148	0.970	–0.060	–0.080
	(0.179)	(0.051)	(0.099)	(0.104)	(1.114)	(0.059)	(0.073)
Observations	1449	1363	1356	1353	1535	1536	1544
R^2	0.568	0.461	0.605	0.606	0.579	0.619	0.596
Number of clusters	332	325	322	322	337	338	338
$\overline{Y}$ of the comparison group	0.070	0.060	0.712	0.635	11.693	0.787	0.156
p-value	0.459	0.729	0.511	0.569	0.607	0.125	0.048

Notes *, **, and *** indicate significance at 10%, 5%, and 1%, respectively. The main sample of children is divided into two groups by household income level. A household is "low-income" if the net household income is below sample median and "high-income" if otherwise. Each column of each panel represents a separate regression of the outcome variable (shown as the column name) on Tap water IU (availability of a tap water connection in the village of birth in the year of conception). All regressions control for individual and household characteristics, village fixed effects, province-specific cohort fixed effects, and village controls interacted with cohort fixed effects, health programs IU, and other infrastructures IU. $\overline{Y}$ of the comparison group is the mean outcome of children who live in villages without a tap water connection in 2010. The bottom row reports *p*-values from the seemingly unrelated estimations, which test whether the estimated coefficients on "Tap water IU" in Panel A and Panel B of the same column are equal using a generalized Hausman specification test. Standard errors in parentheses are clustered at the village level

We estimate the correlation between height and annual income using a sample of adults in rural areas aged 21–55 in 2014 and allow the height premium to differ for adults younger and older than 30.[29] We find that, holding everything else constant, a 1 cm increase in height is associated with a 21.5 USD (132 CNY) increase in annual income at ages 21–30, and an 8 USD (45 CNY) increase in annual income at ages 31–55. Our main analysis shows that *in utero* exposure to tap water raises average childhood height by 2.6 cm at ages 5–15 (column (2) of Table 2.4). Suppose that the

[29] Other explanatory variables we control for in the regression include gender, number of siblings, whether the person had an agricultural *hukou* at age three, parents' years of schooling, and county-birth year fixed effects.

future height premiums of the children who benefited from the program equals the height premiums of adults aged 21–55 in 2014, and that people work from the ages of 21 to 55. Then we use the height effect at ages 5–15 to calculate the potential increase in income. The present value of the increase in total income between the ages of 21 and 55 is then $\sum_{t=6}^{15} \frac{2.6\times 21.5}{(1+r)^t} + \sum_{t=16}^{40} \frac{2.6\times 8}{(1+r)^t}$ for someone aged 15 in 2014, where r is the discount rate. For an individual aged five in 2014, the present value of the increase in total income between the ages of 21 and 55 is $\sum_{t=16}^{25} \frac{2.6\times 21.5}{(1+r)^t} + \sum_{t=26}^{50} \frac{2.6\times 8}{(1+r)^t}$.

The average cost of constructing the water plants and pipeline systems is approximately 30 USD per capita (Meng et al. 2004). Assuming that the cost is measured in 2004 value, the present value of the cost in 2014 would be $30 \times (1 + r)^{10}$. The internal rate of return (the discount rate that equalizes the present values of costs and benefits) is 0.109 for an individual aged five in 2014 and 0.164 for an individual aged 15. For discount rates below these values, the net present value of expanding tap water connections is positive.

This means that, for all reasonable discount rates, the present value of the benefits exceeds the present value of the costs. Considering the durability of the village water supply system and the benefits associated with the program on multiple dimensions of human capital of adults and children (Zhang 2012; Zhang and Xu 2016; Chen et al. 2022), the total benefits would be even higher than our estimates. Hence, our study suggests that water infrastructure is a worthwhile investment to promote population health and long-term development.

2.12 Conclusion

This study documents and explains the positive effect of *in utero* exposure to tap water on childhood health in rural China. Exploiting variation in the timing of the first tap water connection across villages, we show that *in utero* exposure to tap water increases height-for-age during childhood: a 0.3 standard deviation increase in height at ages 1–11, and a 0.2 standard deviation increase in height at ages 5–15. *In utero* exposure to tap water also improves various health outcomes measured at birth, during infancy, and in childhood. Examining children's most severe diseases since birth by cause, we find that *in utero* exposure to tap water significantly reduces the incidence of non-waterborne digestive diseases, whereas the incidence of other disease types including waterborne diseases is not affected. These findings are in line with the common practice of boiling water before drinking in China and suggest that the effect on health is most likely driven by the removal of chemical pollutants but not disease-causing microorganisms from drinking water.

The heterogeneity analysis by maternal education shows that children born to low-educated mothers benefit significantly more from *in utero* exposure to tap water than children of high-educated mothers. The mechanism analysis suggests that two channels are at play behind the considerably larger effect of *in utero* tap water exposure on children of low-educated mothers: a direct channel by improving health at birth and in the first year of life, and a behavioral channel by inducing more subsequent health investments.

Understanding the effects of *in utero* conditions on height and other health outcomes during childhood is at the heart of designing intelligent policies. In this study, we focus not on finalized outcomes in adulthood but rather on childhood outcomes, which are more relevant for the typically short timelines of policy decisions. Along with Zhang and Xu (2016) and (Chen et al., 2022), we find that *in utero* exposure to tap water plays a significant role in shaping the developmental trajectories of human capital. Hence, we confirm that the construction of water infrastructures has the potential to be employed as a method to enhance rural children's human capital development.

More importantly, our study shows that public water infrastructure may play a role in increasing social mobility. Under the rural drinking water program in China, water treatment plants and water pipes were built to supply treated tap water to all rural households. The public provision of treated tap water reduces the inequality in access to safe drinking water across different socioeconomic backgrounds. Children from disadvantaged backgrounds often have poorer health and receive fewer investments from their parents. Our results show that *in utero* exposure to treated tap water under the program improves the health of children from disadvantaged backgrounds more and prevents parental disadvantages from being passed on to children. This finding implies that building water infrastructure in rural areas not only offers contemporaneous benefits, but it could also go a long way toward narrowing the gap in health stocks between children of different socioeconomic backgrounds and fostering social mobility in the long run.

References

State Planning Committee and Ministry of Water Resources (2000) Regulations on construction of rural drinking water projects. Beijing

Ministry of Water Resources and Electric Power (1984) Interim provision on rural drinking water. Beijing

Patriotic Public Health Committee and Ministry of Heath (1991) Implementation guidelines for the "sanitary standard for drinking water quality" in rural areas. Beijing

Adhvaryu A, Fenske J, Nyshadham A (2019) Early life circumstance and adult mental health. J Polit Econ 127(4):1516–1549

Adhvaryu A, Nyshadham A (2016) Endowments at birth and parents' investments in children. Econ J 126(593):781–820

Adukia A, Asher S, Novosad P (2020) Educational investment responses to economic opportunity: evidence from Indian road construction. Am Econ J: Appl Econ 12(1):348–376

Agency for Toxic Substances and Disease Registry (ATSDR) (2003) Toxicological profile for fluorides, hydrogen fluoride, and fluorine. Technical report, Department of Health and Human Services, Public Health Service, Atlanta, GA

Almond D (2006) Is the 1918 Influenza Pandemic over? Long-term effects of In Utero influenza exposure in the post-1940 U.S. population. J Polit Econ 114(4):672–712

Almond D, Currie J (2011) Killing me softly: the fetal origins hypothesis. J Econ Perspect 25(3):153–172

Almond D, Currie J, Duque V (2018) Childhood circumstances and adult outcomes: Act II. J Econ Literat 56(4):1360–1446

Almond D, Edlund L, Palme M (2009) Chernobyl's subclinical legacy: Prenatal exposure to radioactive fallout and school outcomes in Sweden. Quart J Econ 124(4):1729–1772

Almond D, Mazumder B (2005) The 1918 influenza pandemic and subsequent health outcomes: An analysis of SIPP data. Am Econ Rev 95(2):258–262

Almond D, Mazumder B (2013) Fetal origins and parental responses. Ann Rev Econ 5(1):37–56

Almond D, Mazumder B, van Ewijk R (2015) 01). In Utero Ramadan exposure and children's academic performance. Econ J 125:1501–1533

Alsan M, Goldin C (2019) Watersheds in child mortality: the role of effective water and sewerage infrastructure, 1880–1920. J Polit Econ 127(2):586–638

Anderson ML (2008) Multiple inference and gender differences in the effects of early intervention: a reevaluation of the abecedarian, perry preschool, and early training projects. J Am Stat Assoc 103(484):1481–1495

Apelberg BJ, Witter FR, Herbstman JB, Calafat AM, Halden RU, Needham LL, Goldman LR (2007) Cord serum concentrations of perfluorooctane sulfonate (PFOS) and perfluorooctanoate (PFOA) in relation to weight and size at birth. Environ Health Perspect 115(11):1670–1676

Attanasio O, Meghir C, Nix E (2020) Human capital development and parental investment in India. Rev Econ Stud 87(6):2511–2541

Barr DB, Bishop A, Needham LL (2007) Concentrations of xenobiotic chemicals in the maternal-fetal unit. Reprod Toxicol 23(3):260–266

Beckett M, Vanzo JD, Sastry N, Panis C, Peterson C (2001) The quality of retrospective data: an examination of long-term recall in a developing country. J Human Resourc 36(3):593–625

Benjamini Y, Hochberg Y (1995) Controlling the false discovery rate: a practical and powerful approach to multiple testing. J R Stat Soc. Ser B (Methodol) 57(1):289–300

Bertrand M, Duflo E, Mullainathan S (2004) How much should we trust differences-in-differences estimates? Quart J Econ 119(1):249–275

Bhalotra, S. R., A. Diaz-Cayeros, G. Miller, A. Miranda, and A. S. Venkataramani (2021, November). Urban water disinfection and mortality decline in lower-income countries. Am Econ J: Econ Policy 13(4):490–520

Black SE, Bütikofer A, Devereux PJ, Salvanes KG (2019) This is only a test? Long-run and intergenerational impacts of prenatal exposure to radioactive fallout. Rev Econ Stat 101(3):531–546

Bove FJ, Fulcomer MC, Klotz JB, Esmart J, Dufficy EM, Savrin JE (1995) Public drinking water contamination and birth outcomes. Am J Epidemiol 141(9):850–862

Brainerd E, Menon N (2014) Seasonal effects of water quality: The hidden costs of the Green Revolution to infant and child health in India. J Dev Econ 107:49–64

Brown J, Sobsey MD (2012) Boiling as household water treatment in Cambodia: a longitudinal study of boiling practice and microbiological effectiveness. Am J Trop Med Hygiene 87(3):394–398

Callan A, Rotander A, Thompson K, Heyworth J, Mueller J, Odland J, Hinwood A (2016) Maternal exposure to perfluoroalkyl acids measured in whole blood and birth outcomes in offspring. Sci Total Environ 569–570:1107–1113

Case A, Paxson C (2008) Height, health, and cognitive function at older ages. Am Econ Rev 98(2):463–467

Case A, Paxson C (2008) Stature and status: height, ability, and labor market outcomes. J Polit Econ 116(3):499–532

Chen JY, Li L, Xiao Y (2022) Early-life exposure to tap water and the development of cognitive skills. J Human Resourc 57(6):2113–2149

Chen M-H, Ha E-H, Wen T-W, Su Y-N, Lien G-W, Chen C-Y, Chen P-C, Hsieh W-S (2012) Perfluorinated compounds in umbilical cord blood and adverse birth outcomes. PLOS ONE 7(8):1–8

Chen Y, Zhou L-A (2007) The long-term health and economic consequences of the 1959–1961 famine in China. J Health Econ 26(4):659–681

Concha G, Vogler G, Lezcano D, Nermell B, Vahter M (1998) Exposure to inorganic arsenic metabolites during early human development. Toxicol Sci 44(2):185–190
Cunha F, Heckman J (2007) The technology of skill formation. Am Econ Rev 97(2):31–47
Cunha F, Heckman JJ, Schennach SM (2010) Estimating the technology of cognitive and noncognitive skill formation. Econometrica 78(3):883–931
Currie J (2011) Inequalities at birth: Some causes and consequences. Am Econ Rev: Papaers & Proceedings 101(3):1–22
Currie J, Graff Zivin J, Meckel K, Neidell M, Schlenker W (2013) Something in the water: contaminated drinking water and infant health. Can J Econ 46(3):791–810
Currie J, Vogl T (2013) Early-life health and adult circumstance in developing countries. Ann Rev Econ 5(1):1–36
Currie J, Zivin JG, Mullins J, Neidell M (2014) What do we know about short- and long-term effects of early-life exposure to pollution? Ann Rev Resourc Econ 6:217–247
Cutler D, Miller G (2005) The role of public health improvements in health advances: the twentieth-century United States. Demography 42:1–22
de Chaisemartin C, D'Haultfœuille X (2020) Two-way fixed effects estimators with heterogeneous treatment effects. Am Econ Rev 110(9):2964–2996
de Onis M (2000) Measuring nutritional status in relation to mortality. Bull World Health Organ 78(10):1271–1274
DEEOH and NJDHSS (2003) Case-control study of childhood cancers in Dover Township (Ocean County), New Jersey. Technical Report January, Div. of Epidemiology, Environmental and Occupational Health, NJ Dept. of Health and Senior Services
Devoto F, Duflo E, Dupas P, Parienté W, Pons V (2012) Happiness on tap: Piped water adoption in urban Morocco. Am Econ J Econ Pol 4(4):68–99
Ebenstein A (2012) The consequences of industrialization: Evidence from water pollution and digestive cancers in China. Rev Econ Stat 94(1):186–201
Fernandez ID, Himes JH, de Onis M (2002) Prevalence of nutritional wasting in populations: Building explanatory models using secondary data. Bull World Health Organizat 80(4):282–291
Galiani S, Gertler P, Schargrodsky E (2005) Water for life: The impact of the privatization of water services on child mortality. J Polit Econ 113(1):83–120
Gamper-Rabindran S, Khan S, Timmins C (2010) The impact of piped water provision on infant mortality in Brazil: A quantile panel data approach. J Dev Econ 92(2):188–200
Gentzkow M, Shapiro JM (2008) Preschool television viewing and adolescent test scores: Historical evidence from the Coleman study. Quart J Econ 123(1):279–323
He G, Perlof JM (2016) Surface water quality and infant mortality in China. Econ Dev Cult Change 65(1):119–139
Heckman JJ (2007) The economics, technology, and neuroscience of human capability formation. Proc Natl Acad Sci 104(33):13250–13255
Henneberry YK, Kraus TE, Fleck JA, Krabbenhoft DP, Bachand PM, Horwath WR (2011) Removal of inorganic mercury and methylmercury from surface waters following coagulation of dissolved organic matter with metal-based salts. Sci Total Environ 409(3):631–637
Hill EL, Ma L (2022) Drinking water, fracking, and infant health. J Health Econ 82:102595
Hoynes H, Schanzenbach DW, Almond D (2016) Long-run impacts of childhood access to the Safety Net. Am Econ Rev 106(4):903–934
Jalan J, Ravallion M (2003) Does piped water reduce diarrhea for children in rural India? J Economet 112(1):153–173
Karbownik K, Wray A (2019) Long-run consequences of exposure to natural disasters. J Law Econ 37(3):949–1007
Kippler M, Tofail F, Gardner R, Rahman A, Hamadani JD, Bottai M, Vahter M (2012) Maternal cadmium exposure during pregnancy and size at birth: A prospective cohort study. Environ Health Perspect 120(2):284–289
Kosec K (2014) The child health implications of privatizing Africa's urban water supply. J Health Econ 35:1–19

La Ferrara E, Chong A, Duryea S (2012) Soap operas and fertility: evidence from Brazil. Am Econ J Appl Econ 4(4):1–31

Lundborg P, Nystedt P, Rooth D-O (2014) Height and earnings: The role of cognitive and noncognitive skills. J Human Resourc 49:141–166

Mangyo E (2008) The effect of water accessibility on child health in China. J Health Econ 27(5):1343–1356

Meeks R (2017) Water works: The economic impact of water infrastructure. J Human Resourc 52(4):1119–1153

Meng S, Liu J, Tao Y (2004) Water supply and sanitation environment in rural China: Promote service to the poor. Technical report, Poverty Reduction Conference (Chinese), Shanghai, China

Meng X, Qian N (2009) The long term consequences of famine on survivors: Evidence from a unique natural experiment using China's Great Famine. NBER Working Paper No. 14917

MOH (1985) Sanitary standard for drinking water quality gb 5749–85. Technical report, Ministry of Health, Beijing, China

MOH (2007) Sanitary standard for drinking water quality gb 5749–2006. Technical report, Ministry of Health, Beijing, China

Myllynen P, Pasanen M, Pelkonen O (2005) Human placenta: A human organ for developmental toxicology research and biomonitoring. Placenta 26(5):361–371

NDRC (2007) The eleventh five year plan of rural drinking water program. Technical report, National Development and Reform Commission, Beijing, China

NDRC (2012) The twelfth five year plan of rural drinking water program. Technical report, National Development and Reform Commission, Beijing, China

Orgill-Meyer J, Pattanayak SK (2020) Improved sanitation increases long-term cognitive test scores. World Develop 132:104975

Perera F, Herbstman J (2011) Prenatal environmental exposures, epigenetics, and disease. Reprod Toxicol 31(3):363–373

Persico N, Postlewaite A, Silverman D (2004) The effect of adolescent experience on labor market outcomes: The case of height. J Polit Econ 112(5):1019–1053

Rahman A, Vahter M, Smith AH, Nermell B, Yunus M, El Arifeen S, Persson L-R, Ekström E-C (2009) Arsenic exposure during pregnancy and size at birth: A prospective cohort study in bangladesh. Am J Epidemiol 169(3):304–312

Renzetti S, Just AC, Burris HH, Oken E, Amarasiriwardena C, Svensson K, Mercado-García A, Cantoral A, Schnaas L, Baccarelli AA, Wright RO, Téllez-Rojo MM (2017) The association of lead exposure during pregnancy and childhood anthropometry in the Mexican PROGRESS cohort. Environ Res 152:226–232

Rocha R, Soares RR (2015) Water scarcity and birth outcomes in the Brazilian semiarid. J Dev Econ 112:72–91

Rosales-Rueda M, Triyana M (2019) The persistent effects of early-life exposure to air pollution: Evidence from the Indonesian forest fires. J Human Resourc 54(4):1037–1080

Rossi P, Villar P (2020) Private health investments under competing risks: Evidence from malaria control in Senegal. J Health Econ 73:102330

Rudan I, Chan KY, Zhang JS, Theodoratou E, Feng XL, Salomon JA, Lawn JE, Cousens S, Black RE, Guo Y, Campbell H (2010) Causes of deaths in children younger than 5 years in china in 2008. The Lancet 375(9720):1083–1089

Thomas D, Lavy V, Strauss J (1996) Public policy and anthropometric outcomes in the Côte d'ivoire. J Public Econ 61(2):155–192

UNICEF and WHO (2015) Progress on sanitation and drinking water: 2015 update and MDG assessment. Technical report, United Nations Children's Fund and World Health Organization, New York

UNICEF and WHO (2019) Progress on household drinking water, sanitation and hygiene 2000–2017: Special focus on inequalities. Technical report, United Nations Children's Fund and World Health Organization, New York

WHO (2010) Nutrition landscape information system (NLIS) country profile indicators: Interpretation guide. Technical report, World Health Organization, Geneva, Switzerland

WHO (2015) Technical brief - Boil water. Technical report, World Health Organization, Geneva, Switzerland

WHO (2017) Treatment Methods and Performance. Technical report, World Health Organization, Geneva, Switzerland

Xie J, Liebenthal A, Warford JJ, Dixon JA, Wang M, Gao S, Wang S, Jiang Y, Ma Z (2009) Addressing China's water scarcity: Recommendations for selected water resource management issues. Technical report, World Bank, Washington, DC

Xie Y (2012) China Family Panel Studies (2010) user's manual. Technical report, Institute of Social Science Survey, Peking University

Zhang J (2012) The impact of water quality on health: Evidence from the drinking water infrastructure program in rural China. J Health Econ 31(1):122–134

Zhang J, Xu LC (2016) The long-run effects of treated water on education: The rural drinking water program in China. J Dev Econ 122:1–15

Zhang R, Li H, Wu X, Fan F, Sun B, Wang Z, Zhang Q, Tao Y (2009) Current situation analysis on China rural drinking water quality. J Environ Health (Chinese) 26(1):3–5

Chapter 3
Rural Drinking Water Program and Adolescent Cognitive Skills

Abstract In this study, we exploit the variation in the timing of tap water connection across villages imposed by the rural drinking water program in China. Using data drawn from the China Family Panel Studies, we find that one additional year of exposure to tap water in early life increases the cognitive test score at ages 10–15 by 0.132 standard deviations. The event study estimates confirm that the beneficial impacts of tap water exposure are concentrated in early life. The mechanism analysis reveals two key channels: improving childhood health and increasing maternal time for childcare. The findings suggest that improving access to tap water has considerable potential to increase rural children's cognitive skills, and eventually, to narrow the human capital disparity between rural and urban children in China.

3.1 Background

Cognitive skills are important forms of human capital and are closely linked to long-term educational attainment, labor market outcomes, and overall well-being (Glewwe 2002; Heckman et al. 2013). Skill formation theories suggest that taking the parental environment and other investments as inputs, cognitive skills can be produced at different stages of childhood into adulthood (Cunha et al. 2010). Emerging evidence has suggested that early life, usually covering the prenatal period and early childhood, is the most critical window in the process of cognitive development (Cunha et al. 2006; Attanasio 2015).[1]

Understanding the determinants and mechanisms of cognitive skill formation has profound policy implications for developing countries. First, empirical evidence has shown a strong correlation between cognitive skills and economic growth, even when schooling is controlled for (Hanushek and Woessmann 2008). Second, young children in developing countries are subject to many early-life risk factors related to cognitive skills development, such as malnutrition, infectious disease, and poor

[1] See Almond and Currie (2011), Currie and Almond (2011), and Almond et al. (2018) for extensive reviews of the literature.

© The Author(s), under exclusive license to Springer Nature Singapore Pte Ltd. 2025
L. Li, *The Impacts of Water Reforms in Rural and Urban China*,
https://doi.org/10.1007/978-981-96-6902-8_3

overall physical health. Therefore, policies targeting these risk factors might help mitigate adverse early-life conditions and improve cognitive skills.

The development of tap water infrastructure in rural China in recent decades provides a unique opportunity to evaluate the impact of early-life exposure to tap water on children's cognitive development. Tap water is one of the most important and basic public infrastructures and usually consists of two parts: a water treatment plant with water purification equipment and water pipelines that link directly to end users. Connecting households to tap water may improve drinking water quality and reduce the time burden of water collection. In 1990, only 11% of households in rural China had access to on-premise tap water (UNICEF and WHO 2015). To enhance access to safe drinking water in rural areas, the Chinese government has gradually implemented the rural drinking water program since the 1980s, primarily focusing on constructing water plants and pipelines to provide tap water to rural residents. For more details on this program, see Sect. 2.1.2. By 2015, 55% of rural households had access to on-premise tap water (UNICEF and WHO 2015).

Tap water is expected to be of better quality than untreated water, as strict regulations are imposed on tap water in terms of its source selection, process, quality control, and distribution. Existing studies in China have generally shown that the water quality of tap water is better than that of untreated water (Zhang et al. 2009). Evaluating the same rural drinking water program, Zhang (2012) finds that the positive health effects of the program come from improved water quality rather than increased access to water. Ebenstein (2012) finds that water quality and digestive cancer rates is much less strongly linked in areas with tap water connections than areas without.

Besides improved water quality, rural residents' access to safe drinking water has greatly improved, following the implementation of this program. As shown in Fig. 2.1, the share of households using tap water for cooking in villages with a tap water connection in 2010 is around 40% higher than that in villages without a connection. Enjoying the ease of getting water at the turn of a tap also affects the time use pattern of rural residents. Taking women aged 20–45 who have one or more children aged 0–5 in the 2010 wave of the China Family Panel Studies (CFPS) as an example, those living in villages with tap water are found to spend more time caring for family members than those living in villages without tap water (see Sect. 3.9.1 for a detailed discussion on time use).

3.2 Results Preview

We examine the effect of improved access to tap water from one year before birth through the first five years of life on cognitive skills in adolescents (10–15 years old). The data used for the analysis are drawn from the baseline survey of the China Family Panel Studies (CFPS) conducted in 2010. The level of cognitive skills is measured by scores from a word and a math test administered to all children above 10 years of age in the CFPS survey. These questions assess the abilities of word recognition and quantitative reasoning. We exploit the gradual rollout of the rural drinking water program across villages and use a difference-in-differences (DID) approach for estimation. We find that exposure to tap water in early life significantly improves children's cognitive skills in adolescence. In our preferred specification, one additional year of early-life exposure to tap water increases the average cognitive test scores of children between the ages of 10 and 15 by 0.132 standard deviations.

Our findings have profound policy implications in China, where the gap between urban and rural human capital per capita is large and still widening (Human Capital in China, 2016). Comparing the average cognitive test score for rural children aged 10–15 with that of their urban counterparts in the CFPS 2010, we find that, for each cohort, urban children outperform their rural counterparts by around 0.5 standard deviations. Our study reveals that full exposure to tap water in early life (six years) increases the average cognitive test score by 0.792 standard deviations. This implies that improving access to tap water has considerable potential to increase rural children's cognitive skills, and eventually, to narrow or mitigate the growing human capital gap between rural and urban children in China.

We support the validity of our DID identification strategy using a battery of validity checks. First, we use an event study model to rule out the possibility that our estimates are identified by cohort trends within villages. The event study also supports the hypothesis that the beneficial impacts of tap water exposure are concentrated in early life, with limited additional impact after that time window. Second, we show similar pre-intervention trends of outcome variables between villages that received a connection early and those that received a connection late. Finally, in a time-shifted placebo test, we find no effect of a placebo treatment on groups of individuals over 15 years of age in 2010. We also show that our estimates are robust to issues such as potential confounders, sample selection, reporting error, and measurement error.

We find two plausible mechanisms through which tap water access could have affected the development of cognitive skills. First, early-life tap water exposure may increase adolescents' cognitive skills by improving childhood health. Second, our findings also suggest that, for women with young children, the time saved by improved tap water accessibility may have been converted into increased time spent caring for young children, which leads to improved cognitive development.

3.3 Literature Review

Our study is related to four strands of literature. First is the literature on the formation of cognitive skills over a person's life cycle. Previous research has shown that maternal health, early-life conditions, family environment, and schooling are determinants of the development of cognitive skills.[2] Interventions that target specific risk factors, such as malnutrition, infectious disease, and poor sanitation, have also been shown to effectively improve cognitive skills later in life (e.g., Barham 2012; Gertler et al. 2014; Spears and Lamba 2016; Ozier 2018; Vikram and Chindarkar 2020). Our study extends this literature by showing that early-life exposure to one of the most basic and important public infrastructures, tap water, contributes positively to the accumulation of cognitive skills.

Second is the literature on the importance of the early-life environment on later human capital development. Early-life events, such as drought, disease exposure, and income shocks, have been shown to persistently affect human capital development among children and adults (e.g., Cutler et al. 2010; Shah and Steinberg 2017; Adhvaryu et al. 2019).[3] Early-life interventions that are designed to improve children's welfare and development, such as in-kind or cash transfers, health interventions, and preschool programs, have been causally linked with human capital accumulation over a person's life cycle (e.g., Bleakley 2007; Maluccio et al. 2009; Milligan and Stabile 2011; Macours et al. 2012; Bharadwaj et al. 2013; Heckman et al. 2013). Our results add to this literature by showing that early life is the crucial time window for human capital development and that any exposure beyond this window has a limited additional effect on cognitive development.

Third is the literature about the effects of improved access to treated water on human capital development. Access to treated water is generally found to have a contemporaneous impact on children's health and educational outcomes (Jalan and Ravallion 2003; Galiani et al. 2005; Mangyo 2008; Gamper-Rabindran et al. 2010; Zhang 2012; Koolwal and van de Walle 2013; Kosec 2014; Zhang and Xu 2016). The two papers related the most to our study are (Zhang, 2012) and (Zhang and Xu, 2016). (Zhang, 2012) finds that in rural China exposure to treated water improves rural children's height and weight-to-height. (Zhang and Xu, 2016) find that living in villages with treated water is associated with a 1.1 year increase in completed grades of education. We show that tap water exposure in early life leads to better cognitive skills in adolescence. However, the observed effect on cognitive skills is not the result of changes in educational attainment, likely because most of the sampled children had not completed their compulsory schooling. Although education and cognitive skills are likely to be correlated, they are different types of human capital. Educational outcomes, such as completed years of schooling or enrollment status, are indirect measures of cognitive skills that may not reflect what people know, especially if school quality or out-of-school learning varies (Maluccio et al. 2009). Therefore, we argue that the effects of tap water on cognitive skills and educational attainment are two different research questions, both of which are interesting in their own right. As the stock of cognitive skills becomes relatively stable in late childhood (Cunha and

[2] See, e.g., maternal health (Majid 2015; Aizer et al. 2016), birth weight (Black et al. 2007), early-life health (Case and Paxson 2009; Figlio et al. 2014), early-life adverse shocks (Almond et al. 2009; Kelly 2011; Black et al. 2019), family income (Dahl and Lochner 2012), and schooling (Carlsson et al. 2015).

[3] See Almond and Currie (2011), Currie and Almond (2011), and Almond et al. (2018) for extensive reviews of the literature.

Heckman 2006), the improvement in cognitive skills observed in adolescence would affect the overall well-being of these children, including their educational attainment and labor market outcomes, over the course of their lives.

Our study is also related to literature about the microeconomic effects of public infrastructure construction and expansion on human capital development in developing countries. Previous studies have investigated the effects of access to schools, electricity, and roads on various household- and individual-level outcomes (Duflo 2001, 2004; Dinkelman 2011; Banerjee et al. 2020). Our study adds to this stream of literature by examining how constructing tap water infrastructure in less-developed areas affects human capital building. In particular, we address the impact of a health-oriented infrastructure (e.g., safe drinking water) on non-health outcomes (e.g., cognitive skills). Our findings have significant policy implications. About 3.8% of the world's GDP has been spent on economic infrastructure over the last 20 years, an annual amount of around 2,400 billion USD (applied to 2010 GDP) (Inderst 2018). It is estimated that the annual infrastructure spending in developing countries in 2008 was 800–900 billion USD, of which 600–650 billion USD was by the public sector (Fay et al. 2011). However, there is little research on the link between early-life access to public infrastructure and later-life outcomes. Our back-of-the-envelope calculation indicates that the labor market gains from improved cognitive skills far exceed the construction cost of tap water infrastructure; hence, the program passes the cost–benefit analysis.

3.4 Conceptual Framework

In this section, we discuss the link between tap water exposure in early life and the development of cognitive skills. We follow the theoretical model of human capital formation outlined in Cunha and Heckman (2006), Cunha et al. (2010), and Attanasio (2015) to guide our discussion. Skill formation theories suggest that cognitive skills can be produced at different stages of childhood into adulthood, taking parental background and other investments as inputs.

Assume that there are two types of human capital: cognitive skills (c) and health (h). Further suppose that, at any time t, the human capital stock for each child can be written as a vector $H_t = (\theta_t^c, \theta_t^h)$, where θ_t^c and θ_t^h are measures of stocks of cognitive skill and health, respectively. Here, we suppress the individual subscript i for simplicity. Following the literature, we assume that each component of human capital at time $t+1$, i.e., θ_{t+1}^c and θ_{t+1}^h, is determined by the stock of human capital at time t, parental background, and investment inputs as well as a random human capital shock. Hence, the stock of type k human capital at time $t+1$ is given by

$$\theta_{t+1}^k = g_t^k(H_t, Z_t, X_t, e_t^k),\ k \in \{c, h\}, \tag{3.1}$$

where $g_t^k(.)$ is the production function of human capital k at time t. Since H_t consists of both cognitive skills and health, we allow interdependence between the two types of human capital in this setup (e.g., the stock of cognitive skills promotes the production of health and vice versa). Z_t denotes (either fixed or time-variant) parental background variables at time t. Z_t can include mother's background, father's background, household income, and any environmental factors that the child is exposed to. Investment inputs X_t consist of monetary inputs and time inputs. These investments could be general human capital investments or those specific to the human capital type k. We also allow for the effect of e_t^k that reflects a random shock to human capital k. In our context, we can think of period t as the early childhood period and $t + 1$ as the period when cognitive skills are measured (see Sect. 3.5 for definitions of these periods).

Early-life exposure to tap water may affect the development of cognitive skills through its impact on variables in Z_t, such as environmental factors and household income. Evidence in the public health and economics literature suggests that unimproved sources of drinking water with toxic chemicals, such as fluoride, manganese, and arsenic, are associated with worse cognitive outcomes. Children exposed to these chemicals are more likely to have lower IQ scores, cognitive dysfunction, and other behavioral problems (Zoni and Lucchini 2013; Akter 2019; Green et al. 2019). The introduction of tap water might also increase income because of more efficient household production and changes in time allocation (Ilahi and Grimard 2000; Devoto et al. 2012; Koolwal and van de Walle 2013).

The accessibility of tap water may also affect a child's cognitive skills through X_t, particularly the time investment of main caregivers. In developing countries, households without sustainable access to water spend a considerable amount of time collecting water for domestic use, and this task is often designated to women (Devoto et al. 2012; Ashraf et al. 2021). As mothers are usually the primary caregivers of young children, access to tap water could free up mothers' time from water collection to more productive child-rearing activities and hence enhance children's cognitive development.

Last, but not least, tap water exposure may have an indirect effect on the development of cognitive skills through its impact on early childhood health. Equation (3.1) shows that the stock of cognitive skills at time $t + 1$, θ_{t+1}^c, is determined by human capital stock H_t, which includes both early childhood cognitive skills and health. Evidence suggests that early childhood health status is positively associated with cognitive functions in later life (Case and Paxson 2009). If receiving access to tap water improves general physical health in early childhood, then cognitive development could be enhanced.

Because our data set does not include information on the chemical contents of drinking water before and after the program, we cannot evaluate the impact of exposure to the toxic chemicals discussed above. Instead, in Sect. 3.9, we analyze a few ways in which tap water may affect cognitive skills using data on women's time use, child health, and household income.

3.5 Data

3.5.1 Data Source

We draw data from the CFPS survey, which was launched in 2010 by the Institute of Social Science Survey (ISSS) of Peking University, China (Xie 2012). It is a longitudinal study of a nationally representative sample of Chinese communities, families, and individuals. The target sample of CFPS consists of 16,000 households in 25 provinces in China, excluding Hong Kong, Macao, Taiwan, Xinjiang, Tibet, Qinghai, Inner Mongolia, Ningxia, and Hainan. A total of 14,798 households and 42,590 individuals from 645 communities were successfully interviewed in the baseline survey, the source of the data for the main part of our analysis. The survey provides detailed information at the community, household, and individual levels that is essential for our analysis. Our main sample for the analysis includes 2,168 children from 382 villages who were aged 10–15 in 2010.

3.5.2 Outcome Variable

Two tests of cognitive skills, a word recognition test and a math test, were administered to children at least 10 years of age in the CFPS 2010. These questions assess the children's abilities to recognize words and perform quantitative reasoning. Similar tests have been documented in the literature as measures of cognitive skills (Hanushek and Woessmann 2008). The word recognition test includes 34 questions, with the final score ranging from 0 to 34, and the math test includes 24 questions, with the final score ranging from 0 to 24. The questions vary by educational level. To facilitate the comparison of the estimates with other studies of child development (see, e.g., Blau and Grossberg 1992; Parcel and Menaghan 1994; Ruhm 2004), a standardized score is obtained for each test by subtracting the mean and dividing by the standard deviation of those in the same-cohort comparison group who live in villages that had not obtained access to tap water by 2010. An increase of one standard deviation in the math test score is equivalent to answering 4.5 more questions correctly on the test, and an increase of one standard deviation in the word test score is equivalent to correctly answering 7.3 more questions on the test. Our main outcome is the average cognitive test score. It is obtained by first calculating the weighted average of the word recognition and math test scores, with the weights being the inverse of the respective number of questions in each test, and then standardizing the weighted average. All test scores mentioned below are scores after standardization unless otherwise specified. Using the original test scores generates very similar results (see Sect. 3.8.6 for discussion).

3.5.3 Treatment Variable

The treatment variable that we are interested in is the number of years a child was exposed to a village-level tap water connection in early life, spanning from the prenatal period through early childhood. Health at birth can be affected by *in utero* conditions and is an important predictor of long-term outcomes (Aizer and Currie 2014). Early childhood, which is usually defined as the first five years of life, is also believed to be a critical period for human capital accumulation (Currie and Almond 2011; Attanasio 2015). We therefore expect that if tap water exposure has any impact on child cognitive development, the largest magnitude of the effect should occur in utero and during early childhood.

The years of exposure to tap water in early life is jointly determined by the timing of receiving a tap water connection at the village level and the child's year of birth. The information on the availability of a tap water connection and the first year of connection is extracted from the community survey data of the CFPS 2010. The community survey was administered to an individual in each community who knows the community well and has access to community statistical materials, such as the director or the accountant of the community committee or the secretary of the Party branch (Xie 2012). The community survey asks, "Does your community have this facility: *(facility name)*?" If the answer is yes, the survey further asks in which year the facility was first introduced to the community. We use the answer to this question as the year in which the village started to have tap water connections. In Fig. 3.1, we plot the number of new villages connecting to tap water each year and the cumulative distribution of the village-level tap water rollout from 1980 to 2010 among 404 villages in the CFPS 2010. In 1980, less than 5% of the villages had access to tap water. By 2010, over 55% of the villages had received a connection.

3.5.4 Sample

Our main sample includes 2,168 children who were from 382 villages and were aged 10–15 in 2010. As cognitive tests are administered to children who are at least 10 years old in the CFPS 2010, and as the scores of the tests are used to construct the outcome variables, age 10 is chosen as the starting point. We choose age 15 as the ending point because, in general, children complete the nine-year compulsory education at age 15, at which point many rural children choose to leave home to study or work.[4]

One concern about the treatment variable is that it may fail to measure the correct amount of exposure if households choose to move to villages that have recently obtained access to tap water. This movement may bias our estimates if the immigration decision is systematically related to both the timing of the tap water connection

[4] Extending the age range to 17 years of age produces similar results. The results are available in Table 3.6.

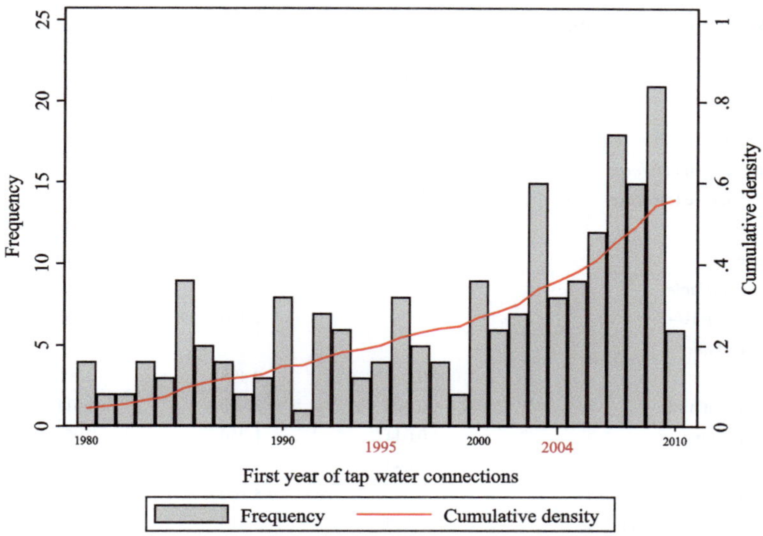

Fig. 3.1 Rollout of the rural drinking water program in China. *Notes* Data from the China Family Panel Studies (CFPS) 2010. The histogram plots the number of new villages connecting to tap water each year, and the red curve plots the cumulative distribution of the village-level tap water rollout during 1980 and 2010 among 404 villages. The variation in the treatment variable in this study comes from the children living in villages that first obtained a tap water connection between 1995 and 2004 (highlighted in red)

and the outcomes. To rule out any potential bias caused by immigration, we restrict the sample to children whose place of birth, place of residence at age three, place of residence in 2010, and place of *hukou* (household registration) in 2010 coincide, so our sample consists of children who are most likely to have resided in the village *in utero* and throughout early childhood. Applying these sample restriction criteria excludes 317 children (12.7%).[5] Regressions without imposing the sample restrictions have results similar to our main findings.

There exists sample selection caused by children leaving home for study or work, household emigration, or other reasons. If the sample selection is systematically related to the treatment variable, our estimates might be biased. In Sect. 3.8.5, we provide evidence that this type of sample selection is unlikely to bias our estimates.

The 2,168 children included in our sample were born between 1995 and 2000. Table 3.1 reports the summary statistics of the sample. Following Deming (2009), we account for missing data by imputing the mean value for the sample and include a dummy variable for the imputed responses in the regressions.

[5] Regarding these 317 children, we know that they migrated from other villages to the surveyed villages after they were born, but we do not know the exact geographic locations of their birthplaces or how long they lived there before migrating. Because we do not have a precise measure of early-life exposure for these children, we exclude them from the main analysis.

Table 3.1 Summary statistics

	Proportion of missing values	Mean	s.d.
	(1)	(2)	(3)
Panel A: Individual characteristics (2,168 children)			
– Outcomes in original form			
Average cognitive test score	0	18.142	6.210
Word score	0	20.913	7.334
Math score	0	10.850	4.514
– Treatment variable			
Exposure to tap IU–5	0	1.326	2.380
– Control variables			
Boy[d]	0	0.498	0.500
Mother's age at birth	0.009	25.702	4.511
Number of siblings	0.044	1.250	0.956
Birth order	0.044	1.761	0.906
Number of household members	0	5.100	1.633
Father's years of schooling	0.017	5.915	3.934
Mother's years of schooling	0.020	4.003	3.932
Exposure to electricity IU–5	0.036	5.362	1.735
Exposure to cable/satellite TV IU–5	0.037	1.688	2.407
Exposure to roads IU–5	0.022	3.451	2.831
Exposure to health facilities IU–5	0.011	2.705	2.930
Exposure to landline phones IU–5	0.036	3.917	2.552
Panel B: Community characteristics (382 villages)			
Suburban village[d]	0	0.217	0.413
Distance to nearest town or city (hours)	0.010	1.091	1.732
Population	0	2,475.686	2,316.092
Area (km^2)	0.081	51.582	412.411
Average years of schooling of 25–55-year-olds	0	5.406	1.971
Net income per capita (yuan)	0.037	3,612.587	3,096.639
Topology: hills[d]	0	0.317	0.466
Topology: mountains[d]	0	0.157	0.364
Topology: plateaus[d]	0	0.045	0.206
Topology: plains[d]	0	0.325	0.469
Topology: others[d]	0	0.157	0.364
Having tap water connection[d]	0	0.550	0.498
Having electricity[d]	0	0.914	0.281
Having cable/satellite TV[d]	0	0.707	0.456
Having road connection[d]	0	0.856	0.352
Having health facilities[d]	0	0.584	0.494
Having landline phone[d]	0	0.872	0.335

Notes The main sample for analysis consists of 2,168 children. We account for missing data by imputing the mean value for the sample, and include a dummy variable for imputed responses in the regressions. Column (1) reports the proportion of missing values for each variable. [d] denotes dummy variables

3.5.5 The Reliability of the Reported Data

We provide three pieces of empirical evidence to support the reliability of the reported data on tap water availability. First, we show that the time use pattern differs for women aged 20–45 by tap water availability. When having one or more children aged 0–5, women living in villages with tap water spent more hours taking care of family members than those in villages without tap water. In contrast, when having no children aged 0–5, women in villages with tap water spent the same amount of time on family care as those without tap water but more time on labor market activities and housework. A detailed discussion on the time use pattern is provided in Sect. 3.9.1.

Second, the household-level tap water penetration rate differs based on tap water availability in the village. As shown in Fig. 2.1, in villages that had not obtained a tap water connection by 2010, less than 10% of the households were using tap water for cooking in 2010, while the share of households using tap water for cooking falls in the range of 50% to 80% in villages that had received a connection before 2010. The large gap in the tap water penetration rates between villages with and without tap water connection in 2010 supports the validity of the survey question on tap water availability in the CFPS.

Third, the tap water availability among CFPS villages is very close to the national level. According to the 2010 China Urban-Rural Construction Statistical Yearbook, 52.3% of the 294,749 villages nationwide had obtained a tap water connection by 2010, whereas 56% of the 404 villages in the CFPS survey had a tap water connection in 2010.

Moreover, we argue that the reported data on the introduction year of a tap water connection in the village are reliable for two reasons. First, receiving a tap water connection is a salient and socially desirable event for rural residents. Hence, the introduction year is likely to be accurately reported even many years later (Beckett et al. 2001). Second, the connection and coverage rate of tap water is standard information in village statistical materials, such as village chronicles of events. Respondents could retrieve the information with ease by referring to these materials. Nevertheless, reporting error, if any, may bias our estimates. We address the issue of reporting error in Sect. 3.8.3. We also show in Sect. 3.8.1 that replacing the village measure with the county-level tap water coverage rate generates a comparable estimate.

In the absence of the exact month of receiving the connection, we define the period of interest as one year before birth through the first five years of life (spanning six years) and assume that the treatment starts counting from the first year of the village's access to tap water. To illustrate this, consider a child born in 1999 in a village that received a tap water connection in 2000. The child's exposure to tap water begins counting in 2000, and the child is considered to receive four years of exposure during the period of interest. This measure assumes that the tap water connection occurs at the beginning of a year. In reality, the connection's timing may be spread out over the year. The possible impact of the measurement error on our estimation is discussed in Sect. 3.8.4.

3.6 Empirical Specification

The human capital indicator Y_{ict} in 2010 for child i from village c and born in year t can be expressed as

$$Y_{ict} = \phi \text{Exposure to tap IU-5}_{ct} + X_{ict}\beta + g_c + \gamma_t + \epsilon_{ict}, \tag{3.2}$$

where $\text{Exposure to tap IU-5}_{ct}$ measures the years of exposure to tap water in early life for children from village c born in year t. It takes discrete values from zero to six.[6] X_{ict} is a vector of basic individual and household characteristics, including gender, number of siblings, birth order, mother's age at birth, number of household members, and parents' years of schooling.[7] g_c is the village fixed effects that control for time-invariant village-level characteristics that may be associated with both the timing of the tap water connection and the outcomes. γ_t is the unrestricted cohort effects at the national level. ϵ_{ict} is the random error term.

This empirical specification is essentially a DID model, where we identify the impact of exposure to tap water, represented by ϕ, from the variation across birth cohorts within villages. If cohort trends are the same for all villages conditional on observables X_{ict}, the difference in outcomes of children from villages that experienced a new connection to tap water between 1995 and 2004 (the treatment group) captures the joint impact of tap water connection and the cohort fixed effects. As shown in Fig. 3.1, the fraction of villages with a tap water connection increases by around 20 percentage points during 1995 and 2004, providing a substantial variation in the treatment variable. Cohort fixed effects can be identified from the control group, consisting of children from villages that had a tap water connection before 1995 or had not received a connection by 2004. Children from villages that were not connected by 2004 had no exposure to tap water in early life. For children from villages that received a tap water connection before 1995, their early-life exposure to tap water is six years.

Taking into account the possibility that cohort effects may vary across provinces, we replace the cohort fixed effects γ_t with province-specific cohort fixed effects, denoted by δ_{pt}. To acknowledge the possible differences in cohort or time trends across villages with different characteristics, we follow Gentzkow and Shapiro (2008) and Hoynes et al. (2016) and include a set of village characteristics W_c that interact

[6] The baseline specifications assume a linear relationship between cognitive skills and years of exposure to tap water. In Sect. 3.8.6, we explore alternative non-linear specifications. We find evidence in support of the baseline linear specifications.

[7] Adding household income and an indicator of a household's engagement in non-farm work collected in 2010 to the regressions does not affect our estimates. The results are available in Table 3.8. The early life of the 10–15-year-olds ranges from 1994 to 2004, all of which are years before 2010. Consequently, household income and engagement in non-farm work may have been altered by a child's early-life exposure to tap water. Thus, we do not control for them in the baseline specifications.

with a cohort-specific coefficient vector θ_t.[8] The validity of our identification strategy then relies on the parallel trends assumption that, in the absence of tap water exposure, the changes in cognitive skills across cohorts would be the same for villages with similar characteristics within a given province. The DID estimator ϕ could be biased if tap water exposure varies simultaneously with other factors that affect children's cognitive development. For example, other concurrent government programs might have driven the effects instead of tap water exposure. Hence, we additionally control for years of exposure to electricity, cable/satellite TV, roads, health facilities, and landline phones in early life (denoted by $\text{Other exposure IU-5}_{ct}$) in our preferred specification. To summarize, our preferred specification becomes:

$$Y_{ict} = \phi \text{Exposure to tap IU-5}_{ct} + X_{ict}\beta + g_c + \delta_{pt} + \theta_t W_c + \text{Other exposure IU-5}_{ct}\tau + \epsilon_{ict}. \quad (3.3)$$

We provide evidence to support the validity of our identification strategy in Sects. 3.7.2 and 3.7.3. In Sect. 3.8.1, we show that accounting for sanitation facilities at the county level does not affect our estimates. We also show that the estimates are not affected by other potential confounding factors, including migration, school supply, the one-child policy, real income, urbanization, and the prevalence of left-behind children (Sect. 3.8.2). To account for any serial correlation across different cohorts within the same village, standard errors are clustered at the village level.

3.7 Main Results

3.7.1 The Effect of Tap Water Exposure on Cognitive Skills

Table 3.2 reports the estimation results for the average cognitive test score as well as the individual scores of the word recognition and math tests. We find strong evidence that exposure to tap water in early life has a positive and significant effect on a child's cognitive skills in adolescence.

Assuming common time trends nationwide, column (1) reports the results in which the individual and household characteristics, cohort fixed effects, and village fixed effects are controlled for. One additional year of early-life tap water exposure is associated with a 0.108 standard deviation increase in children's average cognitive test scores. By augmenting the specification with the province-specific cohort effects and the interactions of village characteristics and cohort dummies, column (2) relaxes the assumption of nationwide common trends and allows the time trends to vary by province and across villages with different characteristics. The estimated effect goes up to 0.126, suggesting that the latent cohort or time trends in cognitive skills may vary across provinces and across villages with different characteristics.

[8] The village characteristics used to construct interactions are an indicator of suburban village, log of distance to nearest town or city, log of area, average years of schooling of 25–55-year-olds, and topographic characteristics. See Sect. 2.1.2 for the definitions. Considering the endogeneity of a village's population size in 2010, we do not include the interactions of population and cohort dummies in the baseline analysis. Our results remain unchanged when including the interactions.

To address the concern that the effect of tap water exposure is driven by other concurrent government programs, we further include the years of exposure in early life to a series of other public facilities—electricity, cable/satellite TV, roads, health facilities, and landline phones—as control variables in our preferred specification in column (3).[9] The point estimate shows that one additional year of early-life exposure to tap water leads to a 0.132 standard deviation increase in the average cognitive test score. This evidence suggests that the effect of early-life exposure to tap water is unlikely to be driven by other public programs.

Applying the same specification as in column (3), we look at the word recognition test and the math test separately in columns (4) and (5). We find that tap water exposure has positive effects on both test scores. One additional year of early-life tap water exposure increases a child's word recognition test score by 0.073 standard deviations and math test score by 0.162 standard deviations, although only the latter increase is statistically significant.[10] Here, an increase of one standard deviation is equivalent to answering 4.5 more questions correctly on the math test or 7.3 more questions on the word recognition test. Taking the math test as an example, one additional year of early-life exposure results in correctly answering 0.7 more questions on the test. It also means that a child receiving full exposure in early life would answer around four more questions correctly than an otherwise similar child with no exposure.

There is little evidence on how early-life conditions or interventions affect children's cognitive development in China. To provide a better sense of the magnitude of the estimated impact, we compare our results with the findings from two recent studies in other developing countries. Maluccio et al. (2009) examine the intention-to-treat effect of a nutritional intervention during the period from birth to 36 months of age in rural Guatemala. The intervention is estimated to increase reading comprehension and non-verbal cognitive test scores in adulthood by 0.25 standard deviations. Hence, the long-term return of a one-year intervention is a 0.08 standard deviation increase in cognitive ability. In another study, Barham (2012) finds that the Matlab Maternal and Child Health and Family Planning (MCH-FP) program in Bangladesh increases cognitive test scores at ages 8–14 by 0.39 standard deviations. Because the program provides health interventions to children under the age of five, the estimated effect of a one-year intervention is approximately 0.08 standard deviations. Our estimated effect of one year of tap water exposure, a 0.132 standard deviation increase in the cognitive test score, is therefore of a reasonable magnitude and tends to mildly exceed the effects of the above-mentioned early-life interventions.

---

[9] The estimates remain almost unchanged when we additionally control for any one of the other public programs at a time or control for all the other public programs at the same time. The results are available from the authors upon request.

[10] A similar pattern is observed in the effects of other early childhood conditions (Almond et al. 2009; Majid 2015). For example, Almond et al. (2009) find that, in Sweden, prenatal exposure to Chernobyl fallout lowers students' mathematics performance more than their performance in Swedish in secondary school. We cannot provide a convincing explanation for this pattern, and it is a direction for future research.

Table 3.2 The impact of tap water exposure on cognitive skills

Dep. var.:	Average cognitive test score			Word	Math
	(1)	(2)	(3)	(4)	(5)
Exposure to tap IU–5	0.108*** (0.034)	0.126*** (0.045)	0.132*** (0.046)	0.073 (0.049)	0.162*** (0.050)
Boy	–0.109** (0.050)	–0.098* (0.054)	–0.105* (0.054)	–0.166*** (0.057)	0.004 (0.049)
Mother's age at birth	0.005 (0.006)	0.008 (0.006)	0.008 (0.006)	0.011 (0.007)	0.003 (0.007)
Number of siblings	–0.022 (0.052)	–0.020 (0.055)	–0.022 (0.055)	0.018 (0.052)	–0.071 (0.060)
Birth order	–0.064 (0.045)	–0.076 (0.047)	–0.074 (0.047)	–0.083* (0.047)	–0.037 (0.049)
Number of household members	0.005 (0.018)	0.009 (0.019)	0.007 (0.020)	–0.001 (0.019)	0.018 (0.022)
Father's years of schooling	0.036*** (0.007)	0.037*** (0.007)	0.037*** (0.007)	0.037*** (0.007)	0.025*** (0.008)
Mother's years of schooling	0.010 (0.007)	0.010 (0.008)	0.010 (0.008)	0.006 (0.008)	0.011 (0.008)
Observations	2,168	2,168	2,168	2,168	2,168
R^2	0.409	0.447	0.448	0.444	0.396
Number of clusters	382	382	382	382	382
Cohort FE	Y	N	N	N	N
village FE	Y	Y	Y	Y	Y
Province-cohort FE, village controls × cohort FE	N	Y	Y	Y	Y
Early-life exposure to other public facilities	N	N	Y	Y	Y

Notes * means significant at 10%, ** significant at 5%, and *** significant at 1%. Each column represents a separate regression with a sample of children aged 10–15 from the CFPS 2010. Test scores are standardized measures with a mean of zero and a standard deviation of unity. In column (2), the village characteristics used to construct interactions with cohort dummies are an indicator of suburban village, log of distance to nearest town or city, log of area, average years of schooling of 25–55-year-olds, and topographic characteristics (hills, mountains, plateaus, plains, and others). Columns (3)–(5) also include early-life exposure to other public facilities, including electricity, cable/satellite TV, roads, health facilities, and landline phones. Standard errors in parentheses are clustered at the village level

3.7.2 Does the Timing of Treatment Matter?

The treatment thus far is the number of years that a village-level tap water supply system is available in early life. However, our estimates may pick up treatment effects beyond early life, as a child is definitely exposed to tap water in later life if the child receives any exposure in early life and stays in the same village. An event study model would allow us to explore the relationship between the timing of the initial exposure and the cognitive outcomes. In addition, the validity of our identification strategy relies on the parallel trends assumption, the violation of which would lead to spurious findings. We can also use the results from the event study to evaluate the validity of the research design.

The event time is defined as the difference between the first year of a tap water connection at the village level and the year of birth.[11] An event time less than or equal to -1, between 0 and 4, and greater than 4 indicates full exposure, partial exposure, and no exposure, respectively. We generate a series of dummies based on two-year intervals of event time. We re-estimate Equation (3.3) but replace the treatment variable $\text{Exposure to tap IU-5}_{ct}$ with the dummies. In doing so, we allow the effect of tap water exposure to vary with age at initial exposure. An event time of 5 to 6 is used as the base group. The end points are open brackets (event time below -7 on the left, and event time over 10 on the right), which helps reduce the collinearity between event time and birth year. Because the sample is unbalanced with respect to event times, we follow Hoynes et al. (2016) and focus on the event study coefficients inside these unbalanced endpoints. We present the results in Fig. 3.2. Each dot indicates the coefficient of interest, and the 95-percent confidence interval is plotted by the vertical line segments.

We test three hypotheses in the event study. The first hypothesis is that tap water exposure in later life has little impact. Since children with an event time above 4 are not treated during early life (no exposure), this hypothesis would be supported if the estimates for any event time beyond 4 are similar and the lowest overall. Second, if the exposure starts during early life, the later a child is exposed to tap water, the smaller the improvement in cognitive skills. To support this hypothesis, the estimate would get smaller as the event time moves from -1 to 4.[12] Finally, additional years of exposure prior to an event time of -1 has little effect on cognitive development. If this hypothesis is true, we expect the estimates for event times less than -1 to be similar and the largest overall due to the cumulative effect of full exposure during early life. Figure 3.2 supports all three hypotheses very well, revealing early life as the crucial time window for cognitive development. Moreover, the findings of similar estimates for event times above 4 and similar estimates for event times less than -1 (the evidence supporting the first and third hypotheses) help to rule out that our estimates are driven by cohort trends within villages, confirming the validity of our identification assumption.

[11] For example, a child born in 2000 in a village that first got a tap water connection in 2002 would have an event time of 2. The child would have an event time of -2 if tap water was first connected to their birth village in 1998.

[12] We thank an anonymous referee for pointing out that the testing of the second hypothesis is also a specification test, which examines whether the baseline linear specification is rejected. More discussions on specification tests can be found in Sect. 3.8.6.

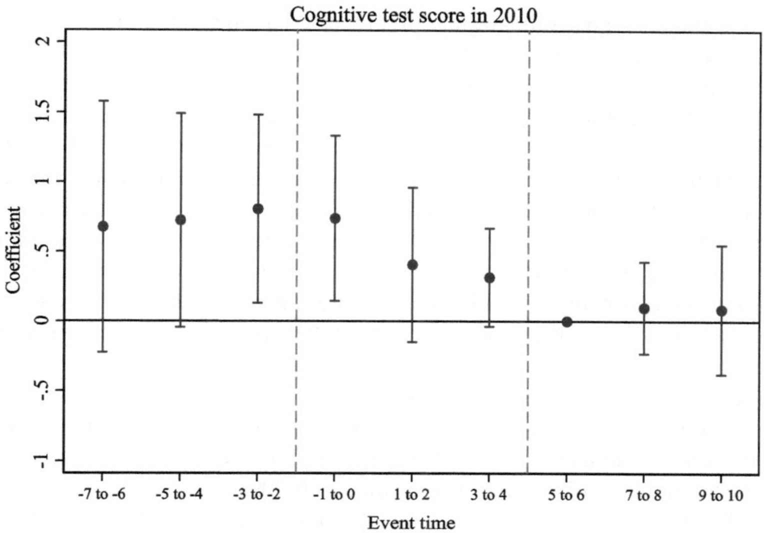

Fig. 3.2 Event study estimates of the impact of tap water exposure. *Notes* The figure plots coefficients (dot) and 95-percent confidence intervals (vertical line) from an event study analysis. The event time is defined as the difference between the first year of a tap water connection at the village level and the year of birth. For example, a child born in 2000 in a village that first got tap water connection in 2002 would have an event time of 2. The child would have an event time of −2 if tap water was first connected to the birth village in 1998. A negative event time indicates full exposure in early life. The event time of 5 to 6 is taken as the base group, so the estimates for the other groups are relative to that point. See Sect. 3.7.2 for a description of the model

3.7.3 Validity of DID Strategy

In this section, we further assess the validity of our identification strategy in two ways. First, we compare the characteristics of villages in the treatment and control groups. Then, we conduct a time-shifted placebo test.

The comparability between the treatment and control groups

In the main analysis, children from villages that first obtained a tap water connection between 1995 and 2004 serve as the treatment group, and those from villages that connected before 1995 or after 2004 constitute the control group. In order to compare the trends in the pre-intervention characteristics across these two groups of villages, we derive from the CFPS 2010 the average height, average years of schooling, sex ratio, and fertility rate at the village level for every five adjacent cohorts born between 1955 and 1984.[13] We do not include villages that received access before 1995, as the trends for the above-mentioned cohorts in those villages may actually reflect

[13] The calculation of village averages is done by five-year period. For example, the value in 1955 is in fact the average for individuals born between 1955 and 1959, and the value in 1980 is the average for individuals born between 1980 and 1984.

post-intervention trends. Villages that first received a tap water connection between 1995 and 2004 are considered to have early access.

In the regressions, we use the aggregated village characteristics as the dependent variables and control for the interactions between the five-year cohort dummies and the indicator of early access, village fixed effects, five-year cohort fixed effects, and other control variables. The coefficients on the interactions are plotted in Fig. 3.3. Most of the coefficients on the interactions are insignificant. The only exception is the fertility rate. For women born after 1960, those from villages that were connected earlier had fewer births than those from villages that were connected later, but the gap has not been growing or shrinking for cohorts since 1960. Hence, the comparison of pre-trends provides strong evidence for parallel trends in the outcome variables for pre-treatment cohorts regardless of connection time.

We re-run the regressions using children from these two types of villages to see if the choice of control group matters for our estimates. The effect of early-life tap water exposure remains positive and significant on the average cognitive test score (a point estimate of 0.137 with p-value equal to 0.009). This exercise suggests that our conclusion still holds after excluding children from villages that first obtained a tap water connection before 1995.

Time-shifted placebo test

To rule out the possibility that other sources of unobserved trends drive the results, we conduct a placebo test using five groups of individuals, who were 16–21, 18–23, 20–25, 22–27, and 24–29 years old in 2010. We uniformly shift their birth year backwards by 6, 8, 10, 12, and 14 years, respectively, so that they were of the same "age," 10–15 years old in 2010, as the children in our main analysis. A pseudo Exposure to tap IU-5 is calculated using the shifted birth year and the actual first year of a tap water connection in the village. We re-run the regressions for each group with Exposure to tap IU-5 replaced by the pseudo Exposure to tap IU-5. The estimates from the placebo tests are plotted in Fig. 3.4 by shifted birth years. They are consistent with the main results; the only positive and significant coefficient is where the birth year is not shifted (the birth year shifted being "0" in the graph), which corresponds to the main specification. For all the other groups, the pseudo tap water exposure in early life is found to have little or no effect on the average cognitive test score. Overall, the findings from the placebo tests suggest that the main results are unlikely to be driven by unobserved trends.

3.7.4 Heterogeneous Effects

In this section, we investigate whether the effect of early-life tap water exposure varies by socioeconomic status (gender, mother's schooling, and household income) or the status of baseline water sources (source, amount, and quality). Dummy variables are generated accordingly. Interactions of these dummy variables with years of exposure in early life are added to the preferred specification, respectively. A mother

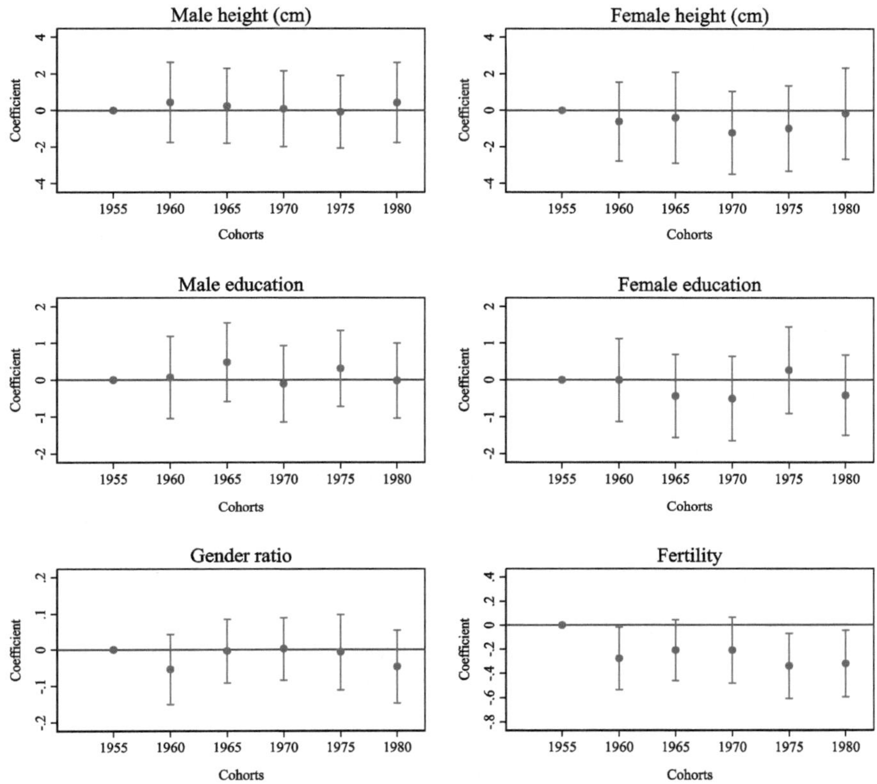

Fig. 3.3 Comparing pre-trends between villages connecting earlier and later. *Notes* The figure plots pre-intervention characteristics by every five-year period for males and females born between 1955 and 1984 from villages receiving a tap water connection between 1995 and 2004 (early access) and villages that did not receive a tap water connection before 2005 (late access). Each small figure is from a separate regression. Each dot on the solid line is the estimated coefficient on the interactions between the five-year-cohort dummies and a binary variable indicating whether the village receiving tap water connection early, and the 95-percent confidence interval is plotted by solid lines. The cohort of 1955 is taken as the base group. In addition to the above mentioned interactions, the model controls for village fixed effects, five-year-cohort fixed effects, province specific five-year-cohort fixed effects, and interactions between village characteristics and five-year-cohort dummies. The village characteristics used to construct interactions include an indicator of suburban village, log of distance to nearest town or city, log of area, and topographic characteristics (hills, mountains, plateaus, plains, and others). Standard errors are clustered at the village level

is considered to have a low education level if she has less than nine years of schooling, and a household is considered to be low-income if the household income is lower than the median level in the same village.

Next, we detail our approach for constructing the measures for the status of baseline water sources. In the CFPS 2010 family questionnaire, households are asked to report the source of water for cooking from a list: river/lake water, well/spring

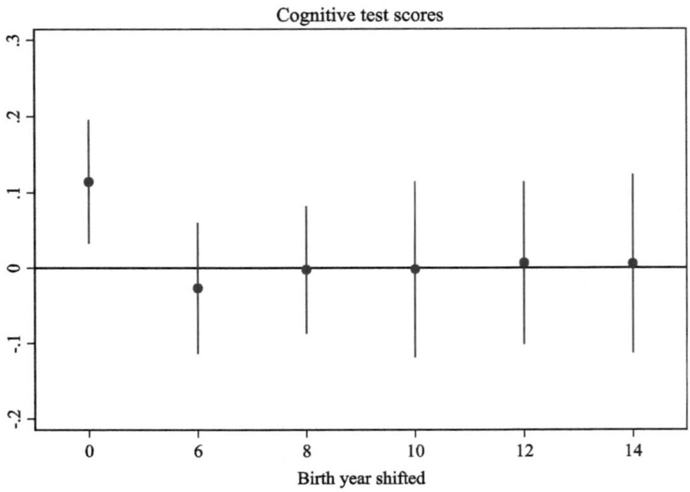

Fig. 3.4 Placebo tests using older cohorts. *Notes* In the placebo test, we uniformly shift the birth year of five groups of individuals who were 16–21, 18–23, 20–25, 22–27, and 24–29 years old in 2010 backwards by 6, 8, 10, 12, and 14 years, respectively, so that they were of the same "age", 10–15 years old in 2010, as the children in our main analysis. We generate pseudo Exposure to tap IU-5 for the individuals and estimate the effect for each of the five groups. Each dot on the solid line is the coefficient of interest, and the 95-percent confidence interval is plotted by solid lines. The estimates for the birth year shifted by "0" come from column (3) in Table 3.2

water, tap water, mineral/purified/filtered water, rainwater, cellar water, pond water, and other. We calculate the fraction of households using each water source within each village. The most frequently used water source other than tap water and mineral/purified/filtered water is the baseline water source. In each village, sources used by less than 10% of residents are excluded. Based on our definition, we find that well or spring water is the baseline water source in 320 of 345 villages (92.8%), water from a river, lake, or pond is used in five villages (1.5%), and rainwater or cellar water is used in 20 villages (5.8%). We generate a dummy indicator that takes on the value one if well or spring water is not the baseline water source (not using underground water) and zero otherwise.

We take precipitation amount as an indicator of the availability of water resources. A high precipitation amount suggests abundant water resources. We extract precipitation data from the National Centers for Environmental Information and map the data to the counties. We calculate the average annual precipitation between 1951 and 2010 using the monthly data of the 221 weather stations nationwide. Then we identify the centroid and five nearest weather stations of each county and use the Inverse Distance Weighting (IDW) interpolation method to calculate the annual precipitation amount at the county level. We match the imputed county-level precipitation data to our main sample in the CFPS 2010 and generate a dummy indicator equal to one if the precipitation amount is above the median (800mm) and zero otherwise.[14]

To obtain water quality at the county level, we follow Ebenstein (2012) and merge the water grade readings with the river basin data. We first draw data from the surface water quality readings of 484 geographic points across China's nine river systems in 2004. Each reading contains information about a set of monitored chemicals. The overall water grade is measured on a six-point scale, from Grade I (best) to Grade VI (worst). Ebenstein (2012) provides data on China's river basins created by the Hydro1k project conducted by the U.S. Geological Survey. Based on the data set, China can be separated into 989 basins (level 6) and a smaller set of larger basins (level 5 and level 4). For each county, we assign the average water grade reading from the smallest basin in which a monitoring station is observed. Among the 2,876 counties, 1,340 are observed within a level-6 basin in which we also observe at least one water quality monitoring station. The remaining counties are assigned the average of water grade readings of larger basins. With this algorithm, we assign water grade readings to 2,197 out of the 2,876 counties. We categorize the six water grades into three types: best (Grade I–II), medium (Grade III–IV, base group), and worst (Grade V–VI). Among the 135 CFPS counties, 95 counties have water quality data matched: 13 counties have the best water quality, 41 counties have the worst water quality, and the rest of the 41 counties have medium water quality.

Column (1) of Panel A in Table 3.3 shows that one additional year of exposure to tap water in early life is found to increase girls' cognitive test scores by 0.129 standard deviations, but the gender interaction term is small and statistically insignificant. Hence, we do not detect any gender difference in the effect of early-life tap water exposure. Similarly, columns (2) and (3) do not detect a significant difference in the effect by mother's schooling and household income. Our findings thus suggest no heterogeneous effects of early-life tap water exposure by socioeconomic status. It is likely that households have poor access to safe drinking water before a tap water connection, and the introduction of tap water to a village provides equal access to safe drinking water to all households, regardless of household characteristics.

We also check if the effect varies according to the alternative source of water used for cooking, the amount of rainfall, and the quality of surface water. Although none of the interactions are significant (Panel B of Table 3.3), we detect some evidence that the effect of early-life exposure to tap water may vary based on the status of baseline water sources. The effect is larger if underground water is not the alternative source of water, the precipitation amount is above the median, or the water quality is the worst. To conclude, children from areas with poorer access to underground water, a higher precipitation amount, and/or lower-quality surface water are likely to benefit more from early-life exposure to tap water.

[14] As counties in the CFPS are not identifiable, we run regressions with county-level variables matched to our main sample at the CFPS data center in Peking University, China. All county-level variables used for the analysis throughout this study are matched in the same way unless otherwise specified.

Table 3.3 Heterogeneous effects of tap water exposure by socioeconomic status and status of baseline water sources

	Dep. var.: Average cognitive test score		
	(1)	(2)	(3)
Panel A. Socioeconomic status			
	Gender	Mother's schooling	Household income
Exposure to tap IU–5	0.129*** (0.047)	0.131*** (0.049)	0.124*** (0.048)
Exposure to tap IU–5 × boy	0.005 (0.020)		
Exposure to tap IU–5 × low-educated mother		0.010 (0.019)	
Exposure to tap IU–5 × low-income household			0.003 (0.015)
Observations	2,168	2,125	2,069
R^2	0.448	0.452	0.454
Panel B. Status of baseline water sources			
	Water source	Water amount	Water quality
Exposure to tap IU–5	0.103** (0.047)	0.097 (0.070)	0.115* (0.061)
Exposure to tap IU–5 × not using underground water	0.044 (0.326)		
Exposure to tap IU–5 × rainfall above median		0.058 (0.094)	
Exposure to tap IU–5 × best water quality			0.016 (0.147)
Exposure to tap IU–5 × worst water quality			0.095 (0.160)
Observations	1,798	2,164	1,540
R^2	0.458	0.448	0.483

Notes * means significant at 10%, ** significant at 5%, and *** significant at 1%. Each column in each panel represents a separate regression with a sample of children aged 10–15 from the CFPS 2010. The same specification as in column (3) of Table 3.2 is applied for estimation. Standard errors in parentheses are clustered at the village level

Panel A: "Low-educated mother" equals one if the mother has less than nine years of schooling and zero otherwise. "Low-income household" equals one if the household income is lower than the median level in the same village and zero otherwise

Panel B: "Not using underground water" equals one if well or spring water is not the baseline water source and zero otherwise. "Rainfall above median" equals one if the average annual precipitation amount is above 800mm and zero otherwise. Water quality of baseline water sources is categorized into three types: best (grade I–II), medium (grade III–IV), and worst (grade V–VI). The type of medium is taken as the base group

3.8 Robustness Checks

3.8.1 The Effect of Sanitation

Evidence from other countries has pointed to the roles of sewerage and sanitation infrastructures in child outcomes. For example, Alsan and Goldin (2019) show that the combination of clean water and effective sewerage systems accounts for approximately one-third of the decline in log child mortality in Massachusetts between 1880 and 1920. Watson (2006) shows that improving sanitation infrastructure on Native American reservations leads to sharp reductions in both waterborne gastrointestinal disease and infectious respiratory disease among Native American infants. Hence, our estimated impact of early-life exposure to tap water may be confounded by the improvement in sewerage and sanitation systems.

A sewerage system is a network of pipes, pumps, and force mains for the collection of wastewater or sewage from a community (Encyclopedia Britannica).[15] The sewerage system is underdeveloped in rural China. A survey conducted by the Ministry of Construction on 74 villages located in 43 counties within nine provinces in 2005 shows that the sewage system and wastewater treatment system were absent in 96% of the villages (Ministry of Construction 2005). Consequently, wastewater from different sources was discharged directly into underground or surface water. According to the China Urban-Rural Construction Statistical Yearbooks (2006–2010), the wastewater treatment rate in villages was as low as 1% nationwide in 2006. It increased to 6% by 2010 but is still very low compared to the tap water coverage rate in villages in 2010 of 52.3%. As we are exploring the variation in tap water connections between 1995 and 2004, the general absence of sewerage and wastewater treatment systems suggests that our estimated effect of tap water exposure is unlikely to be driven by these systems.

We then investigate whether our estimates of the impact of tap water exposure would be confounded by the construction of sanitation facilities. Specifically, we would like to know whether our results are driven by the construction and usage of toilets. In rural China, the construction of toilets is independent of the availability of tap water and a sewerage system. Unlike the tap water system and sewerage system, the decision to construct toilets is more likely to be decentralized to the household level. As a result, we find that, in villages without a tap water connection, the share of children having a toilet at home is as high as 81.8%, only slightly lower than the share in villages with a connection, which is 83.7%. As the information on household accessibility to a toilet is only available for the year 2010 in our data, we are not able to identify the impact of early-life exposure to a toilet at the household or village level. Instead, we estimate the separate effects of tap water and toilet coverage rates during early life at the county level.

We obtain the rural tap water and toilet coverage rates at the county level in 2000 and 2005 by aggregating the accessibility of tap water and toilets among rural

---

[15] See online source at: https://www.britannica.com/technology/sewerage-system.

Table 3.4 Possible confounding effect of sanitation

	Dep. var.: Average cognitive test score		
	(1)	(2)	(3)
Panel A. Separately identifying the effects of tap water and sanitation			
Average county tap coverage rate IU–5	0.760** (0.381)	0.760** (0.381)	0.336 (0.442)
Average county toilet coverage rate IU–5		0.060 (0.346)	–0.030 (0.383)
Average county tap coverage rate IU–5 × average county toilet coverage rate IU–5			0.657 (0.655)
Observations	1,853	1,853	1,853
R^2	0.341	0.341	0.341
Panel B. Accounting for sanitation in the baseline specification			
	+ County toilet coverage rate in 2000 × cohort	+ Change in county toilet coverage rate × cohort	+ County toilet coverage rate in 2000 × cohort
			+ Change in county toilet coverage rate × cohort
Exposure to tap IU–5	0.097* (0.051)	0.101* (0.052)	0.098* (0.051)
Observations	1,884	1,884	1,884
R^2	0.446	0.447	0.447

Notes * means significant at 10%, ** significant at 5%, and *** significant at 1%. Each column in each panel represents a separate regression with a sample of children aged 10–15 from the CFPS 2010. The county-level tap water and toilet coverage rates are aggregated from the 1% sample of the 2000 China Population Census and the 20% sample of the 2005 China 1% Population Sample Survey. Only counties with more than 100 observations in both samples are included

In Panel A, a county fixed-effects model is applied for estimation. For each child, we extrapolate the county-level average tap water and toilet coverage rates during early life. We control for individual and household characteristics, province-specific cohort fixed effects, and interactions of county characteristics and cohort fixed effects. The individual and household characteristics include gender, number of siblings, birth order, mother's age at birth, number of household members, and parents' years of schooling. The county characteristics used to construct interactions include GDP per capita in 2000, share of urban population in 2000, and their changes from 2000 to 2010. Standard errors in parentheses are clustered at the county level

In Panel B, the same specification as in column (3) of Table 3.2 is applied for estimation. Additional controls are described in column titles. Standard errors in parentheses are clustered at the village level

households in the 1% sample of the 2000 China Population Census and the 20% sample of the 2005 China 1% Population Sample Survey.[16] During 2000 and 2005, the average tap water coverage rate increases from 30% to 36%, and the average toilet coverage rate increases from 70% to 77%. The children in our sample were born between 1995 and 2000. By our definition, their early life spans from 1994 to 2004. For each child, we extrapolate the average tap water and toilet coverage rates at the county level during early life. Years in early life falling between 1994 and 2000 are assigned the coverage rate in 2000, and years falling between 2001 and 2004 are assigned the coverage rate in 2005. If a child's early life contains the year 2000, the average coverage rate during early life is then the weighted average of the coverage rates in 2000 and 2005.

In order to estimate the effects of tap water and toilet coverage at the county level during early life on cognitive development, we estimate a DID model similar to our preferred specification in column (3) of Table 3.2. Because the variation in exposure is now measured at the county level, we include county fixed effects, province-specific cohort fixed effects, as well as the interactions of cohort fixed effects and county characteristics (including GDP per capita in 2000, share of urban population in 2000, and their changes from 2000 to 2010). Column (1) of Panel A in Table 3.4 shows that full tap water coverage at the county level during early life significantly increases the average cognitive test score by 0.760 standard deviations. Our main results show that children receiving full village-level exposure could attain an average score 0.792 standard deviations higher than a child with no exposure. Using the county-level coverage rate, therefore, generates a comparable estimate to our baseline estimated effect of village-level exposure, providing support to the validity of our measure of early-life exposure at the village level. In column (2) of Table 3.4, we further add the county-level toilet coverage rate into the regression, and the estimate of the effect of tap water coverage does not change. In column (3), we control for the interaction of tap water and toilet coverage rates. The result indicates that the effect of the tap water coverage rate is higher when the toilet coverage rate is high, although the estimate is insignificant.

In Panel B of Table 3.4, we address the concern about the confounding impact of sanitation facilities in our preferred specification in column (3) of Table 3.2. We add controls for the interactions of the county toilet coverage rate in 2000 and cohort fixed effects and the interactions of changes in the county toilet coverage rate from 2000 to 2005 and cohort fixed effects, both separately and jointly. The point estimates of tap water exposure remain significant and positive. We have confirmed that the differences between the point estimates here and the baseline estimate are due to the smaller sample size caused by missing values in tap water and toilet coverage rates.

[16] Here we aggregate microdata to get county-level measures. To ensure precise county-level measures, we only include the counties having more than 100 observations in both samples of census data. We apply the same restrictions throughout the study when aggregating data from censuses unless otherwise specified. Removing the restrictions does not affect our results.

In sum, we find strong evidence that our baseline estimate of the impact of early-life exposure to tap water is unlikely to be confounded by the development of sanitation facilities.

3.8.2 *Other Potential Confounding Factors*

In this section, we show that the observed effect of tap water on cognitive skills is not driven by other confounding factors, such as other governmental programs, migration, school supply, the one-child policy, real income, urbanization, and the prevalence of left-behind children. We construct measures for these potential confounding variables at the village level whenever data are available and only use county-level measures when village data are not available.

Village macro factors

Although the villages in the CFPS 2010 are not identifiable, we can use the recalled data on the first year of having infrastructure in the community survey of the CFPS 2010 to shed some light on the macro trends in the sampled villages. In Fig. 3.5, we plot the rollout of six types of public infrastructure between 1980 and 2010. Panel 1) plots tap water (same as Fig. 3.1); panels 2)–6) plot electricity, cable/satellite TV, road, health facility, and landline phone, respectively. Access to tap water, cable/satellite TV, and landline phone was underdeveloped in 1980. Less than 5% of the villages had a tap water connection or cable/satellite TV, and only 20% of the villages had landline phones. All three of these types of infrastructure experienced rapid grown during 1980 and 2010 with the share of villages having each type of infrastructure increasing by over 50%. Although electricity had been introduced to 63% of the villages by 1980, we still observe a 28% increase in the share in the next 30 years. Both the share of villages having roads and having a health facility reached 38% in 1980. However, the expansion of roads is much faster than the expansion of health facility, with an increase of 47% compared to 19%. Note that in our study the variation in years of exposure to tap water comes from the children living in villages that first received a tap water connection between 1995 and 2004 (highlighted in red).

To address the concern that government programs other than tap water may have driven our estimates, we control for early-life exposure to all these public infrastructures in our preferred specification (column (3) of Table 3.2). Our estimates remain positive and significant after controlling for the exposure to other public infrastructure.

In the following, we further account for some other village macro factors, including migration workers, school supply, and the one-child policy.

Migration workers—The CFPS 2010 asks each child aged 6–16 "What is the longest time (in weeks) before age three that both parents are not around?" A longer absence period of parents indicates less time with parents for the children but may also suggest better nutrition supported by remittances from parents. Since this measure

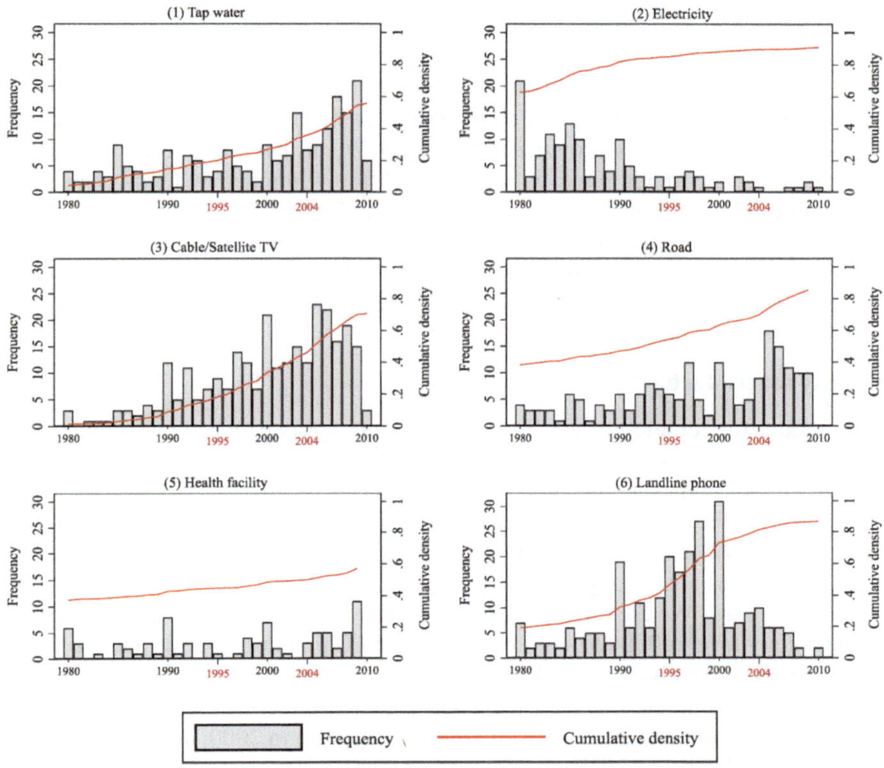

Fig. 3.5 Trends of infrastructure construction in villages in China. *Notes* Data from the China Family Panel Studies (CFPS) 2010. X-axis indicates the first year of connection at the village level. The histogram plots the number of new connections each year, and the red curve plots the cumulative distribution of the village-level rollout during 1980 and 2010 among 404 villages. The variation in the treatment variable in this study comes from the children living in villages that first obtained a tap water connection between 1995 and 2004 (highlighted in red)

is endogenous, we calculate the village's average by every two adjacent cohorts exclusive of their own households, which captures the prevalence of migrant workers in early life at the village level. We then add this new control variable to our preferred specification in column (3) of Table 3.2. The results reported in Panel A1 column (1) of Table 3.5 show that adding this control does not change our baseline results.

School supply—In the absence of a direct measure of school supply, we use a household's distance to the nearest high school from the CFPS 2010 as a proxy. We augment our preferred specification in column (3) of Table 3.2 with (1) the household-reported distance to the nearest high school, (2) the interactions of village average distance to the nearest high school (own household inclusive) and cohort dummies, and (3) the interactions of the village average distance (own household exclusive) and cohort dummies. Panel A1 columns (2)–(4) of Table 3.5 show that the estimated effects seldom change.

The one-child policy—Existing literature (e.g., Ebenstein 2010) uses the variation of the one-child policy intensity across provinces and years. Since we have controlled for province-cohort fixed effects in our preferred specification, the possible confounding effect of the one-child policy has been captured if the variation of the policy comes from the province-cohort level. We further account for the possible difference in time trends across villages with different implementations of the one-child policy. The community survey of the CFPS 2010 collected the details on the implementations of the one-child policy at the community level. We add the interactions of the number of births allowed and the cohort fixed effects to our preferred specification in column (3) of Table 3.2. The estimate in Panel A1 column (5) of Table 3.5 remains positive and significant.

County macro factors

Even though the counties in the CFPS are not identifiable, we seek the assistance of the CFPS data center to merge the county-level data to our sample for analysis. The 2,168 children in our main sample come from 382 villages located in 135 counties. In the following, we discuss the trends of real income, urbanization, migration (immigration and emigration), and left-behind children in the 135 counties and present the results from regressions accounting for the county macro factors.

Real income—We use GDP per capita as a proxy of real income. GDP per capita at the county level (2000–2010) is extracted from China Data Online and the China City Statistical Yearbooks (2001–2011). GDP deflators from the China Statistical Yearbooks are applied to obtain the 2000 constant price. The GDP per capita is 8,720 Chinese Yuan on average in the sampled counties in 2000, and it increases by 36% between 2000 and 2010.

Urbanization—The extent of urbanization is measured by the share of urban residents among the total population. In China, most urban residents reside in urban districts, while a minority of them live in the urban areas of the counties. Urbanization in the counties is lower and progresses slower than that in urban districts. Using the county-level assemblies of the 2000 and 2010 China Population Census, we find that the share of urban residents in the 135 sampled counties increases by 2% from 24% in 2000 to 26% 2010.

Migration—We consider immigration (migrants who come to a county from other counties) and emigration (migrants who have an *hukou* in a county but leave the county for other counties) separately. We obtain the immigration rate from the county-level assemblies of the 2000 and 2010 China Population Census. The share of immigrants among the total population decreases from 20% in 2000 to 18% in 2010. The share of emigrants among households with *hukou* in the county is calculated to be 9% using the county-level assemblies of the 2000 China Population Census. In the absence of emigration information in the county-level assemblies of the 2010 China Population Census, we are not able to determine the change between 2000 and 2010. Using the 1% sample of the 2000 China Population Census and the 20% sample of the 2005 China 1% Population Sample Survey, we find that the share of emigrants drops from 9% in 2000 to 4% in 2005.

Table 3.5 Other robustness checks

	(1)	(2)	(3)	(4)	(5)
Panel A. Other confounding factors					
A1. At village level (Dep. var.: Average cognitive test score, data from CFPS 2010)					
	Migrant workers	School supply			One-child policy
	+ Prevalence of migrant workers	+ Household reported distance to high school	+ village average (own inclusive) × cohort	+ village average (own exclusive) × cohort	+ Number of births allowed × cohort
Exposure to tap IU–5	0.133*** (0.046)	0.131*** (0.046)	0.138*** (0.046)	0.138*** (0.046)	0.115** (0.051)
Observations	2,168	2,168	2,168	2,168	2,153
R^2	0.449	0.449	0.450	0.450	0.452
A2. At county level (Dep. var.: Average cognitive test score)					
	GDP per capita[a] + GDP pc in 2000 × cohort + GDP pc growth rate × cohort	Share of urban[b] + Share of urban in 2000 × cohort + Change in share of urban × cohort	Emigration[c] + Emigration rate in 2000 × cohort + Change in emigration rate × cohort	Immigration[b] + Immigration rate in 2000 × cohort + Change in immigration rate × cohort	Left-behind[c] + Left-behind rate in 2000 × cohort + Change in left-behind rate × cohort
Exposure to tap IU–5	0.145*** (0.052)	0.130*** (0.046)	0.134*** (0.047)	0.131*** (0.049)	0.102* (0.052)
Observations	2,133	2,164	2,098	2,164	1,946
R^2	0.452	0.450	0.453	0.450	0.456
Panel B. Reporting error (Dep. var.: Average cognitive test score)					
	≥1994	≥1996	≥1998	Reliable answers	
Exposure to tap IU–5	0.134** (0.052)	0.137*** (0.052)	0.147** (0.060)	0.170*** (0.061)	
Observations	1,866	1,832	1,742	1,317	
R^2	0.443	0.443	0.448	0.448	
Panel C. Measurement error (Dep. var.: Average cognitive test score)					
Exposure to tap IU–5 (Mid-year connection)	0.127*** (0.044)				
Exposure to tap IU–5 (Year end connection)		0.110*** (0.040)			
Observations	2,168	2,168			
R^2	0.448	0.448			

(continued)

Table 3.5 (continued)

	(1)	(2)	(3)	(4)	(5)
Panel D. Sample selection (Dep. var. shown as column name)					
	Not in the final sample in 2010	Not living at home in 2010	Not surveyed in 2010	No test scores in 2010	Not surveyed in 2012
Exposure to tap IU–5	–0.002 (0.020)	0.006 (0.015)	–0.009 (0.015)	0.003 (0.010)	–0.002 (0.007)
Observations	2,700	2,700	2,539	2,251	3,367
Observations with dep. var.=1	532	161	288	83	519
Observations with dep. var.=0	2,168	2,539	2,251	2,168	2,848
R^2	0.391	0.346	0.451	0.366	0.447

Notes * means significant at 10%, ** significant at 5%, and *** significant at 1%.
[a]Data from China Data Online (CDO) and the China City Statistical Yearbooks
[b]Data from the county-level assemblies of the 2000 and 2010 China Population Census
[c]Data from the 1% sample of the 2000 China Population Census and the 20% sample of the 2005 China 1% Population Sample Survey. Only counties with more than 100 observations in both samples are included
Each column in each panel contains estimates from a separate regression with the same specification as in column (3) of Table 3.2. Standard errors in parentheses are clustered at the village level
In Panel D, each dependent variable is a dummy variable. Among the 2,700 children aged 10–15 in 2010, 161 children were not at home, 288 children were at home but did not participate in the survey, and 83 children did the child survey but did not take the cognitive tests

Left-behind children—We use the 1% sample of the 2000 China Population Census and the 20% sample of the 2005 China 1% Population Sample Survey to calculate the share of left-behind children. Individuals aged below 18 years are considered as children. Children are considered to be left behind if both parents are not living at home at the time of census and half left behind if at least one parent is not living at home at the time of census. We exclude 22 counties with less than 100 children in the samples. Among the remaining 113 counties with over 100 children, the share of left-behind children increases from 2% in 2000 to 6% in 2005, and the share of half left-behind children increases from 4% in 2000 to 19% in 2005.

To account for the possible impact of macro trends on our estimation, we add the interactions of cohort fixed effects and the measures of county-level macro factors as well as their changes into our preferred specification in column (3) of Table 3.2. Panel A2 of Table 3.5 shows that the estimated effects remain positive and significant.

To summarize, the exercise of accounting for the macro trends at the village and county levels provides supporting evidence that our estimates are not driven by these macro trends.

3.8.3 Reporting Error

As mentioned in Sect. 3.5, in the CFPS 2010, a knowledgeable individual who has access to statistical materials in each community was invited to complete the community questionnaire. As part of the survey, they were asked to provide the first year that the community received a tap water connection, the answer to which is used to construct the treatment variable in this study. Since receiving a tap water connection is a salient and socially desirable event in the community, and as the information is available in community statistical materials such as community chronicles of events, the knowledgeable respondents are likely to report accurate years (Beckett et al. 2001). However, reporting error, if it exists and is correlated with the introduction year of tap water in the community, would bias our estimates.

We address the issue of reporting error in two ways. First, Beckett et al. (2001) suggest that data quality likely deteriorates with the length of the recall period, so we exclude villages whose reported connection year is more than 16 years, 14 years, or 12 years ago (the reported year of first connection before 1994, 1996, or 1998). The results presented in Panel B columns (1)–(3) of Table 3.5 show that the exclusion of "vulnerable" observations results in similar estimates to the main results, suggesting that reporting error, if any, is not driving our results.

Second, we account for the correlation between interviewers' impressions of the quality of the respondents' answers and the quality of the data (Beckett et al. 2001). After each community survey of the CFPS 2010, interviewers evaluated the reliability of the respondent's answers on a scale of 1 to 7, with 1 being very unreliable and 7 very reliable. We construct a binary reliability measure and estimate our results using the subsample of children in the reliable villages only (with a score of at least 6). The estimated effect remains positive and significant, as indicated by column (4) in Panel B of Table 3.5.

To further rule out potential misreporting, we replace exposure to tap water at the village level with exposure at the county level. This results in an estimate comparable with the baseline estimate, providing support to the validity of our measure of early-life exposure at the village level. These discussions are detailed in Sect. 3.8.1.

3.8.4 Measurement Error

In our main analysis, we define early life as the period covering one year before birth through the first five years of life. Without information on the exact tap water connection time, we construct the treatment variable, namely, the early-life years of exposure to tap water, using children's birth year and the tap water connection year at the village level. We start counting early-life exposure in the first year of connection. By doing this, we assume that all the connections occur at the beginning of a year. The observed exposure, i.e., $\text{Exposure to tap IU-5}$ in Equation (3.3), is computed under this assumption.

In reality, however, the connection time may be spread out over a year. Suppose we know the exact date of connection, and hence the actual exposure is $\text{Exposure to tap IU-5}^*$. The measurement error $e = \text{Exposure to tap IU-5} - \text{Exposure to tap IU-5}^*$. If e is uncorrelated with the observed exposure, i.e., $\text{Cov}(e, \text{Exposure to tap IU-5}) = 0$, our estimate will remain consistent in the presence of the measurement error. Otherwise, our estimate will be subject to biases. If we know the distribution of the exact connection time, we can test whether $\text{Cov}(e, \text{Exposure to tap IU-5}) = 0$ holds. The magnitude of biases generated due to the measurement error will depend on the imposed distributional assumptions of the connection time.

To check if our estimates would be affected by a non-random connection time, we rerun the regressions considering two extreme cases. In the first case, we assume all the connections happen in the middle of a year, and the early-life exposure in the first year of connection is counted as 0.5 year. In the second case, we assume that all the connections happen at the end of a year, and we start counting early-life exposure in the second year of connection. The results are reported in Panel C of Table 3.5. In both extreme cases, we get results close to our baseline estimate. We also check the scenario in which the connection timing is uniformly distributed throughout the year, and the results do not change (available upon request).

Although we find that using the county tap water coverage rate generates comparable results to the baseline estimate (see Sect. 3.8.1), we prefer to use early-life exposure to tap water at the village level for two reasons. First, it is more relevant to policy to understand the effect of exposure at the village level, as the construction of tap water infrastructure is decentralized, and the timing of connection could vary across villages within a county. To get a sense of the size of the variation in tap water connection year across villages in the same county, we examine the difference between the earliest and latest connection years for villages within counties. The children in the baseline analysis come from 382 villages in 135 counties. We exclude 18 counties that have only one village surveyed by the CFPS 2010. Each of the remaining 117 counties has 2–5 villages covered in the survey. The difference in connection years can be categorized into eight types: no connection within the county by 2010, 0–4 years, 5–9 years, 10–14 years, 15–19 years, 20–24 years, 25–29 years, and 30+ years. Note that the difference here is underestimated for counties in which not all villages had received a connection by 2010. Figure 3.6 plots the distribution of the difference. Around 19% of the counties had no connection for all sampled villages. For 21% of the counties, the difference ranges from zero to four years. In over 60% of the counties, the difference is at least five years. The plotting suggests that using the county-level coverage rate would smooth out the variation across villages.

Second, the measure of county-level tap water coverage rate has a few drawbacks. Censuses are available for every five years, but tap water coverage rate of rural population can only be calculated using the 1% sample of the 2000 China Population Census and the 20% sample of the 2005 China 1% Population Sample Survey. If the expansion of tap water is not linear, the weighted average of the county tap water coverage rate during early life calculated using two waves of censuses may be a poor measure of the actual exposure. Without information on the tap water coverage rate in other periods of life for the children aged 10–15 in 2010, we are unable to prove that early life is the most critical time window in the process of cognitive development. Moreover, the county-level aggregated data from the samples of census data might be imprecise measures of the true coverage rates. To obtain precise measures, we have to drop counties with too few observations and reduce the sample size.

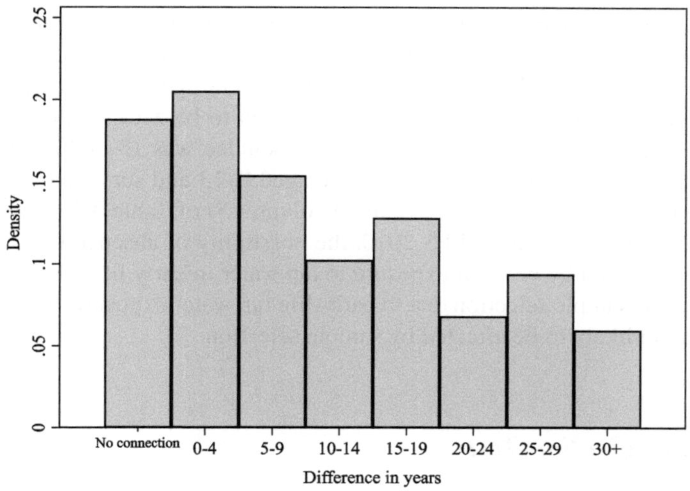

Fig. 3.6 Difference between earliest and latest connection years within counties. *Notes* Data from the China Family Panel Studies (CFPS) 2010. "Difference in years" indicates the gap between the earliest tap water connection year and the latest tap water connection year (or the year of 2010 if having no connection by 2010) among villages in a county. "No connection" indicates no tap water connection by 2010 for all sampled villages within a county

3.8.5 Sample Selection

Our sampled children may not be randomly selected. Children may be absent in the CFPS 2010 due to leaving home for study or work, household emigration, or other reasons. If the absence of the children in the survey is affected by the introduction of tap water in the village, our estimates may be biased. For instance, having access to tap water may improve children's school performance, which in turn may increase their probability of being admitted to prestigious middle schools outside their villages and consequently their probability of leaving home. Since the CFPS does not track children who have moved out of the community, we cannot test the above possibility directly. Instead, we rely on the existing data to shed some light.

Of the 2,700 children aged 10–15 in the CFPS 2010, there are 449 children whose families were surveyed while they themselves were not: 161 of them had left home, and the remaining 288 children were living at home but were not surveyed. There are another 83 children who completed the child survey but did not take the cognitive test. For these 532 children, we are able to calculate their actual years of exposure to tap water based on their parents' reporting of their basic information, such as gender and birth date. We estimate the effect of early-life exposure to tap water on the likelihood of the children not being included in the final sample, the likelihood of leaving home, the likelihood of not completing the child survey, and the likelihood of not taking cognitive tests in 2010. Panel D columns (1)–(4) of Table 3.5 show that early-life exposure to tap water does not affect any of these likelihoods.

Children could also be absent in the survey due to household emigration and other reasons. To check this, we examine the sample attrition between two adjacent CFPS waves, 2010 and 2012. We choose children who were aged 0–13 and participated in the survey in 2010. The starting point is chosen to be zero, as the information on fetuses is absent in 2010. The oldest child included was 13 in 2010 and turned 15 in 2012. Of the 3,367 children who were aged 0–13 and surveyed in 2010, 519 (15%) were not surveyed in 2012. Panel D column (5) of Table 3.5 shows that, for the children surveyed in the CFPS 2010, the possibility of absence from the CFPS 2012 is not affected by years of exposure to tap water in early life. Overall, we find no evidence of sample selection due to early-life tap water exposure. Therefore, our findings are unlikely to be affected by sample selection.

3.8.6 Specification Tests

In our main analysis, the test scores are standardized to facilitate comparison with other child development studies. In this section, we investigate whether the results are sensitive to the transformation of test scores. As there are 34 questions in the word recognition test and 24 questions in the math test, we get the average score by first multiplying the math test score by 34/24 and then taking the average. The highest possible average score is 34. The same specification as in column (3) of Table 3.2 is applied for estimation. The results are reported in Panel A of Table 3.7. One additional year of tap water exposure during early life increases the average test score by 0.618 (out of 34). Similar to the main results, only the math test score is significantly increased (by 0.512 out of 24 and significant at the 1% level), while the effect on the word recognition test score is insignificant. Taking the math test for example, a child receiving full exposure during early life (six years) would answer three more questions correctly in the math test than a child without any exposure, comparable to the estimate of four when the scores are standardized. In general, we find that our results are robust to the transformation of the cognitive test scores.

In Panel B of Table 3.7, we explore alternative non-linear specifications. The baseline specifications assume a linear relationship between cognitive skills and years of exposure to tap water, which is supported by the results from the event study. We conduct three additional specification tests: (1) replacing years of exposure with dummies of full exposure, partial exposure, and no exposure; (2) replacing years of exposure with dummies of years of exposure; and (3) additionally controlling for the square of years of exposure. The findings from the specification tests provide support to the baseline linear specifications.

Table 3.6 The impact of tap water exposure on cognitive skills for children aged 10–17

Dep. var.:	Average cognitive test score			Word	Math
	(1)	(2)	(3)	(4)	(5)
Exposure to tap IU–5	0.050** (0.025)	0.056* (0.031)	0.056* (0.031)	0.016 (0.033)	0.085** (0.034)
Boy	–0.101** (0.039)	–0.103** (0.043)	–0.107** (0.043)	–0.139*** (0.044)	–0.030 (0.040)
Mother's age at birth	–0.004 (0.005)	–0.004 (0.005)	–0.004 (0.005)	–0.002 (0.005)	–0.004 (0.005)
Number of siblings	–0.049 (0.034)	–0.054 (0.035)	–0.054 (0.036)	–0.022 (0.035)	–0.078** (0.038)
Number of household members	0.012 (0.017)	0.016 (0.017)	0.015 (0.018)	0.006 (0.017)	0.023 (0.019)
Father's years of schooling	0.033*** (0.006)	0.032*** (0.006)	0.032*** (0.006)	0.031*** (0.006)	0.025*** (0.006)
Mother's years of schooling	0.016*** (0.006)	0.015** (0.006)	0.015** (0.006)	0.010* (0.006)	0.018*** (0.007)
Observations	2,782	2,782	2,782	2,782	2,782
R^2	0.380	0.430	0.431	0.427	0.370
Number of clusters	388	388	388	388	388
Cohort FE	Y	N	N	N	N
Village FE	Y	Y	Y	Y	Y
Province-cohort FE, village controls × cohort FE	N	Y	Y	Y	Y
Early-life exposure to other public facilities	N	N	Y	Y	Y

Notes * means significant at 10%, ** significant at 5%, and *** significant at 1%. In addition to the 2,168 children aged 10–15 in the main sample, we include 615 children aged 16–17 in 2010 for analysis. In column (2), the village characteristics used to construct interactions with cohort dummies are an indicator of suburban village, log of distance to nearest town or city, log of area, average years of schooling of 25–55-year-olds, and topographic characteristics (hills, mountains, plateaus, plains, and others). Columns (3)–(5) also include early-life exposure to other public facilities, including electricity, cable/satellite TV, roads, health facilities, and landline phones. Standard errors in parentheses are clustered at the village level

3.9 Potential Mechanisms

As discussed in Sect. 3.4, early-life exposure to tap water could directly affect the development of cognitive skills and could also indirectly affect cognitive development through a variety of channels. In this section, we examine four of the most well-known channels documented in the literature: maternal time investment, childhood health, income and educational expenditure, and educational attainment.

Table 3.7 Specification tests

	(1)	(2)	(3)
Panel A. Test scores in original form			
Dep. var.:	Average cognitive test score (original)	Word (original)	Math (original)
Exposure to tap IU–5	0.618***	0.510	0.512***
	(0.215)	(0.313)	(0.168)
Observations	2,168	2,168	2,168
R^2	0.650	0.566	0.646
Panel B. Exposure in other forms			
	Dep. var.: Average cognitive test score		
Full exposure to tap IU–5	0.576** (0.244)		
Partial exposure to tap IU–5	0.291** (0.145)		
One year tap IU–5		0.100 (0.203)	
Two years tap IU–5		0.412* (0.210)	
Three years tap IU–5		0.559** (0.238)	
Four years tap IU–5		0.210 (0.310)	
Five years tap IU–5		0.612* (0.319)	
Six years tap IU–5		0.774*** (0.271)	
Exposure to tap IU–5			0.154 (0.095)
(Exposure to tap IU–5)^2			–0.004 (0.013)
Observations	2,168	2,168	2,168
R^2	0.448	0.450	0.448

Notes * means significant at 10%, ** significant at 5%, and *** significant at 1%. In Panel A, each column is estimated from a separate regression with the same specification applied as in column (3) of Table 3.2. All test scores are in the original form. "Average cognitive test score (original)" is obtained by first multiplying the math test score by 34/24 and then taking the average

In Panel B, each column is estimated from a separate regression with Exposure to tap IU-5 in column (3) of Table 3.2 replaced by exposure in other forms. "No exposure to tap IU–5" is omitted in both columns (1) and (2)

In both panels, standard errors in parentheses are clustered at the village level

Table 3.8 The impact of tap water exposure on cognitive skills (adding household income and household doing non-farm work)

	Dep. var.: Average cognitive test score		
	(1)	(2)	(3)
Exposure to tap IU–5	0.125*** (0.047)	0.121*** (0.047)	0.121*** (0.046)
Log of household gross income last year (yuan)	0.007 (0.041)		0.011 (0.041)
Household doing non-farm work		0.166** (0.084)	0.167** (0.084)
Boy	–0.113** (0.056)	–0.111** (0.056)	–0.112** (0.056)
Mother's age at birth	0.010 (0.007)	0.010 (0.007)	0.010 (0.007)
Number of siblings	–0.015 (0.059)	–0.011 (0.060)	–0.011 (0.060)
Birth order	–0.089* (0.048)	–0.089* (0.048)	–0.089* (0.048)
Number of household members	0.009 (0.021)	0.011 (0.021)	0.010 (0.021)
Father's years of schooling	0.032*** (0.008)	0.031*** (0.008)	0.031*** (0.008)
Mother's years of schooling	0.016* (0.008)	0.014* (0.008)	0.014* (0.008)
Observations	2,069	2,069	2,069
R^2	0.454	0.456	0.456

Notes * means significant at 10%, ** significant at 5%, and *** significant at 1%. The same specification as in column (3) of Table 3.2 is applied for estimation. Standard errors in parentheses are clustered at the village level

3.9.1 *Time Use*

Evidence suggests that the burden of water collection in developing countries is borne primarily by women and girls (Devoto et al. 2012; Ashraf et al. 2021). According to the theoretical framework developed by Koolwal and van de Walle (2013), an improvement in water accessibility increases the labor productivity of water-related domestic activities (e.g., cleaning and cooking). The substitution effect would lead to an increase in the consumption of these domestic goods, although the time devoted to producing these goods may or may not increase (Koolwal and van de Walle 2013). Therefore, the time freed up from water management could be spent on other domestic activities (e.g., family care), the labor market, or leisure. While the evidence is rare, we would like to know whether accessibility to tap water increases the time spent on family care, which includes taking care of young children. If access to tap water increases maternal time investment, it might indirectly improve children's short- and long-term development, as maternal time is a key input for child development (Ruhm 2004, 2008; Miller and Urdinola 2010).

Because the historical time use data of mothers of the sampled children in our baseline analysis are not available from the CFPS 2010, we examine the effect of a village-level tap water connection on time use for a sample of rural women aged 20–45 years in the CFPS 2010. We divide them into two groups: those who have at least one child between the ages of zero and five in 2010 and those who do not. We divide each woman's time use into four sections: family care (including maternal time investment), paid work, housework (including time spent on water collection), and other activities.[17] We estimate the following equation:

$$Y_{ic} = \phi \text{Tapwater}_c + X_{ic}\beta + g_d + W_c\gamma + \epsilon_{ic}, \tag{3.4}$$

where Y_{ic} denotes the time use of woman i living in village c. There are three time-use outcomes: the number of hours spent taking care of family members in a week, the number of hours spent on paid work in a week, and the number of hours spent on housework in a week. Tapwater_c is a dummy indicating whether village c has a tap water connection in 2010. X_{ic} is a vector of variables measuring individual and family characteristics. g_d is the vector of county fixed effects. W_c denotes a series of village characteristics including the availability of many other public facilities (see the table notes of Table 3.9). The estimates of ϕ reveal the correlation between tap water availability and the time-use pattern.[18]

Column (1) of Table 3.9 shows that, when having one or more children aged 0–5, women living in villages with tap water indeed spent more hours taking care of family members than those in villages without tap water. However, the time spent on other household chores or in the labor market does not differ based on water accessibility, as shown in columns (2) and (3). In contrast, when having no children aged 0–5, women in villages with tap water spent the same amount of time on family care as those without (see column (4)). For these women, access to tap water is associated with more time spent in the labor market and other household chores (columns (5) and (6)), which is consistent with the findings of Ilahi and Grimard (2000). The divergent pattern between women with and without young children reflects different marginal returns of time for various household and labor market activities for women of these two groups.

In summary, our evidence suggests that the enhanced cognitive development of children with early-life exposure to tap water may in part stem from the increased time women spend caring for young children.

[17] For the details of the time use module, please refer to the China Family Panel Studies (2010) User's Manual (Xie 2012).

[18] Here we are comparing the time-use pattern of women from villages with tap water with that of their same-county counterparts from villages without tap water.

Table 3.9 Tap water access and women's time use

	Have child aged 0–5			Have no child aged 0–5		
Dep. var.:	Family care	Work	Housework	Family care	Work	Housework
	(1)	(2)	(3)	(4)	(5)	(6)
Tap water in village	6.240** (2.659)	−2.878 (2.818)	0.713 (0.870)	−0.101 (0.510)	3.975** (2.015)	1.480** (0.693)
Observations	1,233	1,238	1,232	3,127	3,138	3,124
R^2	0.269	0.293	0.282	0.199	0.215	0.251

Notes * means significant at 10%, ** significant at 5%, and *** significant at 1%. Each column represents a separate regression with a sample of women who were 20–45 years old in 2010. A county fixed-effects model is applied for estimation. "Tap water in village" equals one if the village has a tap water connection in 2010 and zero otherwise. The dependent variable is measured as the number of hours spent on each activity. Individual-level control variables include age of the respondent and its quadratic form, years of schooling, an indicator of living with the spouse, number of household members, and an indicator of farm household. Village-level controls include an indicator of suburban village, log of distance to nearest town or city, log of population, log of area, average years of schooling among the 25–55 years old residents, topographic characteristics of the village, share of labor force working outside of village, log of annual income per capita, and village accessibility to other facilities (kindergarten, primary school, health facility, electricity, road, cable/satellite TV, landline phone, and mobile signal). Standard errors in parentheses are clustered at the village level

3.9.2 Health

Better access to clean water is found to have first-order effects on childhood health by reducing the incidence of waterborne disease and improving nutritional status (Jalan and Ravallion 2003; Zhang 2012). It has also been documented that childhood health and circumstances have continuing and lasting effects on later outcomes (see, e.g., Case et al. 2005). Hence, we would like to know whether better access to tap water increases children's cognitive skills by improving children's health.

Unfortunately, health status *in utero* or during the early childhood period for children in our sample is not available. Instead, we investigate the effect of having a tap water connection on early childhood health using a sample of children aged 0–5 in 2010. We only include villages that received a tap water connection before 2005 or after 2010 to focus on the children who are either fully exposed since the year prior to birth or are never exposed.[19] We estimate the following equation:

$$Y_{ict} = \phi \text{Tapwater}_c + X_{ict}\beta + g_{dt} + W_c\gamma + \epsilon_{ict}, \quad (3.5)$$

[19] Our results are robust when including the villages getting access between 2005 and 2010.

where Y_{ict} denotes the health outcomes of child i born in year t and living in village c. It takes six measures of health status, including the number of illness incidences and the number of doctor visits the previous month; the number of doctor visits the previous year and whether total health expenditure for the previous year fell in the top quintile; and the number of illness incidences and doctor visits in the first 12 months after birth. Tapwater_c is a dummy indicating whether village c is connected to tap water before 2005. We do not use years of exposure, as it is highly correlated with the children's age. X_{ict} is a vector of variables measuring individual and family characteristics. g_{dt} is the vector of county-cohort fixed effects. W_c denotes a series of village characteristics including the availability of many other public facilities (see the table notes of Table 3.10). The estimates of ϕ reveal the correlation between tap water exposure and the childhood health outcomes. We show in Panel A of Table 3.10 that the early-life health of children from villages with a tap water connection is better than those without a connection on all six measures: fewer illness incidences and doctor visits and lower total health expenditures.

We further examine the effect of early-life exposure to tap water on height-for-age z-scores and the probability of stunting for a sample of children aged 6–15. The same specification as column (3) of Table 3.2 is applied, and the results are presented in Panel B of Table 3.10. One additional year of early-life tap water exposure leads to a 0.056 standard deviation increase in height and lowers the probability of stunting by 0.027. However, only the effect on stunting is statistically significant.

To summarize, we find supporting evidence showing that early-life exposure to tap water leads to better health in both early and late childhood. As childhood health is shown to be related to cognitive functions in later life (Case and Paxson 2009), our evidence suggests that childhood health might be a channel through which tap water connections improve cognitive skills.

3.9.3 Alternative Mechanisms

In this section, we consider the possibility that tap water exposure affects child cognitive skills through its impact on household income and educational attainment.

We first examine the effect of tap water exposure on household income and educational expenditure. We apply our preferred specification in column (3) of Table 3.2 to the sample of children aged 6–15 in 2010.[20] The results are reported in Table 3.11. We find a small and insignificant effect of early-life tap water exposure for all four income measures—(log of) household income, (log of) educational expenditure on the child, (log of) total household educational expenditure, and (log of) household

[20] Household income *in utero* or during the early childhood period is not available for children in our main sample (aged 10–15 in 2010). Instead, we can investigate the relation between tap water availability and household income using a sample of children aged 0–5 in 2010 and from villages that either received tap water before 2005 (full exposure) or after 2010 (no exposure). However, since we can only control for county-cohort fixed effects in this regression, we cannot rule out the possibility that any correlation we find is a result of village-level unobservables.

Table 3.10 Tap water access and health of children

	(1)	(2)	(3)	(4)	(5)	(6)
Panel A. Tap water access and health of children aged 0–5						
	Last month		Last year		First 12 months after birth	
Dep. var.:	# illness	# doctor visits	# doctor visits	Top 20% expenditure	# illness	# doctor visits
Tap water in village	–0.376*** (0.115)	–0.219** (0.100)	–1.007** (0.482)	–0.078* (0.042)	–1.443** (0.616)	–1.354*** (0.517)
Observations	2,036	2,049	1,952	1,996	1,641	1,635
R^2	0.425	0.436	0.428	0.437	0.424	0.448
Panel B. Tap water access and health of children aged 6–15						
Dep. var.:	Height-for-age z-score		Stunting			
Exposure to tap IU–5	0.056 (0.061)		–0.027* (0.014)			
Observations	3,253		3.253			
R^2	0.424		0.383			

Notes * means significant at 10%, ** significant at 5%, and *** significant at 1%. Each column in each panel represents a separate regression

In Panel A, the sampled children are from villages that either received tap water before 2005 or after 2010 and were aged 0–5 in 2010. "Tap water in village" equals one if the village first got a tap water connection before 2005 and zero otherwise. A county-cohort fixed-effects model is applied for estimation. Individual- and household-level control variables include the child's gender, age, age squared, number of siblings, mother's age at birth, parents' years of schooling, number of household members, an indicator of farm household, and log of family income. Village-level controls include an indicator of suburban village, log of distance to nearest town or city, log of population, log of area, average years of schooling among the 25–55 years old residents, topographic characteristics of the village, share of labor force working outside of village, log of annual income per capita, and village accessibility to other facilities (kindergarten, primary school, electricity, cable/satellite TV, road, health facility, landline phone, and mobile signal)

In Panel B, the same specification as in column (3) of Table 3.2 is applied for estimation. The WHO Child Growth Standards are used to calculate "Height-for-age z-score". "Stunting" takes on the value one if height is less than -2 standard deviations of the WHO Child Growth Standards median and zero otherwise

In both panels, standard errors in parentheses are clustered at the village level

educational expenditure on members other than the child. The exercise suggests that household income and monetary inputs are unlikely to be the channel through which early-life tap water exposure affects cognitive development.

Next, we examine the hypothesis that cognitive development increases as a result of changes in children's educational attainment. In this study, we use cognitive test scores rather than educational attainment to measure children's cognitive skills. Zhang and Xu (2016) find that the rural drinking water program in China increases youths' educational attainment, and Carlsson et al. (2015) show that improvement in educational attainment increases cognitive test scores. Thus, tap water exposure may increase cognitive test scores through improving educational attainment. To test this,

Table 3.11 Tap water access and household income/educational expenditure

Dep. var.:	Logarithm of			
	Family income	Educational exp on the child	Household educational exp	Educational exp on members other than the child
	(1)	(2)	(3)	(4)
Exposure to tap IU–5	0.003 (0.019)	0.030 (0.056)	0.009 (0.054)	0.006 (0.080)
Observations	3,380	3,511	2,685	2,685
R^2	0.494	0.517	0.568	0.458

Notes * means significant at 10%, ** significant at 5%, and *** significant at 1%. Each column in each panel represents a separate regression with a sample of children aged 6–15 from the CFPS 2010. The same specification as in column (3) of Table 3.2 is applied for estimation. Standard errors in parentheses are clustered at the village level. In columns (3) and (4), children whose total household expenditure is less than individual expenditure are dropped

Table 3.12 Tap water access and educational attainment

Dep. var.:	Years of schooling	Grade-for-age	School enrollment
	(1)	(2)	(3)
Exposure to tap IU–5	–0.016 (0.054)	0.003 (0.028)	0.001 (0.010)
Observations	2,184	2,246	2,246
R^2	0.807	0.432	0.356

Notes * means significant at 10%, ** significant at 5%, and *** significant at 1%. Each column in each panel represents a separate regression with a sample of children aged 6–15 from the CFPS 2010. The same specification as in column (3) of Table 3.2 is applied for estimation. Standard errors in parentheses are clustered at the village level. "Grade-for-age" takes on the value one if the child was enrolled in the supposed grade for his/her age and zero otherwise. "School enrollment" equals one if the child was enrolled in school at the survey time and zero otherwise

we estimate the treatment effects of early-life exposure to tap water on children's educational attainment, measured by completed years of schooling, grade-for-age status, and school enrollment status in 2010. The results are shown in Table 3.12. We find no significant impact of early-life access to tap water on later educational attainment. This finding implies that the positive effect of tap water exposure on cognitive test scores is unlikely to be because of increased educational attainment. A possible explanation for this is that the nine-year compulsory education is strictly followed in these villages, and consequently children automatically progress every year.

3.10 Cost–Benefit Analysis

In addition to showing that early-life exposure to tap water has significantly improved rural children's cognitive skills, we examine whether the rural drinking water program initiated by the Chinese government passes a cost–benefit analysis. China's fiscal expenditures have experienced a dramatic increase over the years. According to the 2011 China Statistical Yearbook, total government expenditures soared to roughly nine trillion Chinese yuan (equivalent to 1.34 trillion USD) in 2010 from 601 billion yuan (89.7 billion USD) in 1980 (all numbers in 2010 values). Given this significant growth in government spending, it is essential to understand what returns the fiscal expenditures have generated. To this end, we conduct a back-of-the-envelope calculation of the benefits and costs of the rural drinking water program.

Following the method proposed by Lindqvist and Vestman (2011), we estimate the returns to cognitive skills using a sample of rural residents aged 25 to 35 in the CFPS 2010. The average annual income for these individuals is 10,729 yuan (1,601 USD) in 2010. A simple OLS regression reveals that a one standard deviation increase in cognitive skills is associated with an increase of 1,054 yuan (157 USD) in annual income for these individuals.[21] Our baseline estimate implies that one additional year of early-life tap water exposure increases the average test score by 0.132 standard deviations. The baseline estimate and the estimated return to cognitive skills imply that one additional year of exposure to tap water in early life would lead to an increase of 139 yuan (21 USD) in annual income. The average cost of constructing the water plants and pipeline systems is approximately 30 USD per capita (Meng et al. 2004), so the income increase for an individual receiving merely one year of early-life exposure would cover the cost in two years. Considering the durability of the village water supply system and the benefits associated with the program on health (Zhang 2012) and educational attainment (Zhang and Xu 2016), the total benefits should be significantly larger. Hence, our analysis reveals that the benefits of the program greatly outweigh the costs.

3.11 Conclusion

In this study, we examine the impact of access to tap water in early life on the cognitive skills of rural children in adolescence (10–15 years old). Using a DID approach, we find that early-life exposure to tap water has a positive and significant effect on rural children's cognitive test scores. An additional year of exposure to tap water from one year before birth through the first five years of life is found to increase a rural child's average cognitive test score by 0.132 standard deviations. The estimate implies that children with full exposure to tap water during early life

[21] Other explanatory variables we control for in the regression include gender, number of siblings, parents' years of schooling, cohort dummies, county fixed effects, and whether the person lives in a suburban village, does farm work, or has a wage job.

answer five more math questions correctly or read three more words correctly than children with no exposure during the same period.

The event study reveals that the timing of initial exposure to tap water is crucial. The effect of tap water on cognitive skills is largest for children whose exposure starts at least one year before birth. The effect becomes smaller as the initial intervention lags behind the birth year and becomes trivial if the first exposure kicks in after early life. We provide several pieces of evidence supporting the validity of our research design. Our results also survive a series of robustness tests. Finally, the mechanism analysis suggests that early-life exposure to tap water increases cognitive skills by improving childhood health and increasing maternal time investment.

Our study reveals the essential role of early-life exposure to tap water in the development of cognitive skills. A tap water supply system is one type of public infrastructure. Similarly, cognitive development, although crucial, is just one dimension of human capital development. As the construction of public infrastructure always involves large fiscal expenditures, future work should examine the effects of exposure to various types of public infrastructure on the development of multiple dimensions of human capital in children and at different growth stages. These findings will reveal the role of public infrastructure in human capital development and the importance of intervention timing. They could also provide guidance for distributing fiscal resources across regions or customizing government spending based on local conditions to achieve maximum benefits for society.

References

Adhvaryu A, Fenske J, Nyshadham A (2019) Early life circumstance and adult mental health. J Polit Econ 127(4):1516–1549

Aizer A, Currie J (2014) The intergenerational transmission of inequality: Maternal disadvantage and health at birth. Science 344(6186):856–861

Aizer A, Stroud L, Buka S (2016) Maternal Stress and Child Outcomes: Evidence from Siblings. Journal of Human Resources 51(3):523–555

Akter S (2019) Impact of drinking water salinity on children's education: Empirical evidence from coastal Bangladesh. Sci Total Environ 690(10):1331–1341

Almond D, Currie J (2011) Killing me softly: the fetal origins hypothesis. J Econ Perspect 25(3):153–172

Almond D, Currie J, Duque V (2018) Childhood circumstances and adult outcomes: Act II. J Econ Literat 56(4):1360–1446

Almond D, Edlund L, Palme M (2009) Chernobyl's subclinical legacy: Prenatal exposure to radioactive fallout and school outcomes in Sweden. Quart J Econ 124(4):1729–1772

Alsan M, Goldin C (2019) Watersheds in child mortality: The role of effective water and sewerage infrastructure, 1880–1920. J Polit Econ 127(2):586–638

Ashraf N, Glaeser E, Holland A, Steinberg BM (2021) Water, health and wealth: the impact of piped water outages on disease prevalence and financial transactions in Zambia. Economica 88:755–781

Attanasio OP (2015) The determinants of human capital formation during the early years of life: theory, measurement, and policies. J Eur Econ Assoc 13(6):949–997

Banerjee A, Duflo E, Qian N (2020) On the road: access to transportation infrastructure and economic growth in China. J Dev Econ 145:102442

Barham T (2012) Enhancing cognitive functioning: medium-term effects of a health and family planning program in Matlab. Am Econ J: Appl Econ 4(1):245–273

Beckett M, Vanzo JD, Sastry N, Panis C, Peterson C (2001) The quality of retrospective data: an examination of long-term recall in a developing country. J Human Resourc 36(3):593–625

Bharadwaj P, Løken KV, Neilson C (2013) Early life health interventions and academic achievement. Am Econ Rev 103(5):1862–1891

Black SE, Butikofer A, Devereux PJ, Salvanes KG (2019) This is only a test? Long-run and intergenerational impacts of prenatal exposure to radioactive fallout. Rev Econ Stat 101(3):531–546

Black SE, Devereux PJ, Salvanes KG (2007) From the cradle to the labor market? The effect of birth weight on adult outcomes. Quart J Econ 122(1):409–439

Blau FD, Grossberg AJ (1992) Maternal labor supply and children's cognitive development. Rev Econ Stat 74(3):474–481

Bleakley H (2007) Disease and development: evidence from hookworm eradication in the American South. Quart J Econ 122(1):73–117

Carlsson M, Dahl GB, Öckert B, Rooth D-O (2015) The effect of schooling on cognitive skills. Rev Econ Stat 97(3):533–547

Case A, Fertig A, Paxson C (2005) The lasting impact of childhood health and circumstance. J Health Econ 24:365–389

Case A, Paxson C (2009) Early life health and cognitive function in old age. Am Econ Rev 99(2):104–09

China Center for Human Capital and Labor Market Research, Central University of Finance and Economics (2016) Human capital in China. Technical report, Beijing, China

Cunha F, Heckman JJ (2006) Formulating, identifying and estimating the technology of cognitive and noncognitive formation. J Human Resourc 43(4):738–782

Cunha F, Heckman JJ, Lochner L, Masterov DV (2006) Interpreting the evidence on life cycle skill formation, Volume 1 of Handbook of the economics of education, Chapter 12. Elsevier, pp 697–812

Cunha F, Heckman JJ, Schennach SM (2010) Estimating the technology of cognitive and noncognitive skill formation. Econometrica 78(3):883–931

Currie J, Almond D (2011) Human capital development before age five, Volume 4 of handbook of labor economics, Chapter 15. Elsevier, pp 1315–1486

Cutler D, Fung W, Kremer M, Singhal M, Vogl T (2010) Early-life malaria exposure and adult outcomes: evidence from malaria eradication in India. Am Econ J: Appl Econ 2(2):72–94

Dahl GB, Lochner L (2012) The impact of family income on child achievement: evidence from the Earned Income Tax Credit. Am Econ Rev 102(5):1927–1956

Deming D (2009) Early childhood intervention and life-cycle skill development: evidence from Head Start. Am Econ J Appl Econ 1(3):111–134

Devoto F, Duflo E, Dupas P, Parientó W, Pons V (2012) Happiness on tap: piped water adoption in urban Morocco. Am Econ J Econ Pol 4(4):68–99

Dinkelman T (2011) The effects of rural electrification on employment: new evidence from South Africa. Am Econ Rev 101(7):3078–3108

Duflo E (2001) Schooling and labor market consequences of school construction in Indonesia: Evidence from an unusual policy experiment. Am Econ Rev 91(4):795–813

Duflo E (2004) The medium run effects of educational expansion: Evidence from a large school construction program in Indonesia. J Dev Econ 74(1):163–197

Ebenstein A (2010) The "Missing GirlsâŁž of China and the unintended consequences of the One Child Policy. J Human Resourc 45(1):87–115

Ebenstein A (2012) The consequences of industrialization: evidence from water pollution and digestive cancers in China. Rev Econ Stat 94(1):186–201

Fay M, Toman M, Benitez D, Csordas S (2011) Infrastructure and sustainable development. In: Fardoust S, Yongbeom K, Sepúlveda C (eds) Post-crisis growth and development, Chapter 8. World Bank, Washington, DC, pp 329–382

Figlio D, Guryan J, Karbownik K, Roth J (2014) The effects of poor neonatal health on children's cognitive development. Am Econ Rev 104(12):3921–55
Galiani S, Gertler P, Schargrodsky E (2005) Water for life: the impact of the privatization of water services on child mortality. J Polit Econ 113(1):83–120
Gamper-Rabindran S, Khan S, Timmins C (2010) The impact of piped water provision on infant mortality in Brazil: a quantile panel data approach. J Dev Econ 92(2):188–200
Gentzkow M, Shapiro JM (2008) Preschool television viewing and adolescent test scores: historical evidence from the Coleman study. Quart J Econ 123(1):279–323
Gertler P, Heckman J, Pinto R, Zanolini A, Vermeersch C, Walker S, Chang SM, Grantham-McGregor S (2014) Labor market returns to an early childhood stimulation intervention in Jamaica. Science 344(6187):998–1001
Glewwe P (2002) Schools and skills in developing countries: education policies and socioeconomic outcomes. J Econ Literat 40(2):436–482
Gordon B, Mackay R, Rehfuess E (2004) Fluoride and arsenic in drinking water. In Inheriting the World: The Atlas of Children's health and the environment. Myriad Editions Limited, Brighton, UK
Green R, Lanphear B, Hornung R, Flora D, Martinez-Mier EA, Neufeld R, Ayotte P, Muckle G, Till C (2019) Association between maternal fluoride exposure during pregnancy and IQ scores in offspring in Canada. JAMA Pediatr 173(10):940–948
Hanushek EA, Woessmann L (2008) The role of cognitive skills in economic development. J Econ Literat 46(3):607–668
Heckman J, Pinto R, Savelyev P (2013) Understanding the mechanisms through which an influential early childhood program boosted adult outcomes. Am Econ Rev 103(6):2052–2086
Henneberry YK, Kraus TE, Fleck JA, Krabbenhoft DP, Bachand PM, Horwath WR (2011) Removal of inorganic mercury and methylmercury from surface waters following coagulation of dissolved organic matter with metal-based salts. Sci Total Environ 409(3):631–637
Hoynes H, Schanzenbach DW, Almond D (2016) Long-run impacts of childhood access to the Safety Net. Am Econ Rev 106(4):903–934
Ilahi N, Grimard F (2000) Public infrastructure and private cost: water supply and time allocation of women in rural Pakistan. Econ Dev Cult Change 49(1):45–75
Inderst G (2018) Infrastructure investment, private finance, and institutional investors: Asia from a global perspective. In: Helble M, Abidhadjaev U (eds) Yoshino N. Financing infrastructure in Asia and the Pacific, Capturing Impacts and New Sources, Asian Development Bank Institute, pp 401–447
Jalan J, Ravallion M (2003) Does piped water reduce diarrhea for children in rural India? J Economet 112(1):153–173
Kelly E (2011) The scourge of Asian flu: In utero exposure to pandemic influenza and the development of a cohort of British children. J Human Resourc 46(4):669–694
Koolwal G, van de Walle D (2013) Access to water, women's work, and child outcomes. Econ Dev Cult Change 61(2):369–405
Kosec K (2014) The child health implications of privatizing Africa's urban water supply. J Health Econ 35:1–19
Leong C, Howlett M (2017) On credit and blame: Disentangling the motivations of public policy decision-making behaviour. Policy Sci 50:599–618
Lindqvist E, Vestman R (2011) The labor market returns to cognitive and noncognitive ability: evidence from the Swedish enlistment. Am Econ J Appl Econ 3:101–128
Macours K, Schady N, Vakis R (2012) Cash transfers, behavioral changes, and cognitive development in early childhood: evidence from a randomized experiment. Am Econ J: Appl Econ 4(2):247–273
Majid MF (2015) The persistent effects of in utero nutrition shocks over the life cycle: Evidence from ramadan fasting. J Dev Econ 117:48–57

Maluccio JA, Hoddinott J, Behrman JR, Martorell R, Quisumbing AR, Stein AD (2009) The impact of improving nutrition during early childhood on education among Guatemalan adults. Econ J 119(537):734–763

Mangyo E (2008) The effect of water accessibility on child health in China. J Health Econ 27(5):1343–1356

Meng S, Liu J, Tao Y (2004) Water supply and sanitation environment in rural China: promote service to the poor. Technical report, Poverty Reduction Conference (Chinese), Shanghai, China

Miller G, Urdinola BP (2010) Cyclicality, mortality, and the value of time: The case of coffee price fluctuations and child survival in Colombia. J Polit Econ 118(1):113–155

Milligan K, Stabile M (2011) Do child tax benefits affect the well-being of children? Evidence from Canadian child benefit expansions. Am Econ J Econ Pol 3(3):175–205

Ministry of Construction (2005) The current situation and problems of village living environment. Technical report, Village and Town Construction Office, Ministry of Construction, Beijing, China

Ministry of Health (1985) Sanitary standard for drinking water quality gb 5749–85. Technical report, Beijing, China

Ministry of Health (2007) Sanitary standard for drinking water quality gb 5749–2006. Technical report, Beijing, China

Morales-Suarez-Varela MM, Llopis-Gonzalez A, Tejerizo-Perez ML (1995) Impact of nitrates in drinking water on cancer mortality in Valencia. Spain. European J Epidemiol 11(1):15–21

National Development and Reform Commission (2007) Rural Drinking Water Program The Eleventh Five Year Plan. Technical report, Beijing, China

National Development and Reform Commission (2012) Rural drinking water program the twelfth five year plan. Technical report, Beijing, China

Ozier O (2018) Exploiting externalities to estimate the long-term effects of early childhood deworming. Am Econ J Appl Econ 10(3):235–262

Parcel TL, Menaghan EG (1994) Early parental work, family social capital, and early childhood outcomes. Am J Sociol 99(4):972–1009

Ruhm CJ (2004) Parental employment and child cognitive development. J Human Resourc 39(1):155–192

Ruhm CJ (2008) Maternal employment and adolescent development. Labour Econ 15(5):958–983

Shah M, Steinberg BM (2017) Drought of opportunities: contemporaneous and long-term impacts of rainfall shocks on human capital. J Polit Econ 125(2):527–561

Spears D, Lamba S (2016) Effects of early-life exposure to sanitation on childhood cognitive skills: evidence from India's Total Sanitation Campaign. J Human Resourc 51(2):298–327

UNICEF and WHO (2015) Progress on sanitation and drinking water: 2015 update and MDG assessment. Geneva, Switzerland, Technical report, UNICEF and World Health Organization, New York, United States

Vikram K, Chindarkar N (2020) Bridging the gaps in cognitive achievement in india: the crucial role of the integrated child development services in early childhood. World Development 127:104697

Watson T (2006) Public health investments and the infant mortality gap: Evidence from federal sanitation interventions on U.S. Indian reservations. J Public Econ 90(8–9):1537–1560

World Health Organization (2017) Treatment methods and performance (4 ed). Guidelines for drinking-water quality. WHO Press, Geneva, Switzerland, pp. 485–503

Xie J, Liebenthal A, Warford JJ, Dixon JA, Wang M, Gao S, Wang S, Jiang Y, Ma Z (2009) Addressing China's water scarcity: recommendations for selected water resource management issues. World Bank, Washington, DC

Xie Y (2012) China family panel studies (2010) user's manual. Institute of Social Science Survey, Peking University. http://www.isss.edu.cn/cfps/d/file/EN/Documentation/js/2014-09-18/bedee4470e0469260939e40eac2415c9.pdf

Zhang J (2012) The impact of water quality on health: evidence from the drinking water infrastructure program in rural China. J Health Econ 31(1):122–134

Zhang J, Xu LC (2016) The long-run effects of treated water on education: the rural drinking water program in China. J Dev Econ 122:1–15

Zhang R, Li H, Wu X, Fan F, Sun B, Wang Z, Zhang Q, Tao Y (2009) Current situation analysis on china rural drinking water quality. J Environ Health (Chinese) 26(1):3–5
Zoni S, Lucchini RG (2013) Manganese exposure: cognitive, motor and behavioral effects on children: a review of recent findings. Curr Opin Pediatr 25(2):255–260

Part II
Water Management in Urban Domestic Sector

Chapter 4
Private Sector Participation and Performance of County Water Utilities

Abstract In the early 1990s, China opened its urban water sector to private investors to secure the country's growing urban water demand. In Chinese counties which accommodated around 195 million urban population in 2012, private sector participation (PSP) has progressed slowly but steadily among the county-level water utilities. Using a panel data set extracted from the annual surveys conducted by the National Bureau of Statistics of China (1998–2006), we exploit the changes in the PSP status of water utilities and apply a fixed-effects model to identify the causal effects of PSP on 12 performance indicators. We find that utilities with private investment enjoyed significant performance improvement in three areas: output, financial performance and profitability, and efficiency. Using supplementary data from population censuses and statistical yearbooks, we find that water quality is slightly lowered under PSP, while no significant effect is detected for the other service outcomes. The findings suggest that a greater role of PSP in the urban water supply sector of Chinese counties could be promoted.

4.1 Private Sector Participation in Public Utilities in China

China's economic boom of the past three decades has been accompanied by an unprecedented scale of urbanization, characterized by a rapid expansion of urban areas and significant rural-urban migration. Statistics from the China Statistical Yearbooks show that in 2014, 750 million people lived in urban China (55% of the total population), an increase from 170 million in 1978 (18% of the total population at the time). Such rapid urbanization has brought enormous pressure on the public services, including transportation, water supply, wastewater treatment, and solid waste treatment, all of which remained under the government's control following the onset of economic reforms in the late 1970s. Inspired by the experience from developed countries (including England and Wales, France, Germany, and Spain) and other developing countries (including Chile, Malaysia, and Philippines), the Chinese government considers private sector participation (PSP) as one of the solutions to meet

© The Author(s), under exclusive license to Springer Nature Singapore Pte Ltd. 2025
L. Li, *The Impacts of Water Reforms in Rural and Urban China*,
https://doi.org/10.1007/978-981-96-6902-8_4

the tremendous financial needs to invest in and maintain public infrastructure and to improve the economic performance of the state-owned enterprises.[1]

The sector of urban water supply sector, in particular, is challenged by an obsolete water supply system, general water shortages, and a severe deterioration in water quality. This sector was closed to private investment until 1992, when Sino French Water and the water utility of Zhongshan City jointly established Zhongshan Tanzhou Water Supply Company Limited, the first Sino-foreign joint venture in water supply in China. The first legal grounds for PSP in urban infrastructure were formed in the mid-1990s, when the Chinese government promulgated the *Circular on Attracting Foreign Investment through BOT Approach* (Ministry of Foreign Trade and Economics Cooperation 1994) and the *Circular on Major Issues of Approval Administration of the Franchise Pilot Projects with Foreign Investment* (National Development and Planning Commission et al. 1995). Thereafter, Sino French Water and other international water groups such as Veolia and ThamesWater began to actively engage in the operation and management of China's urban water sectors.

The formal opening of the public utilities to private investment occurred following the *Guidelines on Encouraging and Guiding Nongovernment Investment* (State Planning Committee 2001), and the *Opinions on Accelerating the Marketization of Public Utilities* (Ministry of Construction 2002). The subsequent *Management Measures on Public Utilities Concession* (Ministry of Construction 2004) specifies the roles of enterprises and government agencies in the concessionary operation of public utilities. On reviewing the issues raised in the course of the marketization of public utilities, the *Opinions on Strengthening Regulation of Public Utilities* (Ministry of Construction 2006) emphasized the importance of governmental regulation in securing public good supply for the welfare of the public. These government documents laid the groundwork for private investors to play a role in the urban water sector. In practice, however, there is not yet a systematic and comprehensive regulatory framework for the Chinese urban water sectors (Zhong et al. 2008).

During the marketization process of urban water supply in China, a number of international investors (*e.g.*, Sino French Water, Veolia, and ThamesWater) and domestic private investors (*e.g.*, Beijing Capital Group, General Water of China, and Shenzhen Water Group) have actively participated in the market of water supply through PSP. There are more than ten models of PSP in the water supply sector, including share transfer, joint venture, BOT (Build-Operate-Transfer), TOT (Transfer-Operate-Transfer), BT (Build-Transfer), ROT (Renovate-Operate-Transfer), BOO (Build-Own-Operate), Operation & Maintenance Contract, Operation Outsourcing, etc (Zhang 2006). Among them, share transfer, joint venture, BOT, and TOT are dominant ones (Zhang 2006; Fu and Chang 2006).

---

[1] Yet neither theoretical nor empirical literature regarding the relation between privatization and efficiency has led to a definitive conclusion. A detailed survey of the theoretical literature on privatization and efficiency can be found at Cavaliere and Scabrosetti (2008). Megginson and Netter (2001) provided a comprehensive survey of the empirical literature on privatization. In particular, Parker and Kirkpatrick (2005) and Estrin et al. (2009) reviewed the empirical literature in developing and transition economies, respectively.

The share transfer and joint venture models make changes in the ownership of the water utility. Under share transfer, the government sells part of the water utility's ownership to private investors. For example, Changshu Water Utility in Jiangsu Province sold 49% of its shares to Sino French Water in 2006; in 2010, Water Conservancy Investment of Jiangxi Province acquired 84.67% of the shares of the Xiushui Water Utility; in 2012, Jintang Water Utility in Sichuan Province sold all its shares: 51% to Chengdu Water Utility, 39% to Dujiangyan Water Conservancy, and the rest 10% to Hitachi Plant Technologies. In a joint venture, the government establishes a joint company to own and run the water utility. The government contributes the existing fixed assets, while private investors usually contribute cash. One example is a joint venture by Yuyao City Investment & Development (accounting for 20% of the shares of the joint venture) and Beijing Capital Group (accounting for 80% of the shares of the joint venture) in Yuyao, a county in Zhejiang Province. A franchise agreement was granted by the local government for the joint venture to provide water supply service in the region for 25 years. A 2005 study on the marketization of urban infrastructure by the Ministry of Construction found that share transfer and joint venture are the dominant PSP models in the urban water supply sector. Among the 129 water supply projects involving private investors that were surveyed, 94.6% follow the share transfer or joint venture model (Fu and Chang 2006).

In PSP models other than share transfer and joint venture, the government retains ownership of the water utilities. In a BOT arrangement, the private investor is in charge of facility financing and construction, and owns and operates the utility under the government concession for a specified time period. When the concession expires, the private investor is required to transfer the facility to the water utility. One example is the BOT of Pei Xian water supply in Jiangsu Province in 2016. A joint company set up by Pei Xian City Investment & Development (accounting for 90% of the shares) and Xingrong Group (accounting for 10% of the shares) receives a concession to construct and operate water facilities for 30 years. In a TOT arrangement, the private investor pays a transfer fee to the government to obtain the rights to operate the facilities for a specified time period and returns the facilities when the contract expires. In 2006, Shenzhen Water Facility Investment acquired the 28-year water service franchise via TOT in Anji, Zhejiang Province. BOT and TOT approaches dominate China's wastewater sector in China according to the 2005 survey by the Ministry of Construction, but only a few water supply projects adopted these approaches (Fu and Chang 2006).

The privatization of the prefecture-level water utilities, which mainly serve an urban population residing at the centers of municipalities or prefecture-level cities, is the focus of a number of existing studies on PSP in the Chinese water supply industry (Jiang and Zheng 2014; Wang et al. 2011).[2] While the majority of the urban population resides in city centers, the counties or county-level cities in China have also experienced rapid urbanization and are accommodating a considerable number of urban residents. According to the China County Statistical Yearbooks, the size of the urban

[2] Please refer to Fu and Chang (2006) and Zhang (2006) for typical cases of PSP in urban water utilities at prefectural cities.

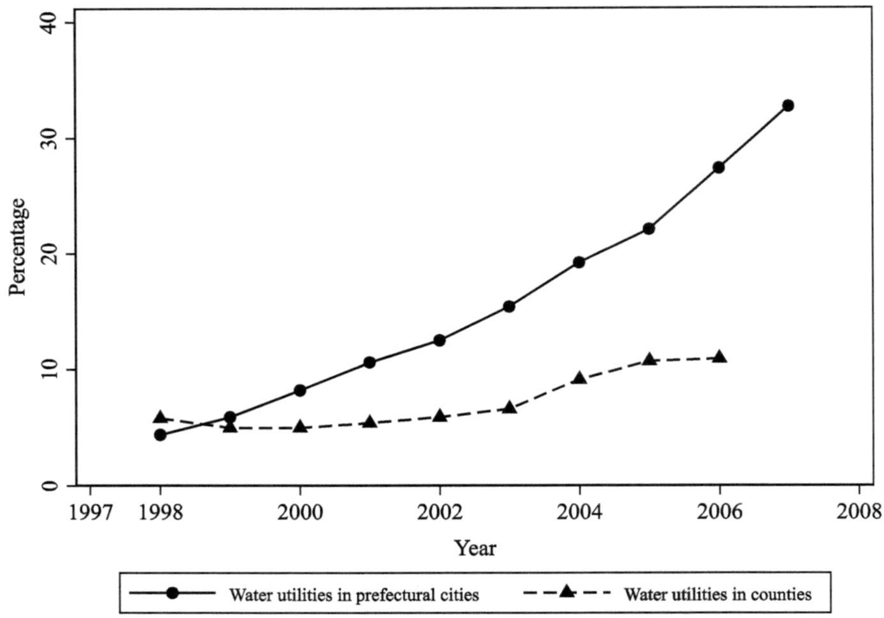

Fig. 4.1 PSP progress among prefecture-level and county-level water utilities. *Sources* PSP data of water utilities at the prefecture level are from Jiang and Zheng (2014). PSP data on county-level water utilities are assembled from the Annual Industrial Firm Surveys (1998–2006), National Bureau of Statistics.

population residing in counties in China grew by 67% over the last two decades, from 117 million in 1992 to 195 million in 2012. PSP is progressing slowly but steadily among the county-level water utilities, which serve the urban population in counties with treated water. Figure 4.1 compares PSP progress in county-level and prefecture-level utilities (Jiang and Zheng 2014). In 1998, a higher proportion of county-level water utilities were practicing PSP (5.7% compared to 4.4%), but their progress in the following years lagged behind that of prefecture-level utilities. While the share of prefecture-level water utilities with PSP involvement surged from 4.4% in 1998 to 32.7% in 2007, only 10% of county-level utilities had nonstate capital in 2006.[3]

The service population of county-level water utilities is expected to continue growing. In 2011, the Chinese government announced the *Decision on Propelling the Water Reform and Development* (CPC Central Committee and the State Council 2011). This policy prioritized expanding urban water supply to peri-urban populations in counties to achieve "integration of urban and rural water supply," generating significant opportunities for both county-level water utilities and private investors. Nevertheless, we know little about the performance of county-level water utilities and the details of PSP in the water supply sector of Chinese counties.

[3] We discuss the possible reasons for the slower PSP progress in county-level water utilities in Sect. 4.10.

4.2 Results Preview

In this study, we take the first step in unveiling the progress and impact of PSP on the performance of small-sized county-level water utilities in China. A unique panel data set of 1,123 county-level water utilities (1998–2006) is assembled from the Annual Industrial Firm Surveys data in China. We exploit the changes in PSP status of water utilities over time and apply a utility fixed-effects model to identify the causal effects of PSP on utility performance. To address the potential bias in selection into PSP, we directly control for utility and county characteristics that may correlate with water demand or supply in the model, to capture the effects of time-variant utility characteristics and contemporaneous shocks at the county level. To allow the time trends in outcome variables to vary by province and county characteristics, we additionally control for province-specific year fixed effects and interactions of county characteristics in 1998 and linear time trends.

We find that PSP improved the performance of county-level water utilities in three areas: output, financial performance and profitability, and efficiency. In particular, PSP is found to raise water utilities' sales revenues by 3.6%, value added by 10%, profit-sales ratio by 5.9 percentage points, and average revenue product of labor by 3,583 Chinese yuan (CNY, in 1998 constant price). PSP is also found to lower the liability ratio by 0.048 and the managerial expense ratio by 0.031. The estimates pass a series of robustness tests, including addressing the concern on possible coding errors in PSP and using a sample with the year 2007 included.

Heterogeneity analysis shows that water utilities with any extent of PSP (both PSP-majority and PSP-minority) and any source of PSP (collective, legal entity, individual, and other nonstate) have the potential to outperform state-owned utilities. By examining the long-term effect of PSP, we find that the effects of PSP on financial performance and profitability, and on labor productivity, remained after three years of PSP, and the effect size gets larger as years of PSP increases.

By merging baseline sample with supplementary data from population censuses and statistical yearbooks, we test whether PSP had any effect on service outcomes, including water tariffs (domestic and industrial), non-revenue water, water pressure, water quality, household access to tap water, and child mortality. We find that PSP led to a 0.9 percentage point decrease in the average pass rate of water quality tests, and the effect is marginally significant, suggesting that water quality got slightly worse under PSP. No significant effect is detected for the other service outcomes.

4.3 Literature Review

Our study is related to four strands of literature. First is the broad literature on the effect of PSP on the performance of water utilities. Earlier empirical studies generally use the methods of data envelopment analysis and stochastic cost frontier analysis to evaluate the effect. A mixed picture has been presented for developed economies, including the United States (Bhattacharyya et al. 1995), England and

Wales (Saal and Parker 2001; Saal et al. 2007), and Spain (Benito et al. 2010), and developing economies in the Asia and Pacific region (Estache and Rossi 2002) and Africa (Estache and Kouassi 2002; Kirkpatrick et al. 2006). Recent empirical studies have used large samples and controlled for utility fixed effects. For instance, using a multi-country panel data set of water utilities, Gassner et al. (2009) showed that PSP in water supply leads to a decrease in employment, but no impact is detected on investment. Using a panel data set of water utilities from 208 prefecture-level cities in China from 1998 to 2007, Jiang and Zheng (2014) found that PSP in water utilities resulted in significant cost savings through employment downsizing and reduced managerial expenses. Also in the context of China, Wang et al. (2011) explored the impact of PSP on performance of urban water supply using panel data for 35 major cities over the period 1998 to 2008. The introduction of PSP is significantly correlated with an improvement in integrated production capacity and water coverage rate, but not with investment in fixed assets. In this study, we compile a panel data set of county-level water utilities in China and provide the first evidence on the performance of these water utilities and the effect of PSP. We find that PSP improves the performance of county-level water utilities in three areas: output, financial performance and profitability, and efficiency.

Second is the literature on the relationship between firm size and the PSP effect. Traditional research in economics has generally found a positive and significant association between firm size and efficiency (Shepherd 1972; Imel and Helmberger 1971; Gale 1972). Applied to the water supply sector, it is suggested that large water utilities enjoy advantages such as economies of scale, bargaining power with suppliers and distributors, brand name recognition, and experience curve effects, and thus are likely to gain higher efficiency than smaller water utilities. In contrast, research in the field of organizational behavior has highlighted the formal and informal structure of a small firm as a source of competitive advantage. The empirical findings of Neilsen (1974) indicate that, small firms, where hierarchy is often tightened up and decision-making is centralized, have greater interaction among departments, thereby increasing synergism and decreasing response time to environmental changes. Empirical evidence suggests that privately owned water utilities tend to be more efficient at smaller scales of operation, whereas publicly owned utilities exhibit greater efficiency at larger scales (Bhattacharyya et al. 1995; Peda et al. 2013). Our study extends the literature by providing evidence from China that small-scale county-level water utilities experienced greater performance improvements following PSP, compared to large-scale prefectural water utilities (Jiang and Zheng 2014).

Third is the literature is on the long-term effect of PSP. Existing studies on the long-term effect of PSP have documented that the positive effect of PSP on performance might appear immediately (Brown et al. 2006) or emerge after several years (Brown et al. 2006; Villalonga 2000), and might be transitory (Frydman et al. 1999; Cook and Uchida 2008) or keep increasing over a long period (Boardman et al. 2016). Our study presents the first evidence from China that the effects of PSP on financial performance and profitability (measured by liability ratio, financial expense ratio, and profit-sales ratio) and labor productivity (measured by average revenue product of labor) are not transitory, and the effect size enlarges over time.

Our study is also related to the literature on the effect of PSP on service outcomes, such as water tariffs, water quality, non-revenue water, access to water, and child mortality. Some studies have pointed out that privatization of water supply is associated with higher water tariffs (Saal and Parker 2001; Chong et al. 2006; García-Valiñas et al. 2013; Ruester and Zschille 2010). Lee (2011) found that privatization of water sector in Malaysia does not improve access to treated water. Using a multi-country panel data set of water utilities, Gassner et al. (2009) showed that PSP in water supply leads to an increase in residential connections, connections per worker, and water sold per worker, but no impact is detected on retail tariffs. Galiani et al. (2005) estimated that child mortality fell 8% in municipalities that privatized their water services in Argentina, with expansion of water services considered to be one of the possible pathways. (Jiang and Zheng, 2014) found that PSP in the prefecture-level water utilities in China does not have a significant effect on total water supply, domestic water supply, and number of domestic water users. Our study adds to this line of literature by showing that PSP in county-level water utilities in China slightly lowered water quality, while no significant effect is detected for the other service outcomes. The exercise suggests that, alongside the encouragement of private investors, a better water quality monitoring system should be set up.

4.4 Data

The data used in this study come from the Annual Industrial Firm Surveys conducted by the National Bureau of Statistics (NBS) of China. These surveys cover all state-owned enterprises, and nonstate enterprises with sales above five million Chinese yuan.[4] They include 39 two-digit industries and over 600 four-digit industries in three broad categories: mining, manufacturing, and public utilities.[5] There are three four-digit industries related to water industry: water production and supply (4610), wastewater treatment and reuse (4620), and other water treatment, utilization, and distribution (4690). This study focuses on water production and supply firms with an industry code of 4610.

The sample is further restricted to county-level water utilities. County here refers to counties and county-level cities. A rapid expansion of urban population has been observed in Chinese counties over the years. According to the China County Statistical Yearbooks, from 1992 to 2012 the size of the urban population residing in counties grew by 67% from 117 million to 195 million.[6]

[4] At the exchange rate of 8.28 CNY per USD (in force between December 1997 and July 2005), this amounts to USD 604,000. As noted by Brandt et al. (2014) and evidenced by the county-level water utilities sampled in this study, inclusion in the annual survey sample does not strictly adhere to the five-million-yuan threshold.

[5] Detailed discussions on the NBS survey data can be found in Nie et al. (2012) and Brandt et al. (2014).

[6] The total number of counties and county-level cities in China is stable over time—2,084 in 2012 compared with 2,081 in 1992.

The sample period in this study covers 1998 to 2006.[7] We construct a balanced panel of water utilities following similar procedures employed by Brandt et al. (2012) and Jiang and Zheng (2014). We first use firm ID to track utilities. Second, we seek to match the same utilities with different IDs across years using an expanded set of criteria, such as firm name, geographic code, and location. For example, if there was only one utility in one county from 1998 to 2006, we check the consistency of the observations in terms of name, size, and address to determine that the observations belong to the same utility.

Unique identifiers are assigned to link utilities over the years. The final data set contains 1,123 water utilities in 1,099 counties from 29 provinces. These counties witnessed rapid urbanization over the years. According to the China Data Online and the China County Yearbooks, the total population in these counties increased from 534 million in 1998 to 555 million in 2006, and the urban population escalated by 63%, from 90 million to 146 million. This urban population approximates the population serviced by utilities in our data.

The NBS surveys collect detailed information on firms' financial status, based on which we define the utilities' ownership types and construct performance indicators. A utility's actual capital sources are categorized as state, collective, legal entity, individual, Hong Kong, Macau, or Taiwan (HMT), and foreign. The ownership defined by the firm's actual capital composition is found to be more accurate than the one defined by a firm's registration type in China (Dollar and Wei 2007). Following the study by Jiang and Zheng (2014) on the impact of PSP on performance of prefecture-level water utilities, we define PSP as an arrangement with any financial sources other than the state.[8] In line with the definition in Bai et al. (2009) and Jiang and Zheng (2014), a water utility is defined as PSP-majority if it has more than 50% nonstate ownership and as PSP-minority if it has more than 50% state ownership. We categorize PSP into four types by the source of private capital: collectives, legal entities, individuals, and other private investors (HMT or foreign). One utility can have more than one source of capital.

Table 4.1 shows the number of water utilities with PSP, the number of water utilities by PSP extent, source, and shifting of status during the sample period. Among the 1,123 county-level water utilities, 64 (5.7%) had PSP in 1998, and 120 (10.7%) had PSP in 2006. Figure 4.2 plots the spatial distribution of the 1,099 counties hosting

[7] The data after the year 2006 are excluded from the analysis, as a substantial fraction of the water utilities (42.5%) with observations available in 2006 are absent beginning in 2007 (the reasons for this are not available from public sources). We do a robustness test in Sect. 4.6.2 based on a sample consisting of the (fewer) water utilities from 1998 to 2007. It shows that our main results are unlikely to be driven by the choices of sample composition and time span.

[8] By defining PSP according to the actual capital structure of the water utilities, in fact we examine the effect of the share transfer and joint venture forms of PSP on utility performance. Utilities that engage private investors through other forms of PSP are still considered to be state owned, as the capital structure is retained. Fu and Chang (2006) find that in the urban water supply sector in China, share transfer and joint venture are the dominant PSP forms. If this same pattern applies for county-level water utilities, the potential biases of the estimates should be small.

Table 4.1 Number of county water utilities having private sector participation (1998–2006)

				By PSP extent		By PSP source				By shifting of status		
Year	All	PSP	% of PSP	PSP-maj	PSP-min	Col	Leg	Ind	Oth	New	Exit	Successor
1998	1,123	64	5.7	29	35	32	27	13	0	–	–	–
1999	1,123	53	4.7	22	31	28	23	16	0	16	27	37
2000	1,123	47	4.2	21	26	23	19	17	0	18	24	29
2001	1,123	58	5.2	26	32	25	27	23	1	24	13	34
2002	1,123	61	5.4	31	30	26	27	22	0	20	17	41
2003	1,123	69	6.1	39	30	20	37	25	0	27	19	42
2004	1,123	97	8.6	59	38	19	54	35	4	41	13	56
2005	1,123	115	10.2	84	31	24	69	41	5	42	24	73
2006	1,123	120	10.7	87	33	23	70	44	4	28	23	92

Notes Data are assembled from the Annual Industrial Firm Surveys (1998–2006), National Bureau of Statistics. The column of "All" provides the total number of county-level water utilities each year. The columns of "PSP" and "% of PSP" present the number and the proportion of water utilities with PSP each year, respectively. The columns of "PSP-maj" and "PSP-min" show the breakdown of water utilities by PSP extent. "PSP-maj" refers to having more than 50% nonstate ownership, and "PSP-min" refers to having more than 50% state ownership. The columns of "Col", "Leg", "Ind", and "Oth" show the breakdown of water utilities by PSP source. "Col" indicates collective, "Leg" indicates legal entity, "Ind" indicates individual, and "Oth" indicates other sources of private capital including Hong Kong, Macau, or Taiwan (HMT), and foreign. The last three columns show the breakdown of water utilities by shifting of status

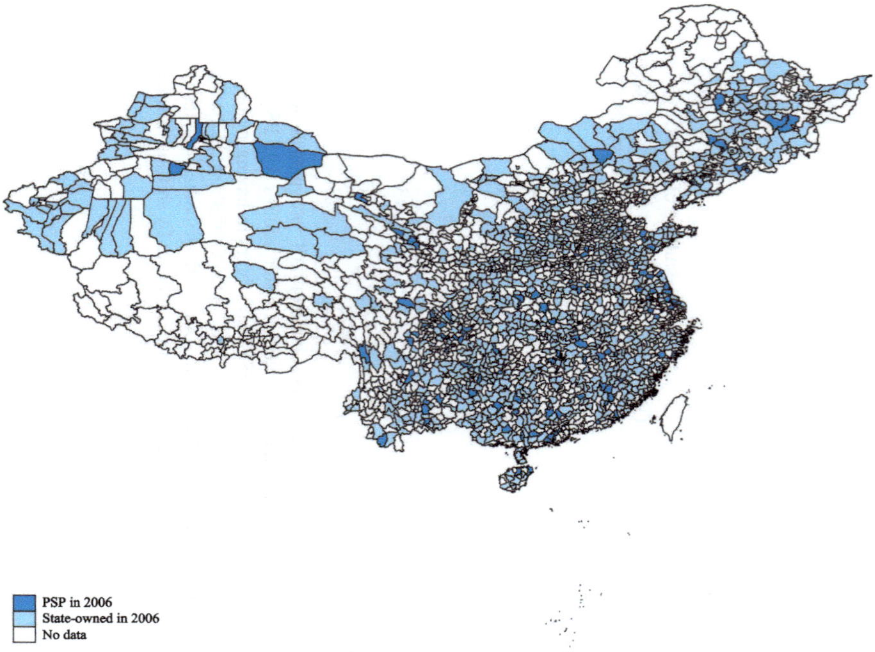

Fig. 4.2 Counties with water utilities receiving private investment in China. *Notes* PSP data of county-level water utilities are assembled from the Annual Industrial Firm Surveys (1998–2006), National Bureau of Statistics.
The 1,099 counties where the 1,123 water utilities are located are shaded in blue. The light blue denotes the counties having non-PSP water utilities in 2006, and the dark blue denotes the counties having PSP water utilities in 2006

the 1,123 county-level water utilities. The light blue denotes the counties with non-PSP water utilities in 2006, and the dark blue denotes the counties with PSP water utilities in 2006. The sampled counties are nationally representative, and the PSP cases are spread nationwide.

Among 64 county-level water utilities involving PSP in 1998, 29 were PSP-majority utilities and 35 were PSP-minority utilities. After 2002, the number of PSP-majority utilities overtook that of PSP-minority utilities. This suggests that private investors are gaining more bargaining power and control in PSP water utilities. To check if the effects of PSP on utility performance vary by the extent of private ownership, we compare and discuss the effects of PSP-majority and PSP-minority utilities in Sect. 4.8.1. In terms of source of private capital, we find legal entity and individual-sourced PSP gradually overtook collective-sourced PSP after 2001. To examine whether the source of financing for PSP exerts a different impact on utility performance, we compare the effects of PSP by the source of capital in Sect. 4.8.2. The breakdown of water utilities by shifting of status suggests that utilities frequently shift between pure state-owned status and PSP status.[9] Each year, more than ten water utilities adopted PSP while more than ten quit PSP. Since 2001, the number of water utilities adopting PSP has overtaken that of those exiting PSP. A similar phenomenon was observed in the PSP of large-sized water utilities in prefecture-level cities (Jiang and Zheng 2014). There are at least two reasons for these frequent shifts. First, they may reflect a lack of certainty and stability for foreign investors due to the fragmented and diverse regulatory system in the urban water supply sector (Zhong et al. 2008). Second, some of the shifts may be due to errors in coding capital sources. In Sect. 4.6.2, we recode the PSP in cases that water utilities switch between state-owned and PSP statuses back and forth in three consecutive years. The performance improvements brought in by PSP to water utilities retain after recoding.

We use the same 12 indicators as in Jiang and Zheng (2014) to assess utility performance in three aspects. Table 4.2 presents the definitions of all 12 indicators.[10] The first set of indicators measures utilities' inputs and outputs, including investment, total employment, sales revenues, and value added. The second set measures utilities' financial performance and profitability. It contains ratios of liability to assets, managerial expenses to sales, financial expenses to sales, profits to sales, taxes paid to sales, and subsidies to sales. The third set of indicators looks at utilities' efficiency, measured by average revenue product of labor and total factor productivity (TFP). The TFP is calculated following the method proposed by Caves et al. (1982), which produces the comparable productivity level across firms within the same industry.[11] To obtain the 1998 constant price, we extract price indices from the China Statistics Yearbooks and apply indices of fixed assets investment to capital, assets, and investment, and indices of industrial products to sales revenues and value added. All nominal figures are expressed in thousands of Chinese Yuan (1,000 CNY) in 1998 value unless otherwise specified.

Compared with the prefecture-level water utilities studied in Jiang and Zheng (2014), the county-level water utilities studied in this study are not only operating on a smaller scale but also performing at a lower efficiency level. Table 4.3 reports the sample means of the performance indicators for the two types of water utilities respectively.[12] For investment, sales revenues, and value added, the average of prefecture-level water utilities is more than 20 times higher than that of the

[9] There are 239 water utilities that ever experienced a change in PSP status during 1998 and 2006. Results from these water utilities are presented in Panel A of Table 4.7. The estimates are consistent with the main results except that the effect on sales revenues becomes small and insignificant.

[10] The discussion on the effect of PSP on service outcomes of water supply is elaborated in Sect. 4.9.

[11] To compare the productivity level across firms within the same industry, Caves et al. (1982) proposed the following multilateral productivity measure:

$$\ln TFP_{it} = \left(\ln VA_{it} - \overline{\ln VA_t}\right) - \widetilde{S_{it}}\left(\ln L_{it} - \overline{\ln L_t}\right) - \left(1 - \widetilde{S_{it}}\right)\left(\ln K_{it} - \overline{\ln K_t}\right),$$

where TFP, VA, L, and K denote total factor productivity, value added, labor, and fixed capital, respectively. $\overline{\ln *}$ is the industry average of logarithm of a variable in year t. $\widetilde{S_{it}} = \left(S_{it} + \overline{S_t}\right)/2$, where S_{it} is the share of wage bill in value added of individual utility in year t, and $\overline{S_t}$ is the industry average of wage bill shares in year t.

[12] The information on prefecture-level water utilities is extracted from Jiang and Zheng (2014).

Table 4.2 Variable definitions

Variable	Definition
Water utility variable	
Private sector participation (PSP)	Dummy variable=1 if state capital share in total capital is less than 1
PSP majority	Dummy variable=1 if state capital share in total capital is equal to or less than 50%
PSP minority	Dummy variable=1 if state capital share in total capital is less than 1 and greater than 50%
PSP collective	Dummy variable=1 if collective capital share in total capital is nonzero
PSP legal entity	Dummy variable=1 if legal entity capital share in total capital is nonzero
PSP individual	Dummy variable=1 if individual capital share in total capital is nonzero
PSP other	Dummy variable=1 if Hong Kong, Macau, or Taiwan (HMT), or foreign capital share in total capital is nonzero
Assets (log)	Logarithm of total assets in 1,000 CNY, in 1998 constant price
Investment	Difference between assets in the end of current year and assets in the end of previous year, both in 1,000 CNY, in 1998 constant price
Employment (log)	Logarithm of number of employees
Sales (log)	Logarithm of sales revenues in 1,000 CNY, in 1998 constant price
Value added (log)	Logarithm of value added in 1,000 CNY, in 1998 constant price
Liability ratio	Ratio of liability to total assets
Managerial expense ratio	Ratio of managerial expenses to sales revenues
Financial expense ratio	Ratio of financial expenses to sales revenues
Profit-sales ratio	Ratio of profits to sales revenues
Tax-sales ratio	Ratio of tax paid to sales revenues
Subsidy-sales ratio	Ratio of subsidy to sales revenues
Average revenue product of labor	Value added in 1,000 CNY, in 1998 constant price, divided by total employment
TFP (log)	Logarithm of total factor productivity, same as in Caves et al. (1982)
County variable	
Population (log)	Logarithm of total population of the county
Population density	Population per square kilometers
Share of rural population in total population	Ratio of rural population to total population
GDP per capita (log)	Logarithm of per capita gross regional product in CNY, in 1998 constant price
Share of agriculture in GDP	Ratio of agriculture in total GDP
Share of industry in GDP	Ratio of industry in total GDP
Public financial deficit as a share of government revenues	Difference between public expenditure and revenues divided by public revenues

Notes In line with Jiang and Zheng (2014), water utility variables are constructed from the Annual Industrial Firm Surveys. County variables come from the China Data Online and the China County Statistical Yearbooks

county-level ones, and county-level water utilities hire on average one eighth of the personnel as prefecture-level ones. A small difference is detected between the two types of utilities in terms of financial performance and profitability (measured by liability ratio, managerial expense ratio, financial expense ratio, and profit-sales ratio),

Table 4.3 Sample mean of utility scale and performance indicators

	County level	Prefecture level
	(1)	(2)
Investment^	1,663.519	38,373.050
Employment	112.751	959.143
Sales^	3,974.967	98,812.610
Value added^	2,025.645	49,377.840
Liability ratio	0.487	0.413
Managerial expense ratio	0.306	0.217
Financial expense ratio	0.050	0.050
Profit-sales ratio	–0.085	–0.027
Tax-sales ratio	0.012	0.073
Subsidy-sales ratio	0.013	0.025
Average revenue product of labor^	18.019	51.340
TFP (log)	–0.087	–0.041

Notes Data on county-level water utilities are assembled from the Annual Industrial Firm Surveys (1998–2006), National Bureau of Statistics. Data on prefecture-level water utilities are extracted from Jiang and Zheng (2014).

^Indicators are in 1,000 CNY and in 1998 constant price

but prefecture-level water utilities outperform county-level water utilities in almost all these dimensions. Furthermore, we find that the efficiency of county-level water utilities (measured by average revenue product of labor and TFP) is much lower than that of prefecture-level utilities.

County-level data on demography and economy, including population, share of rural population in total population, population density, and GDP per capita, are extracted from the China Data Online and the China County Statistical Yearbooks, and merged with the water utility data. These county factors may have affected the performance of water utilities as well as the counties' decision to convert the ownership of their water utilities. Table 4.2 provides definitions of all dependent and explanatory variables. GDP deflators from the China Statistics Yearbooks are applied to GDP to obtain 1998 constant price.

4.5 Drivers of Private Sector Participation in Water Utilities

As China's privatization has been gradual and selective, the impacts of privatization could be due to the characteristics of the state-owned enterprises chosen for privatization rather than the ownership changes themselves (Bai et al. 2009). The decision to involve private investment in water utilities is the outcome of interactions between local government and private investors, and the two sides often have disparate interests. If utilities are under financial burden or an obsolete water supply system fails to meet escalating water demand, local governments are more likely to embrace PSP, while profit-driven private investors are primarily concerned with potential profitability. To address the potential issue of selection bias and determine how different factors have contributed to the adoption of PSP in some water utilities but not others, we identify a list of factors at both the utility and county levels.

First, following Jiang and Zheng (2014), we select six of the 12 utility performance indicators that are available or can be constructed from public information. Employment, assets, and sales revenues measure the scale and capacity of a utility; the ratio of managerial expense to sales revenues indicates a utility's managerial flexibility and competency; the ratio of liability to assets measures the financial risk borne by a utility, and the ratio of profits to sales measures profitability. Since the present values of utility characteristics are likely to be affected by the PSP status of a utility, one-year lags are used.

Second, we control for a set of one-year lags of county characteristics. Total population, proportion of rural population, and GDP per capita are proxies for residential water demand.[13] Population density is the measure of technical difficulty of supplying water. GDP composition by sector and the ratio of fixed assets investment to GDP are proxies for industrial water demand. The ratio of public financial deficit to government revenues measures the capacity of the local government to invest in water supply.

Third, to test the hypothesis that the decision to involve private investment was made in response to a sudden shock to the water utility or county, we include in the regressions the changes in utility characteristics and county characteristics over the last two years—that is, changes from two years ago to one year ago.

We apply both a linear model and a logit model to estimate the probability of a water utility involving PSP in a given year. Since the marginal effects from the logit model are close to the coefficients from the linear model, we report the more intuitive results from the linear model.[14] Columns (1) and (2) of Table 4.4 show the estimation results from the fixed-effects linear model and the random-effects linear model, respectively. In both models, province-specific year dummies are controlled for, and standard errors are clustered at the utility level. We apply a cluster-robust version of Hausman's specification test to compare the estimates from the fixed-effects model and the random-effects model. The null hypothesis that the slope coefficients of the two models do not differ significantly cannot be rejected.[15] Therefore, we make use of the consistent and efficient estimates from the random-effects model.

---

[13] In general, county-level water utilities are not responsible for supplying tap water to rural residents. The coverage rate of tap water in rural China is low. According to China Census 2000, less than 28% of rural households had access to tap water, compared with 82% for urban households.

[14] Another reason for choosing the linear model is that in logit model, observations from a province in one year where every utility has the same PSP status have to be dropped from analysis, leading to a smaller sample size for estimation. Please refer to Caudill (1988) for detailed discussion on this issue. The results from the logit model are available upon request.

[15] We ran the robust Hausman specification test ten times with the number of bootstrap repetitions set to 2,000. The p-value ranges from 0.9630 to 0.9789.

Table 4.4 Determinants of PSP adoption in county-level water utilities

	FE	RE
	(1)	(2)
Utility characteristics		
Employment (log) (lag 1)	–0.059*	–0.048***
	(0.031)	(0.016)
Assets (log) (lag 1)	0.001	0.008
	(0.011)	(0.008)
Liability ratio (lag 1)	–0.009	–0.002
	(0.015)	(0.012)
Sales (log) (lag 1)	–0.004	0.013
	(0.021)	(0.015)
Managerial expense ratio (lag 1)	0.043	0.036
	(0.036)	(0.030)
Profit-sales ratio (lag 1)	0.033	0.029
	(0.023)	(0.021)
Δ Employment (log)	–0.031	–0.036**
	(0.019)	(0.017)
Δ Assets (log)	0.008	0.005
	(0.008)	(0.008)
Δ Liability ratio	0.006	0.003
	(0.012)	(0.011)
Δ Sales (log)	0.002	–0.005
	(0.016)	(0.014)
Δ Managerial expense ratio	–0.025	–0.021
	(0.021)	(0.019)
Δ Profit-sales ratio	–0.014	–0.011
	(0.013)	(0.012)
County characteristics		
Population (log) (lag 1)	–0.011	0.024*
	(0.069)	(0.014)
Population density (lag 1)	–8.94e-07	–1.01e-06
	(8.51e-07)	(8.66e-07)
Share of rural population (lag 1)	0.125	0.027
	(0.082)	(0.055)
GDP per capita (log) (lag 1)	–0.019	0.026
	(0.034)	(0.017)
Share of agriculture in GDP (lag 1)	0.129	0.020
	(0.108)	(0.062)
Share of industry in GDP (lag 1)	0.222**	0.077
	(0.094)	(0.063)
Public financial deficit as a share of government revenues (lag 1)	–0.0002 (0.0002)	–0.0002 (0.0002)

(continued)

Table 4.4 (continued)

	FE	RE
	(1)	(2)
Δ Population (log)	–0.052 (0.095)	–0.068 (0.086)
Δ Population density	2.83e-07 (4.00e-07)	3.37e-07 (4.09e-07)
Δ Share of rural population	–0.060 (0.067)	–0.011 (0.058)
Δ GDP per capita (log)	0.024 (0.029)	–0.002 (0.024)
Δ Share of agriculture in GDP	–0.014 (0.062)	0.050 (0.052)
Δ Share of industry in GDP	–0.077 (0.058)	0.007 (0.052)
Δ Public financial deficit as a share of government revenues	0.00008 (0.00009)	0.00008 (0.00009)
Province-year dummies	Y	Y
Observations	7,643	7,643
R^2	0.067	...

Notes * means significant at 10%, ** significant at 5%, and *** significant at 1%. The dependent variable is PSP dummy, equal to one if there is any nonstate capital in a utility's capital structure. "Δ variable" refers to changes in the variable from $t-2$ to $t-1$. Standard errors clustered at utility level are reported

We find that the probability of privatization is affected by the scale of the water utility. Water utilities employing a large size of personnel in the prior year or those having significantly expanded personnel size over the last two years are less likely to engage in PSP status than others. The other two scale measures, assets and sales revenues, do not have an effect on the likelihood of PSP. Similarly, the profitability of a water utility does not affect the likelihood of PSP adoption. This finding suggests that private investors may value the potential in profitability, so that water utilities with low profitability or experiencing a profit slump may be as attractive to private investors as those with high profitability or rising profit.

The likelihood of PSP is higher in counties with a large population size. This implies that PSP is more likely to happen in counties with a large base of potential water users and a high water demand. None of the county-level shocks are statistically significant, which suggests that the decision to privatize is unlikely to be made in response to shocks at the county level.

The analysis of drivers for PSP detects some factors that may have led to PSP, among a rich list of utility and county characteristics and their changes. The utility's employment size and change in employment size and the county's scale may have been taken into account in the decision-making process. All the models estimated below control for these factors, so the estimated impact of PSP on utility performance will be solely driven by a variation of PSP status orthogonal to these factors. Besides the observable variables, unobservable factors may have also affected the likelihood of PSP adoption, for example, idiosyncratic factors such as the foresight of a local government leader or long-term factors such as the status of a county's water-related infrastructure. While the idiosyncratic factors would not bias the estimation of the impact of PSP, the long-term unobservables correlated with both PSP and utility performance would be addressed by the utility fixed effects.

4.6 Impact of PSP on Water Utility Performance

4.6.1 Empirical Strategy

In this study, we exploit the variation in the adoption of PSP across utilities and time and apply a utility fixed-effects model to identify the causal impact of PSP on utility performance.[16] The empirical specification is given by the following equation:

$$Y_{ict} = \phi PSP_{ict} + X_{ict-1}\alpha + g_i + \gamma_t + Z_{ct}\beta + \theta_{pt} + \delta W_c t + \epsilon_{ict}, \quad (4.1)$$

where Y_{ict} is the performance of utility i in county c in year t. PSP_{ict} is a binary variable which is equal to one if the water utility has nonstate capital in year t and zero otherwise. ϕ is the parameter of interest which quantifies the effect of PSP on utility performance Y_{ict}. X_{ict-1} is a set of time-variant utility characteristics that may affect the performance of the utility. As the analysis in Sect. 4.5 reveals that one-year lag of utility employment and the change of employment from $t-2$ to $t-1$ might have contributed to the adoption of PSP in water utilities, they are included in the estimation to control for possible selection bias. We also include utility sales and assets to capture the scale of utilities. Since contemporaneous utility characteristics may be affected by PSP, all the utility characteristics are one-year lags from year t. Utility fixed effects g_i are included to control for time-invariant observable and unobservable utility characteristics that may affect both PSP adoption and utility performance.[17] Year fixed effects γ_t account for the common time trends of performance for all utilities. ϵ_{ict} is the random error term. We cluster standard

[16] To address the concern on the joint determination of PSP and the effects of PSP on performance, we also employed an endogenous switching regression model in a two-stage estimation (Lee 1978). It is shown that for all 12 performance outcomes, the average increments from the switching regression model are much larger than the main results (column (3) of Table 4.5) in magnitude. It suggests that addressing the selectivity bias, if any, would strengthen our results. However, the average increments of PSP from the switching regression model are likely to be biased for at least two reasons. First, Lee's model is designed for cross-sectional data, while our sample is a panel data set. Second, observations from a province in one year where every utility has the same PSP status have to be dropped from analysis in the random-effects probit model in the first stage, leading to a smaller sample size for estimation (see Caudill (1988) for more details on the discussion). The results from the switching regression model are available upon request.

[17] Since a county-level water utility supplies water to urban population in one county or part of a county, by controlling for utility fixed effects, we have actually controlled for county, prefecture, and province fixed effects.

errors by utility to deal with any potential correlation across years within the same utility (Bertrand et al. 2004).

The identification requires that there are no contemporaneous utility-level trends that are correlated with the adoption of PSP and utility performance outcomes. We address the concern in two ways. First, we directly control for a set of time-variant county characteristics Z_{ct} that may correlate with water demand or supply to capture the effects of contemporaneous shocks at the county level. The vector of county characteristics includes logarithm of population, population density, share of rural population, logarithm of GDP per capita, share of agriculture in GDP, share of industry in GDP, and public financial deficit as a share of government revenues. Second, following Hoynes et al. (2016), we control for province-specific year fixed effects θ_{pt} and interactions of county characteristics in 1998 and linear time trends $W_c t$.[18] Including the variables allows the time trends in outcome variables to vary by province and county characteristics in the initial period, and limits the chance that our results will be confounded by unobserved differences in time trends across provinces and counties of different characteristics.

The estimation of two performance indicators, sales and employment, is done on a dynamic panel model, since lags of the dependent variables (the one-year lags of sales and employment) are controlled for as independent variables. The model used is as follows:

$$Y_{ict} = \rho Y_{ict-1} + \phi PSP_{ict} + X_{ict-1}\alpha + g_i + \gamma_t + Z_{ict}\beta + \theta_{pt} + \delta W_c t + \epsilon_{itc}. \quad (4.2)$$

We apply the Arrelano-Bond method for the estimation and report robust errors for Arrelano-Bond estimation results.

4.6.2 Main Results

Columns (1)–(3) of Table 4.5 present the estimated effects of PSP on each of the 12 performance indicators.[19] Each cell indicates one estimate of PSP's impact on the corresponding performance indicator. Column (1) reports results from the specification with PSP, utility fixed effects, year dummies, and lagged utility characteristics controlled for. In column (2), we further control for county characteristics that may capture the contemporaneous shocks to utility performance at the county level. Column (3) presents results from the augmented specification, which controls for province-year dummies and the interactions of county characteristics in 1998 and linear time trends, so as to allow the time trends to vary across provinces and with

[18] County characteristics in Z_{ct} but from the year of 1998 are used to construct the interactions.

[19] The PSP here is constructed from the raw data. Later, we address the concern on the possible coding errors in PSP and present the results in Panel A of Table 4.6.

Table 4.5 Effects of PSP on water utility performance

		County			Prefecture[a]
Dep. var.	Key var.	(1)	(2)	(3)	(4)
Investment	PSP	–336.555	–296.014	–45.888	10,568
		(1,843.574)	(1,853.654)	(1,798.315)	(19,987)
		7,779	7,779	7,779	1,752
		0.057	0.059	0.095	0.061
Employment (log)	PSP	–0.009	–0.017	–0.008	–0.092**
		(0.012)	(0.012)	(0.012)	(0.040)
		6,648	6,648	6,648	1,547
		–	–	–	0.092
Sales (log)	PSP	0.052**	0.043*	0.036**	0.068
		(0.026)	(0.024)	(0.018)	(0.087)
		6,647	6,647	6,647	1,515
Value added (log)	PSP	0.115***	0.115***	0.100***	0.015
		(0.037)	(0.037)	(0.037)	(0.047)
		7,688	7,688	7,688	1,530
		0.133	0.134	0.179	0.245
Liability ratio	PSP	–0.046**	–0.046**	–0.048***	–0.009
		(0.018)	(0.018)	(0.018)	(0.017)
		7,779	7,779	7,779	1,515
		0.064	0.065	0.094	–
Managerial expense ratio	PSP	–0.034***	–0.033***	–0.031***	–0.027*
		(0.010)	(0.010)	(0.011)	(0.015)
		7,779	7,779	7,779	1,752
		0.013	0.015	0.051	0.027
Financial expense ratio	PSP	–0.004	–0.004	–0.005	–0.007
		(0.007)	(0.007)	(0.007)	(0.008)
		7,779	7,779	7,779	1,752
		0.008	0.009	0.032	0.041
Profit-sales ratio	PSP	0.058***	0.058***	0.059***	0.015
		(0.014)	(0.014)	(0.015)	(0.020)
		7,779	7,779	7,779	1,515
		0.026	0.027	0.064	–

(continued)

county characteristics. Because one-year lag of utility employment and the change of employment over the last two years are controlled for in the regressions, we are actually exploiting the variation in PSP between 2000 and 2006. As a comparison, column (4) reports the estimated effects of PSP on the performance of water utilities at the prefecture level, extracted from Table 5 in Jiang and Zheng (2014).

Table 4.5 (continued)

		County			Prefecture[a]
Dep. var.	Key var.	(1)	(2)	(3)	(4)
Tax-sales ratio	PSP	0.001	0.001	0.0008	0.002
		(0.002)	(0.002)	(0.002)	(0.003)
		7,779	7,779	7,779	1,548
		0.003	0.003	0.036	0.033
Subsidy-sales ratio	PSP	–0.0009	–0.0002	0.0007	–0.009
		(0.008)	(0.007)	(0.007)	(0.009)
		7,779	7,779	7,779	1,752
		0.002	0.003	0.019	0.029
Average revenue product of labor	PSP	4.001***	3.977***	3.583***	6.448
		(1.324)	(1.311)	(1.257)	(5.181)
		7,775	7,775	7,775	1,547
		0.13	0.135	0.211	0.216
TFP (log)	PSP	0.159	0.119	0.164	0.209
		(0.120)	(0.144)	(0.114)	(0.389)
		7,672	7,672	7,672	1,507
		0.002	0.003	0.018	0.110
Utility and year fixedeffects		Y	Y	Y	Y
Lagged utility characteristics		Y	Y	Y	Y
County characteristics		N	Y	Y	N
Province-year dummies, 1998 county char. × year		N	N	Y	N
City characteristics		N	N	N	Y

Notes * means significant at 10%, ** significant at 5%, and *** significant at 1%. Each block corresponding to the dependent variable under each column contains the estimated effect of PSP on the dependent variable, standard errors (in parentheses), number of observations, and R^2. Estimates on effect of PSP on the performance of urban water utilities at the county level are presented in columns (1)–(3). For employment (log) and sales (log), dynamic panel models were estimated using Arellano-Bond method. For the other dependent variables, utility fixed effects panel models were estimated. Robust standard errors are reported for estimates from dynamic panel models. Standard errors clustered at utility level are reported for estimates from fixed-effects models.

[a] Column (4) reports the estimated effects of PSP on the performance of urban water utilities at the prefecture level extracted from Table 5 of Jiang and Zheng (2014)

If PSP improved performance of water utilities, the sign of the effect on investment, employment, sales revenues, value added, profit-sales ratio, average revenue product of labor, and TFP tends to be positive, and the sign of the effect on liability ratio, managerial expense ratio, and financial expense ratio tends to be negative. Yet, we do not have a priori on the sign for tax-sales ratio and subsidy-sales ratio. As shown in columns (1) to (3), the signs are mostly as expected except for investment and employment, which we will elaborate later on. The estimates are by and large stable across specifications in columns (1) to (3), both in magnitude and significance level. The mild decrease in the effect magnitude for sales revenues and average revenue product of labor from column (1) to (2) suggests that certain county characteristics that are correlated with PSP adoption also affect the outcome variables (*e.g.*, one-year lag of population size as shown in Table 4.4). From column (2) to (3), sales revenues, value added, and average revenue product of labor experience a minor drop in the effect magnitude. It is probably that time trends in these outcomes vary across provinces and counties of different characteristics. Our discussion below is based on the estimates from our preferred specification in column (3).

The introduction of PSP significantly raised water utilities' output, measured by sales revenues and value added. PSP increased sales revenues by 3.6% and value added by 10%, respectively. No significant changes are detected in inputs. The effect of PSP on investment is negative and insignificant, which might be attributed to the large standard errors. There is anecdotal evidence that some local governments set a precondition of not laying off redundant labor after privatization (Zhong et al. 2008; Bai et al. 2009), which may explain the finding in Sect. 4.5 that water utilities with more employees or experiencing a positive shock in employment size are less likely to attract private investment. Therefore, it is not surprising that the impact of PSP on employment size of water utilities is small and statistically insignificant. This finding echoes the multitask theory of state-owned enterprises as a second-best way of maintaining social stability (Bai et al. 2006) and the empirical findings from the panel data set of China's state-owned enterprises in Bai et al. (2009).

We find that PSP improved the financial performance of water utilities, cutting the ratio of liability to total assets by 0.048. It is likely that the entry of private investors relieved the utilities' debt burden by improving accessibility to external finance or lifting leverage capability. Moreover, these improvements were probably achieved without imposing an additional financial burden on the utilities, as the impact on the financial expense ratio is small and statistically insignificant.

In line with Bai et al. (2009) and Jiang and Zheng (2014), PSP is found to lower the ratio of managerial expenses to sales revenues by approximately 0.031. Reducing managerial expenses is probably one of the most effective ways to cut costs, as flexible expenses such as employment benefits and travel costs usually take up a large share of managerial expenses. The profitability of water utilities, as measured by profit-sales ratio, increased by 0.059 for PSP utilities. Taking into account the impacts of PSP on raising the output and reducing the liability ratio and managerial expense ratio, this finding is as expected. According to Williamson (1963)'s managerial model, a nonnegligible part of true monopoly profits could be absorbed internally in executive salaries and in perquisites of a variety of sorts. It is possible that the introduction of the PSP interrupted the absorption, and consequently, raised the profitability.[20]

[20] Ownership may also affect profitability via pricing strategy, although mixed evidence has been found in the literature. For instance, using a data set of French water utilities, Porcher (2012) found that private provision of water is more expensive than public provision, although public (private) provision is not directly associated with lower (higher) prices among switchers. One possible reason is that public managers may have a stronger desire to serve the public interest. In contrast, Schargrodsky (2003) showed that, in the U.S. newspaper industry, firms increase their

However, the increase is still not enough to reverse the negative average profit-sales ratio in the county-level water utilities, −0.085 as shown in Table 4.3. It may partially explain the slow PSP progress among the county-level water utilities. Neither the tax-sales ratio nor the subsidy-sales ratio is affected by PSP, suggesting that both government revenues and expenditures may not be affected by PSP.

Finally, PSP is found to raise labor productivity, as measured by the average revenue product of labor. On average, the average revenue product of labor increased by 3,583 CNY (in 1998 constant price) after privatization. This is consistent with the finding that privatization of county-level water utilities had little impact on employment levels, but raised sales revenues. PSP is found to raise TFP by around 16%, although the increase is not significant. It is thus not clear whether PSP brought technological change to the privatized water utilities.

The comparison of the estimates in column (3) with Jiang and Zheng (2014)'s findings on prefecture-level urban water utilities (presented in column (4)) provides two insights. First, among county-level water utilities, six of the twelve indicators are significantly improved by PSP, compared with merely two indicators for prefecture-level utilities. Second, the significant estimates for county-level water utilities are generally larger than the estimates for prefecture-level cities, while the standard errors are close. The only exceptions are the coefficients on sales and average revenue product of labor. The comparison suggests that PSP has more pronounced and more comprehensive impacts on county-level water utilities than on prefecture-level utilities. It is important to note that the greater effects of PSP on county-level water utilities should not be attributed to the larger sample used for analysis in this study. Considering the smaller scale of county-level water utilities than the prefecture-level ones, our results are consistent with the findings of Bhattacharyya et al. (1995) and Peda et al. (2013) that small water utilities would benefit more by engaging with private investors than large water utilities.

4.7 Robustness Checks

We address the concern regarding possible coding errors of capital sources in the raw data. As mentioned in Sect. 4.4, each year some water utilities welcomed private investors, while some others experienced private capital withdrawal. Although the possibility of switching between PSP and pure state ownership cannot be ruled out in reality, frequent switching can be attributed to coding errors. To smooth out the potential coding errors, we recode the key variable, PSP. In the case of PSP, pure state ownership, and PSP in three consecutive years, pure state ownership is recoded as PSP. In the case of pure state ownership, PSP, and pure state ownership in three con-

prices when their ownership structure changes from private to public. A plausible explanation is that private owners may enjoy more freedom than public managers to pursue nonpecuniary benefits of control. We discuss the effect of PSP on water tariffs in Sect. 4.9.

Table 4.6 Sensitivity analysis of PSP on water utility performance

Dep. var.:	Investment	Employment (log)	Sales (log)	Value added (log)	Liability ratio	Managerial expense ratio	Financial expense ratio	Profit-sales ratio	Tax-sales ratio	Subsidy-sales ratio	Average revenue product of labor	TRP (log)
	(1)	(2)	(3)	(4)	(5)	(6)	(7)	(8)	(9)	(10)	(11)	(12)
Panel A. Possible coding errors adjusted												
PSP (recoded)	330.856	–0.021	0.046*	0.104**	–0.049**	–0.030**	–0.011	0.072***	–0.0004	0.009	4.366***	0.207
	(2,268.384)	(0.020)	(0.025)	(0.045)	(0.022)	(0.014)	(0.009)	(0.019)	(0.002)	(0.006)	(1.537)	(0.129)
Observations	7,779	6,648	6,647	7,688	7,779	7,779	7,779	7,779	7,779	7,779	7,775	7,672
R^2	0.095	–	–	0.178	0.094	0.05	0.033	0.065	0.036	0.019	0.212	0.018
Panel B. Sample period 1998–2007												
PSP	–842.052	–0.027	0.030	0.054	–0.058**	–0.025*	–0.0009	0.060***	0.0002	–0.001	4.012**	0.068
	(2,095.180)	(0.153)	(0.218)	(0.035)	(0.023)	(0.013)	(0.010)	(0.019)	(0.001)	(0.008)	(1.641)	(0.085)
Observations	4,474	3,908	3,907	4,439	4,474	4,474	4,474	4,474	4,474	4,474	4,475	4,433
R^2	0.13	–	–	0.335	0.137	0.086	0.049	0.119	0.049	0.082	0.319	0.171

Notes * means significant at 10%, ** significant at 5%, and *** significant at 1%. For employment (log) and sales (log), dynamic panel models were estimated using Arellano-Bond method. For the other dependent variables, utility fixed-effects models were estimated. The same specification as in column (3) of Table 4.5 is applied to all regressions. Robust standard errors are reported for estimates from dynamic panel models. Standard errors clustered at utility level are reported for estimates from fixed-effects models

secutive years, the PSP is recoded as pure state ownership. This adjustment results in 96 corrected cases for 84 water utilities. We further verify the cases one by one by searching information from authoritative sources—the websites of water utilities and local governments. However, only 13 out of the 84 water utilities (15.5%) can be verified.[21] Panel A of Table 4.6 presents the estimation results of the corrected recoding. Compared with the PSP in the original coding in column (3) of Table 4.5, all the performance indicators that are found to be significantly affected by PSP remain significant. In particular, there is no change in the signs of these estimates, and for some indicators, the effects become larger (*e.g.*, sales revenues, liability ratio, profit-sales ratio, and average revenue product of labor). PSP is not found to have significant effect on the indicators that are not significantly affected in the main results. The results suggest that our findings are unlikely to be affected by errors in the coding of capital sources.

A large proportion (42.5%) of the water utilities observed in 2006 have been absent in the NBS surveys since 2007.[22] We exclude the data after the year 2006 from the main analysis for two reasons. First is to have a sample of proper size. We use the balanced sample of 1,123 water utilities (1998–2006) in the main analysis. Keeping records after the year 2006 ends up with a sample of much fewer water utilities—a balanced sample of 563 water utilities (1998–2007). Second is to lower the likelihood of sample selection. The reason for absence of water utilities is not available from public sources. By comparing the sample means, we find that the water utilities that dropped out in 2007 were less likely to be PSP utilities and did worse in almost all 12 outcomes than those retained in 2007, suggesting that many small and low-performance water utilities dropped out of the survey in 2007.[23] To check if our estimates are affected by sample composition and time span, we rerun the regressions on the balanced sample of 563 water utilities (1998–2007), and present the results in Panel B of Table 4.6. The estimates are very close to the main results (column (3) of Table 4.5). The performance indicators that are found to be significantly affected by PSP in the main results mostly remain significant, except that the positive effects of PSP on outputs, measured by sales revenues and value added, become smaller and insignificant. For the indicators that PSP has no significant effect in the main results, the effects of PSP are still insignificant in Panel B. Since extending the time span of the sample by one year at the cost of losing half of the water utilities only makes minor changes to the estimates, our main findings are not likely to be challenged by the choices of sample composition and time span.

---

[21] Only nine of the 84 water utilities (10.7%) have a proper website with ownership information. The ownership information of the rest four water utilities is extracted from government reports on the website of local governments.

[22] The number of county-level water utilities surveyed in 2007 plunged from 1,663 in 2006 to 957 in 2007.

[23] Summary statistics are available upon request from the author.

Table 4.7 Other robustness tests

Dep. var.:	Investment	Employment (log)	Sales (log)	Value added (log)	Liability ratio	Managerial expense ratio	Financial expense ratio	Profit-sales ratio	Tax-sales ratio	Subsidy-sales ratio	Average revenue product of labor	TRP (log)
	(1)	(2)	(3)	(4)	(5)	(6)	(7)	(8)	(9)	(10)	(11)	(12)
A. Utilities ever shifting PSP status during 1998 and 2006												
PSP	856.853	–0.024	0.009	0.113***	–0.053***	–0.037***	–0.005	0.058***	0.001	0.019	3.238**	0.251*
	(1,599.976)	(0.080)	(0.227)	(0.044)	(0.020)	(0.014)	(0.009)	(0.017)	(0.002)	(0.014)	(1.301)	(0.148)
Observations	1,663	1,421	1,421	1,643	1,663	1,663	1,663	1,663	1,663	1,663	1,662	1,638
R^2	0.204	–	–	0.258	0.209	0.164	0.148	0.153	0.108	0.1	0.294	0.154
B. Ratio of PSP as key variable												
Ratio of PSP	–994.125	–0.020	0.035	0.074	–0.066***	–0.032**	–0.011	0.071***	0.0009	0.006	4.152***	0.129
	(2,828.420)	(0.016)	(0.027)	(0.045)	(0.025)	(0.014)	(0.010)	(0.020)	(0.002)	(0.007)	(1.542)	(0.140)
Observations	7,725	6,571	6,571	7,638	7,725	7,725	7,725	7,725	7,725	7,725	7,724	7,624
R^2	0.096	–	–	0.177	0.097	0.052	0.033	0.066	0.038	0.019	0.213	0.018

Notes * means significant at 10%, ** significant at 5%, and *** significant at 1%. For employment (log) and sales (log), dynamic panel models were estimated using Arellano-Bond method. For the other dependent variables, utility fixed-effects models were estimated. The same specification as in column (3) of Table 4.5 is applied to all regressions. Robust standard errors are reported for estimates from dynamic panel models. Standard errors clustered at utility level are reported for estimates from fixed-effects models

4.8 Discussion

4.8.1 The Extent of PSP

One of the consequences of China's gradual and selective approach to privatization is that it is possible to preserve significant state ownership, even after privatization (Bai et al. 2009). PSP-majority ownership may provide private investors more control rights over the water utilities, while private investors in PSP-minority water utilities may have more limited control rights. If we assume that state ownership is the main source of inefficiency in state-owned water utilities, we would expect to find PSP-majority utilities to outperform PSP-minority utilities. An alternative perspective is that PSP-minority utilities perform better than pure state-owned utilities because private investors can play a role as delegates of advanced management concepts in collaborating with state shareholders. U sing all industry data from China NBS surveys, Bai et al. (2009) found that the impacts of privatization on social welfare responsibility were statistically significant only for PSP-majority, and that the effects on firm profitability were more pronounced for PSP-majority. Moreover, the findings by Jiang and Zheng (2014) on the impact of PSP on performance of prefecture-level water utilities point to the importance of control rights obtained by private investors to achieve cost savings and profit increase. It thus would be interesting to investigate if the extent of PSP matters for the performance improvement in county-level water utilities.[24]

We modify model (4.1) by replacing the dummy variable of PSP with two dummy variables, PSP-majority and PSP-minority. The modified model is as follows:

$$Y_{it} = \phi_1 \text{PSP-majority}_{it} + \phi_2 \text{PSP-minority}_{it} + X_{ict-1}\alpha + g_i + \gamma_t + Z_{ct}\beta + \theta_{pt} + \delta W_{c}t + \epsilon_{ict}, \quad (4.3)$$

where ϕ_1 and ϕ_2 measure the effects of PSP-majority and PSP-minority status, respectively, on utility performance relative to that of the pure state-owned utilities. The same list of explanatory variables and estimation methods as in column (3) of Table 4.5 are applied.

The estimation results are presented in Panel A of Table 4.8. Both PSP-majority and PSP-minority water utilities are found to lower managerial expense ratio, and raise value added and profit-sales ratio. In addition, the impacts of both PSP-majority and PSP-minority on sales revenues are positive but insignificant, although PSP in general is found to raise sales revenues (see column (3) of Table 4.5). Financial performance and labor efficiency can be greatly improved only if private investors enjoy higher control rights in PSP. Under majority privatization, the liability ratio was lowered by an average of 6.4 percentage points, and the average revenue product of labor was lifted up by 5,043 CNY. PSP-minority is also found to reduce the liability ratio and raise the average revenue product of labor, but the estimated effects are on

[24] An alternative measure of PSP extent is ratio of nonstate ownership, which takes continuous values from 0 to 1. Panel B of Table 4.7 presents results using this measure. The estimates are in line with main results except that the estimates for sales revenues and value added are insignificant.

Table 4.8 PSP effects by extent and source

Dep. var.:	Investment	Employment (log)	Sales (log)	Value added (log)	Liability ratio	Managerial expense ratio	Financial expense ratio	Profit-sales ratio	Tax-sales ratio	Subsidy-sales ratio	Average revenue product of labor	TRP (log)
	(1)	(2)	(3)	(4)	(5)	(6)	(7)	(8)	(9)	(10)	(11)	(12)
Panel A. PSP extent												
PSP-majority ($e1$)	–1,039.139	–0.020	0.028	0.083*	–0.064***	–0.031**	–0.010	0.064***	0.0008	0.004	5.043***	0.129
	(2,487.503)	(0.016)	(0.023)	(0.042)	(0.022)	(0.013)	(0.010)	(0.019)	(0.002)	(0.006)	(1.617)	(0.129)
PSP-minority ($e2$)	1,706.536	–0.004	0.041	0.131*	–0.020	–0.030*	0.003	0.049**	0.0009	–0.005	1.008	0.227
	(1,262.807)	(0.013)	(0.036)	(0.067)	(0.023)	(0.016)	(0.007)	(0.022)	(0.003)	(0.017)	(1.642)	(0.148)
Observations	7,779	6,648	6,647	7,688	7,779	7,779	7,779	7,779	7,779	7,779	7,775	7,672
R^2	0.096	–	–	0.179	0.095	0.051	0.032	0.064	0.036	0.019	0.212	0.018
p-value ($e1 = e2$)	0.249	0.349	0.757	0.534	0.102	0.965	0.235	0.581	0.978	0.613	0.064	0.528
Panel B. PSP source												
PSP-collective ($s1$)	–210.120	–0.011	0.039	0.084*	–0.048	–0.066***	–0.009	0.040*	0.003	–0.005	2.424	0.125
	(2,042.988)	(0.019)	(0.031)	(0.048)	(0.029)	(0.017)	(0.009)	(0.021)	(0.004)	(0.005)	(2.434)	(0.138)
PSP-legal entity ($s2$)	–797.200	–0.004	0.017	0.087**	–0.053***	–0.013	–0.011	0.042**	0.002	0.008	4.031**	–0.016
	(2,595.458)	(0.012)	(0.022)	(0.044)	(0.020)	(0.013)	(0.010)	(0.017)	(0.002)	(0.007)	(1.637)	(0.093)

(continued)

Table 4.8 (continued)

Dep. var.:	Investment	Employment (log)	Sales (log)	Value added (log)	Liability ratio	Managerial expense ratio	Financial expense ratio	Profit-sales ratio	Tax-sales ratio	Subsidy-sales ratio	Average revenue product of labor	TRP (log)
	(1)	(2)	(3)	(4)	(5)	(6)	(7)	(8)	(9)	(10)	(11)	(12)
PSP-individual ($s3$)	1,551.257	−0.036*	0.034	0.058	0.003	−0.008	−0.0004	0.048**	−0.001	−0.013	1.142	0.215
	(1,828.649)	(0.021)	(0.027)	(0.066)	(0.024)	(0.013)	(0.013)	(0.019)	(0.002)	(0.015)	(2.225)	(0.189)
PSP-other ($s4$)	−570.693	−0.060	0.048	0.115	−0.107	0.029	0.067	0.199***	−0.002	0.042	−1.953	0.977
	(9,019.697)	(0.052)	(0.100)	(0.137)	(0.083)	(0.029)	(0.065)	(0.066)	(0.002)	(0.028)	(2.915)	(0.807)
Observations	7,779	6,648	6,647	7,688	7,779	7,779	7,779	7,779	7,779	7,779	7,775	7,672
R^2	0.096	–	–	0.178	0.095	0.052	0.033	0.065	0.036	0.02	0.211	0.018
p-value ($s1 = s2 = s3 = s4$)	0.912	0.38	0.905	0.977	0.197	0.009	0.424	0.146	0.588	0.235	0.328	0.364

Notes * means significant at 10%, ** significant at 5%, and *** significant at 1%. PSP-majority equals one if a utility has more than 50% nonstate ownership, and zero otherwise. PSP-minority equals one if state ownership is more than 50% in a privatized utility, and zero otherwise.
PSP-collective equals one if a utility has private capital from collective investors, and zero otherwise. PSP-legal entity equals one if a utility has private capital from legal entity investors, and zero otherwise. PSP-individual equals one if a utility has private capital from individual investors, and zero otherwise. PSP-other equals one if a utility has private capital from Hong Kong, Macau, or Taiwan (HMT), or foreign investors, and zero otherwise
For employment (log) and sales (log), dynamic panel models were estimated using Arellano-Bond method. For the other dependent variables, utility fixed-effects models were estimated. The same specification as in column (3) of Table 4.5 is applied to all regressions except that PSP is replaced by corresponding variables. Robust standard errors are reported for estimates from dynamic panel models. Standard errors clustered at utility level are reported for estimates from fixed-effects models

a smaller magnitude and statistically insignificant. We report the p-values from F tests to show if the difference between the effect of PSP-majority and that of PSP-minority is statistically significant. Only the impact on average revenue product of labor is statistically different by the extent of PSP.

The findings from this exercise suggest that utilities with private investors holding different level of control rights may choose to play distinct business strategies, so that PSP-majority and PSP-minority can both positively affect the performance of the water utilities. Furthermore, water utilities which receive a majority of their capital from private investors may enjoy larger and more widespread improvements in performance.

4.8.2 The Source of PSP

As shown in Frydman et al. (1999), privatization may have different effects depending on the types of owners to whom it gives control. By the definition in Sect. 4.4, we do not distinguish the sources of PSP, and water utilities with actual capital from collective, legal entity, individual, HMT, or foreign sources are all considered as PSP utilities. Yet depending on the capital source, nonstate capital may have some similarities to state capital. For example, collective capital could be similar to state capital given that under the *Constitution of the People's Republic of China* (National People's Congress 2004), state ownership and collective ownership comprise the public sector of the economy. On the other hand, a legal entity could represent either private investors or an enterprise with state background. For example, Beijing Capital—a state-controlled shareholding company that has invested in projects on water supply, wastewater treatment, solid waste treatment, and environment management in 54 cities in China by 2015 (Beijing Capital 2016)—would be more likely to be profit driven.

We investigate if different sources of PSP function in distinct ways in reshaping the water utilities. Since only four utilities ever received capitals from HMT and six utilities ever received capital from foreign sources, we categorize them into one type, other private sources. We generate dummies for each specific capital source, PSP-collective, PSP-legal-entity, PSP-individual, and PSP-other. As such, one utility can have more than one source of capital. We replace the dummy variable of PSP in model (4.1) with the dummies. Below is the modified model:

$$\begin{aligned} Y_{it} = {} & \phi_1 \text{PSP-collective}_{it} + \phi_2 \text{PSP-legal-entity}_{it} + \phi_3 \text{PSP-individual}_{it} + \phi_4 \text{PSP-other}_{it} \\ & + X_{ict-1}\alpha + g_i + \gamma_t + Z_{ct}\beta + \theta_{pt} + \delta W_c t + \epsilon_{ict}, \end{aligned} \tag{4.4}$$

where ϕ_1, ϕ_2, ϕ_3, and ϕ_4 measure the effects of PSP ownership type—collective, legal entity, individual, and other, respectively—on utility performance relative to that of the state-owned utilities. Again, the same list of explanatory variables and estimation methods as in column (3) of Table 4.5 are applied.

Panel B of Table 4.8 reports the regression results. Water utilities with any source of private capital outperform state-owned utilities in terms of raising profit-sales ratio. In addition, each private capital exerts a unique impact on performance. For instance, water utilities with collective or legal entity capital outperform state-owned utilities in value-added. Water utilities with collective capital experienced a significant reduction in the managerial expense ratio as opposed to state-owned utilities. Legal entity-sourced PSPs enjoyed a significant decrease in liability ratio and a significant increase in average revenue product of labor. Individual-sourced PSPs experienced a significant employment downsizing. None of the sources of capital significantly increased sales revenues, although PSP in general is found to increase sales revenues. To show if the difference in effects across different sources of PSP is statistically significant, we report the p-values from F tests of equal effects across sources. Only the impact on managerial expense ratio is statistically different by sources of PSP, suggesting that PSP-collective outperform any other source of private capital in lowering managerial expense ratio.

The unveiled heterogeneous effects of PSP by source on improving the performance of water utilities are in accord with the prediction that the strategies played by private investors and thus performance outcomes may vary by source of nonstate capital. The findings suggest that water utilities with any source of private capital have the potential to outperform state-owned utilities in at least one indicator.

4.8.3 Long-Term Effects of PSP

So far, we have assumed that the effect of PSP is uniform across years. The estimated effect of PSP on utilities' performance is thus the average of short-term and long-term effects. Existing studies on the long-term effects of PSP have suggested that the positive effect of PSP on performance might appear immediately (Brown et al. 2006) or emerge after several years (Brown et al. 2006; Villalonga 2000), and might be transitory (Frydman et al. 1999; Cook and Uchida 2008) or keep increasing over a long period (Boardman et al. 2016). We are interested to know if the performance improvement of county-level water utilities brought in by PSP persists in the long run. To obtain a precise measure of years of PSP, we apply two rules. First, we focus on the sample of 1,059 water utilities that did not have PSP in 1998, as for those having PSP in 1998, it is unknown when the PSP started. Hence, the highest number of years of PSP is eight. Second, years of PSP starts counting from one if a water utility had no PSP last year and got PSP this year. If PSP status is not continuous over time, this calculation takes the newly entered PSP as different from the previously exited PSP, and recounts the years of PSP. The model (4.1) is modified with the dummy of PSP replaced by dummies of years of PSP. Since only a small number of water utilities had PSP for more than three years, we take after three years of PSP as one group.

The revised model is as follows:

$$Y_{ict} = \sum_{k=1}^{4} \phi^k YrPSP_{ict}^k + X_{ict-1}\alpha + g_i + \gamma_t + Z_{ct}\beta + \theta_{pt} + \delta W_c t + \epsilon_{ict}, \quad (4.5)$$

where $YrPSP_{ict}^k$ ($k = 1, ..., 3$) equals one if water utility i in county c was in k^{th} year of PSP in year t and zero otherwise, $YrPSP_{ict}^4$ equals one if the water utility was in at least its 4th year of PSP in year t. We apply the same specification as in column (3) of Table 4.5 for estimation.

Table 4.9 shows the estimation results. Managerial expense ratio was lowered for up to three years after PSP. The effects on liability ratio, financial expense ratio, profit-sales ratio, and average revenue product of labor remained after three years of PSP, and the effect size gets larger as years of PSP increases. Although no significant effect is detected for financial expense ratio on average (column (3) of Table 4.5), PSP is found to exert effect since the third year of PSP. PSP is found to have only short-term effects on utilities' output, as measured by sales and value added. The estimates are significant in the 1st year of PSP but not after.

The findings from this exercise reveal that the effects of PSP on financial performance, profitability, and labor productivity are not transitory, and some effects of PSP may not exert until PSP is adopted for a few years.

4.9 The Impact of PSP on Service Outcomes

The above analysis focuses on the impact of PSP on the performance indicators developed from the financial statements of water utilities. It is equally important to examine the effect of PSP on the service outcomes of the water utilities. In this section, we investigate the effect of PSP on water tariffs, non-revenue water, water quality, water pressure, household access to tap water, and child mortality by combining the baseline sample with data sets from other sources.

Water Tariffs, Non-Revenue Water, Water Quality, and Water Pressure

We extract information on water tariffs, non-revenue water (NRW), water quality, and water pressure from the China County and Town Water Supply Yearbooks (1998–2005).[25] We mainly look at two types of water tariffs: tariffs for domestic use and tariffs for industry use. Consumer price indexes (CPI) from the China Statistics Yearbooks are applied to the water tariffs to obtain 1998 constant price. NRW is measured by the ratio of non-revenue water (water produced less water sold) to water produced. Tap water quality is measured by an aggregate indicator which is the average of the pass rates in five water quality tests: national standard 31-item test, bacteria test, coliform bacteria test, chlorine residual test, and turbidity test. A

[25] Unfortunately, the China County and Town Water Supply Yearbook 2006 is not available from public sources.

Table 4.9 Long-term effects of PSP

Dep. var.:	Investment	Employment (log)	Sales (log)	Value added (log)	Liability ratio	Managerial expense ratio	Financial expense ratio	Profit-sales ratio	Tax-sales ratio	Subsidy-sales ratio	Average revenue product of labor	TRP (log)
	(1)	(2)	(3)	(4)	(5)	(6)	(7)	(8)	(9)	(10)	(11)	(12)
1st year of PSP	304.971	0.003	0.058***	0.104***	–0.048**	–0.026*	0.002	0.046**	–0.0005	–0.006	1.488	0.162
	(2,419.693)	(0.015)	(0.019)	(0.037)	(0.022)	(0.014)	(0.009)	(0.018)	(0.002)	(0.011)	(1.180)	(0.127)
2nd year of PSP	1,887.688	0.006	0.045	0.079	–0.027	–0.033*	–0.012	0.056**	0.003	0.002	3.886*	0.277
	(1,701.837)	(0.020)	(0.030)	(0.089)	(0.026)	(0.017)	(0.009)	(0.025)	(0.003)	(0.008)	(2.292)	(0.251)
3rd year of PSP	–96.164	–0.045	0.037	0.034	–0.072**	–0.038**	–0.018*	0.123***	0.004	0.014	7.976**	–0.093
	(2,476.629)	(0.033)	(0.033)	(0.074)	(0.030)	(0.018)	(0.011)	(0.027)	(0.006)	(0.011)	(3.472)	(0.205)
After 3rd year of PSP	412.179	–0.037	0.057	0.016	–0.111***	–0.039	–0.030*	0.110***	–0.003	0.014	12.250**	–0.225
	(2,600.161)	(0.045)	(0.048)	(0.087)	(0.034)	(0.026)	(0.018)	(0.041)	(0.003)	(0.011)	(5.311)	(0.189)
Observations	7,342	6,276	6,275	7,255	7,342	7,342	7,342	7,342	7,342	7,342	7,338	7,240
R^2	0.09	–	–	0.173	0.09	0.052	0.034	0.066	0.039	0.02	0.212	0.019

Notes * means significant at 10%, ** significant at 5%, and *** significant at 1%. Years of PSP starts counting from one if a water utility had no PSP last year and got PSP this year. 1st year of PSP, 2nd year of PSP, 3rd year of PSP, and after 3rd year of PSP are all dummies variables. The former three equal one if a utility is in the kth year of PSP, and the last equals one if a utility has been in PSP for at least 3 years

For employment (log) and sales (log), dynamic panel models were estimated using Arellano-Bond method. For the other dependent variables, utility fixed-effects models were estimated. The same specification as in column (3) of Table 4.5 is applied to all regressions except that PSP is replaced by corresponding variables. Robust standard errors are reported for estimates from dynamic panel models. Standard errors clustered at utility level are reported for estimates from fixed-effects models

Table 4.10 Effect of PSP on service outcomes

	(1)	(2)	(3)	(4)	(5)
Panel A. Yearbook data combined with water utility data					
	Tariff		NRW	Pressure	Quality
Dep. var.:	Domestic (unit: CNY/m^3)	Industrial (unit: CNY/m^3)	Ratio of non-revenue water	Average pressure (unit: MPa)	Average pass rate
PSP	0.406	−0.042	0.008	0.006	−0.009*
	(0.345)	(0.155)	(0.012)	(0.015)	(0.005)
Observations	2,456	2,581	2,713	1,790	1,953
R^2	0.033	0.067	0.202	0.127	0.139
$\overline{Y}$	1.930	1.506	0.230	0.324	0.978
Panel B. Census data combined with water utility data					
	Access		Child mortality		
Dep. var.:	Household having access to tap water		Dead within one year of birth		
Years having PSP (lag 1)	0.003 (0.005)	−0.002 (0.013)			
Years having PSP (lag 1)^2		0.001 (0.003)			
PSP (lag 1)			−0.007 (0.015)		
PSP				0.004 (0.011)	
Observations	971,570	971,570	2,452	2,452	
R^2	0.182	0.182	0.333	0.333	
$\overline{Y}$	0.702	0.702	0.00979	0.00979	

Notes * means significant at 10%, ** significant at 5%, and *** significant at 1%. Each block under each column in each panel contains the coefficient estimate, standard errors (in parentheses) clustered at the county level, and other statistics. A county fixed-effects model is applied for estimation. In all regressions, we include the same set of control variables as in column (3) of Table 4.5. In panel B, we additionally control for number of household members, highest years of schooling, and highest age in the household in columns (1) and (2), and woman's age and years of schooling, spouse's age and years schooling, number of household members, and whether having access to tap water at home in columns (3) and (4). Sampling weights are applied for regressions in panel B

higher rate indicates higher water quality. Water pressure is measured by the average water pressure (unit: MPa) in tests. Both water quality and water pressure are not recorded in the yearbooks before 2001. To prepare the data to merge with our baseline sample, we first identify the county-level water utilities using the name and location. Secondly, to seek a good match of county-level water utility in the two data sets, we exclude those counties with more than one utility in a year. Merging the data set with our baseline sample generates a sample of 714 water utilities with each having at least two observations between 1998 and 2005.

We use a county fixed-effects model for estimation. The same set of control variables as in column (3) of Table 4.5 are included. Standard errors are clustered at the county level. Panel A of Table 4.10 reports the results. We find that PSP raised water tariffs for domestic use by 0.406 yuan per cubic meter (in 1998 constant price), although insignificantly. The effect of PSP on industrial water tariffs is small and insignificant. It suggests that PSP may affect the water tariffs differently across sectors, and that the domestic sector may be more prone to the water tariff increase. However, since the estimate for the domestic sector is insignificant, we should interpret the results with caution. Both non-revenue water and water pressure are not affected by PSP; the estimates are small in magnitude and insignificant. In terms of water quality, we find that PSP led to a 0.9 percentage point decrease in the average pass rate, and the effect is marginally significant (p-value=0.09), suggesting that water quality got slightly worse under PSP.

Household Access to Tap Water and Child Mortality

We next estimate the effect of a county's exposure to privatized water service on access to tap water and child mortality among the urban population. We extract urban households from 1% sample of China Census 2000 and 20% sample of China 1% Census 2005. A household is taken as an urban household if any member of the household holds a non-agriculture *Hukou*.

In both censuses, households were asked, "Does your household use tap water as drinking water?" The household is considered as having a connection to a water network if they answer yes, and considered as having no connection if they answer no. The data set is organized in the following ways. First, to seek a good match of service population and county-level water utility, we exclude counties with more than one utility. Second, again we exclude the water utilities that had PSP in 1998, to avoid the wrong counting of years of exposure to PSP. Third, since the expansion of the water pipeline is a gradual process that may not be affected by PSP concurrently, the key variable, years having PSP (lag 1), is the one-year lag of accumulative years of a water utility in receipt of private capital.[26] In the end, we obtain a pooled sample of 987,620 households. From 2000 to 2005, the average tap water coverage rate increased from 69% to 78%. We use a county fixed-effects model for estimation. Besides the control variables in baseline analysis, we further control for household characteristics, including number of household members, highest years of schooling, and highest age in the household. Sampling weights are applied, and standard errors are clustered at the county level. We report the estimation results in Panel B columns (1) and (2) of Table 4.10. Years having PSP has a minor and insignificant effect on a household's probability of having access to tap water. Adding quadratic years of PSP does not generate a significant effect either, suggesting no nonlinear effect of PSP on coverage. The findings imply that in the context of rapid urbanization, water utilities with PSP and pure state-owned water utilities have performed similarly in increasing tap water coverages among urban population.

[26] The accumulative years of water utility in receipt of private capital is calculated in the same way as in Sect. 4.8.3.

In both censuses, women aged 15 to 50 were asked to report the total number of births they ever gave, the total number of children alive, and whether they gave birth in the past 12 months (and if so, the gender and birth month of the child). We include in the analysis those women who first gave birth in the past 12 months.[27] Child mortality is equal to one if the child is dead and zero if alive. We merge the water utility data into the census data. We keep counties having observations in both censuses and exclude counties with more than one utility in one year. The final sample contains 2,499 women. We use a county fixed-effects model for estimation. Besides the control variables in the baseline analysis, we additionally control for woman's age and years of schooling, spouse's age and years schooling, number of household members, and whether having access to tap water at home. Sampling weights are applied, and standard errors are clustered at the county level. We report the estimation results in Panel B columns (3) and (4) of Table 4.10. Regardless of whether PSP is lagged or not, we do not detect any effect of PSP on child mortality.

4.10 Conclusion

To address the discrepancy between the escalating demand for drinking water in urban China and a lack of capability of urban water utilities, the Chinese government opened the water supply industry to private capital in the 1990s and formalized the reform nationally in 2002. Relying on a unique panel data set of 1,123 county-level water utilities extracted from the annual surveys of industrial firms conducted by the National Bureau of Statistics (NBS) of China from 1998 to 2006, we estimate the impact of PSP on the performance of county-level water utilities. This study provides the first evidence on the performance of the small-sized urban water utilities in China and the impact of PSP.

To deal with the non-randomness issue of PSP adoption, we first estimate a model of PSP probability with lagged utility and county characteristics. The results show that a utility's scale (measured by employment size) and the change in scale, and a county's scale (measured by population size), may have been taken into account in the decision-making process of PSP adoption. A utility fixed-effects model is applied to estimate PSP's effect on utility performance. Utility fixed effects are controlled for to deal with unobserved time-invariant utility characteristics that are correlated with both PSP and performance. We also control for province-year dummies and the interactions of county characteristics in 1998 and linear time trends to allow the time trends in outcome variables to vary by province and county characteristics in the initial period.

The results show that PSP significantly raised county-level water utilities' performance by raising outputs (with increases in both sales and value added), improving financial sustainability (lowering the liability ratio and managerial expense ratio, and

[27] So that the total number of births they ever gave is equal to the number of births they gave in the past 12 months.

raising the profit-sales ratio), and boosting labor productivity (increasing the average revenue product of labor). The findings are generally consistent with the impacts of PSP on China's state-owned enterprises as compiled in Bai et al. (2009). Compared with Jiang and Zheng (2014)'s findings from large-sized urban water utilities in prefecture-level cities, we find that county-level water utilities have achieved more pronounced and comprehensive progress by adopting PSP.

Our results survive a series of sensitivity analyses, including addressing the concern on the possible coding errors in PSP and using a sample with the year 2007 included. Heterogeneity analysis shows that any extent of PSP (both PSP-majority and PSP-minority) and any source of PSP (collective, legal entity, individual, and other private capital) have the potential to outperform state-owned utilities, while the magnitude and area of improvement varies. By examining the long-term effect of PSP, we find that the effects of PSP on financial performance and profitability, and on labor productivity, are not transitory. Using supplementary data from population censuses and statistical yearbooks, we test whether PSP had any effect on service outcomes, including water tariffs, non-revenue water, water quality, water pressure, household access to tap water, and child mortality. We find that water quality is slightly lowered under PSP, while no significant effect is detected for other service outcomes.

Given the results of this study, showing that PSP allows county-level water utilities to outperform state-owned utilities, China should promote further entry of non-state capital to the water supply sector at the county level. Since the magnitude and area of improvement varies by the extent and source of PSP, the selection of the extent and source of PSP could take into account the existing conditions and needs of utilities and counties. Most important, the significant improvement in performance as a result of PSP is achieved harmoniously, without laying off surplus labor or compromising the service outcomes of water supply. It is thus surprising to observe how much slower PSP has progressed among county-level water utilities than among prefecture-level ones. From 1998 to 2006, the percentage of county-level water utilities involving PSP increased from 5.7% to 10.7%, while the percentage of prefecture-level water utilities involving PSP between 1998 and 2007 soared from 4.4% to 32.7% (Jiang and Zheng 2014).

The slower adoption rate of PSP in county-level water utilities as compared to prefecture-level water utilities could be attributed to at least three reasons. First is the lack of a systematic and comprehensive regulatory framework for the Chinese urban water sector in practice. Some local governments rushing to reduce the financial burden of the water supply industry promised a fixed investment return to investors, but the practice was later banned by the central government in 1997, hampering the enthusiasm of private investment and the progress of PSP.[28] The uncertainties that private investors face could also partially explain the frequent entry and exit of nonstate capital observed in this study and in Jiang and Zheng (2014). According to

[28] For instance, Shenyang's water supply sector experienced several failed marketization efforts due to the constantly changing policies and decisions of the local government during 1995–2000 (Zhong et al. 2008).

the *Legislation Law of the People's Republic of China* (National People's Congress 2000, 2015), county governments do not possess the legislative power to make local law or regulation, thus designing local policy papers on specific water projects is not an option for county governments.[29] As strong institutional arrangements generate incentives and opportunities for private investors (Fergusson 2006), building up a consistent and sound national regulatory framework for the privatization of water utilities is required to encourage the entry of hesitant private investors into the water supply sector in Chinese counties.

Second is the smaller scale of water utilities in counties, compared to their counterparts at the prefecture level. As suggested by traditional research in economics, large water utilities enjoy advantages such as economies of scale, bargaining power with suppliers and distributors, brand name recognition, and experience curve effects, which may be attractive for private investors. In fact, the county-level water utilities in China have the potential to increase their service areas and the scale of their operations. In 2011, the Chinese government announced the *Decision on Propelling the Water Reform and Development* (CPC Central Committee and the State Council 2011). One of the policy priorities in the water supply sector is to extend tap water coverage to the peri-urban population to achieve "integration of urban and rural water supply." The expansion of urban water supply to the rural areas will provide new opportunities to the county-level water utilities and to private investors. Therefore, we expect PSP to play an increasingly active role in county-level water utilities.

Third, the negative profit rate even after PSP may have discouraged the private investors. By comparing the average profit-sales ratio (−0.085 in Table 4.3) and the average effect of PSP on profit-sales ratio (0.059 in column (3), Table 4.5), we find that the average profit for a PSP county-level water utility can still be negative. Since PSP had no effect on both tax-sales ratio and subsidy-sales ratio, the county-level government may introduce a tax reduction or a subsidy to attract the entry of private investors.

References

Bai C-E, Lu J, Tao Z (2006) The multitask theory of state enterprise reform: Empirical evidence from China. Am Econ Rev 96(2):353–357

Bai C-E, Lu J, Tao Z (2009) How does privatization work in China? J Comp Econ 37(3):453–470

Beijing Capital (2016). Profile of Beijing Capital Co, Ltd. http://www.capitalwater.cn/html/Profile/ (Accessed on July 18, 2016)

Benito B, Bastida F, García JA (2010) Explaining differences in efficiency: an application to Spanish municipalities. Appl Econ 42(4):515–528

Bertrand M, Duflo E, Mullainathan S (2004) How much should we trust Differences-in-Differences estimates? Quart J Econ 119(1):249–275

[29] To address the concern of private investors, some prefectural governments issued local policy papers on specific water projects. For example, the *Interim Provision on Administrating Concession Right of Chengdu* (Chengdu Municipality 2001) was issued for implementing the BOT project of Chengdu Water Plant No.6 B (Zhong et al. 2008).

Bhattacharyya A, Harris TR, Narayanan R, Raffiee K (1995) Specification and estimation of the effect of ownership on the economic efficiency of the water utilities. Reg Sci Urban Econ 25(6):759–784

Boardman AE, Vining AR, Weimer DL (2016) The long-run effects of privatization on productivity: evidence from Canada. J Policy Model 38(6):1001–1017

Brandt L, Biesebroeck JV, Zhang Y (2012) Creative accounting or creative destruction? Firm-level productivity growth in Chinese manufacturing. J Dev Econ 97(2):339–351

Brandt L, Biesebroeck JV, Zhang Y (2014) Challenges of working with the Chinese NBS firm-level data. China Econ Rev 30:339–352

Brown JD, Earle JS, Telegdy A (2006) The productivity effects of privatization: longitudinal estimates from Hungary, Romania, Russia, and Ukraine. J Polit Econ 114(1):61–99

Caudill SB (1988) Practitioners corner: an advantage of the linear probability model over probit or logit. Oxford Bull Econ Stat 50(4):425–427

Cavaliere A, Scabrosetti S (2008) Privatization and efficiency: from principals and agents to political economy. J Econ Surv 22(4):685–710

Caves DW, Christensen LR, Diewert WE (1982) Multilateral comparisons of output, input, and productivity using superlative index numbers. Econ J 92(365):73–86

Chengdu Municipality (2001). Interim provision on administrating concession right of chengdu. No 131, Chengdu

Chong E, Huet F, Saussier S, Steiner F (2006) Public-private partnerships and prices: Evidence from water distribution in France. Rev Ind Organ 29:149–169

Cook P, Uchida Y (2008) The performance of privatised enterprises in developing countries. J Develop Stud 44(9):1342–1353

CPC Central Committee and the State Council (2011). Decision on propelling the water reform and development. Beijing

Department of Rural Surveys, National Bureau of Statistics (2013) China county statistical yearbook. China Statistics Press, Beijing

Dollar D, Wei S-J (2007). Das (wasted) kapital: Firm ownership and investment efficiency in China. National Bureau of Economic Research

Estache A, Kouassi E (2002) Sector organization, governance, and the inefficiency of African water utilities. World Bank, Washington, DC

Estache A, Rossi MA (2002) How different is the efficiency of public and private water companies in Asia? World Bank Econ Rev 16(1):139–147

Estrin S, Hanousek J, Kocenda E, Svejnar J (2009) The effects of privatization and ownership in transition economies. J Econ Literat 47(3):699–728

Fergusson L (2006) Institutions for financial development: what are they and where do they come from? J Econ Surv 20(1):27–70

Frydman R, Gray C, Hessel M, Rapaczynski A (1999) When does privatization work? The impact of private ownership on corporate performance in the transition economies. Q J Econ 114(4):1153–1191

Fu T, Chang M (2006) Water sector reform in Urban China: practices and cases. China Architecture & Building Press, Beijing (in Chinese)

Gale BT (1972) Market share and rate of return. Rev Econ Stat 54(4):412–423

Galiani S, Gertler P, Schargrodsky E (2005) Water for life: The impact of the privatization of water services on child mortality. J Polit Econ 113(1):83–120

García-Valiñas MDlA, González-Gómez F, Picazo-Tadeo AJ (2013) Is the price of water for residential use related to provider ownership? Empirical evidence from Spain. Utilit Policy 24:59–69. Water utility regulation in developed countries

Gassner K, Popov AA, Pushak N, Bank W (2009) Does private sector participation improve performance in electricity and water distribution? Number 6 in Trends and Policy Options. World Bank, Washington, DC

Hoynes H, Schanzenbach DW, Almond D (2016) Long-run impacts of childhood access to the Safety Net. Am Econ Rev 106(4):903–934

Imel B, Helmberger P (1971) Estimation of structure-profit relationships with application to the food processing sector. Am Econ Rev 61(4):614–627
Jiang Y, Zheng X (2014) Private sector participation and performance of urban water utilities in China. Econ Develop Cult Change 63(1):155–189
Kirkpatrick C, Parker D, Zhang Y-F (2006) An empirical analysis of state and private-sector provision of water services in Africa. World Bank Econ Rev 20(1):143–163
Lee C (2011) Privatization, water access and affordability: evidence from Malaysian household expenditure data. Econ Model 28(5):2121–2128
Lee L-F (1978) Unionism and wage rates: a simultaneous equations model with qualitative and limited dependent variables. Int Econ Rev 19(2):415–433
Megginson WL, Netter JM (2001) From state to market: A survey of empirical studies on privatization. J Econ Literat 39(2):321–389
Ministry of Construction (2002) Opinions on accelerating the marketization of public utilities. No 272, Beijing
Ministry of Construction (2004) Management measures for concession of urban public unities. No 126, Beijing
Ministry of Construction (2006) Opinions on strengthening regulation of public utilities. No 154, Beijing
Ministry of Foreign Trade and Economics Cooperation (1994) Circular on attracting foreign investment through BOT approach. No 89, Beijing
National Development and Planning Commission, Ministry of Electric Power Industry, and Ministry of Communications (1995) Circular on major issues of approval administration of the franchise pilot projects with foreign investment. No 1208, Beijing
National People's Congress (2000). Legislation law of the People's Republic of China. Order No 31 of the President, Beijing
National People's Congress (2015). Legislation law of the People's Republic of China (2015 Amendment). Order No 20 of the President, Beijing
Neilsen EH (1974) Contingency theory applied to small business organizations. Human Relat 27(4):357–379
Nie H, Jiang T, Yang R (2012) A review and reflection on the use and abuse of Chinese industrial enterprises database. J World Econ 5:142–158 (in Chinese)
Parker D, Kirkpatrick C (2005) Privatisation in developing countries: A review of the evidence and the policy lessons. J Develop Stud 41(4):513–541
Peda P, Grossi G, Liik M (2013) Do ownership and size affect the performance of water utilities? Evidence from Estonian municipalities. J Manage Governance 17(2):237–259
Porcher S (2012) Do markets reduce prices? EPPP DP No. 2012-07 (working paper)
Ruester S, Zschille M (2010) The impact of governance structure on firm performance: An application to the German water distribution sector. Utilit Policy 18(3):154–162. The Water Industry, Competition and Climate Change
Saal DS, Parker D (2001) Productivity and price performance in the privatized water and sewerage companies of England and Wales. J Regul Econ 20(1):61–90
Saal DS, Parker D, Weyman-Jones T (2007) Determining the contribution of technical change, efficiency change and scale change to productivity growth in the privatized English and Welsh water and sewerage industry: 1985–2000. J Prod Anal 28:127–139
Schargrodsky E (2003) Do publicly traded firms price differently from private firms? Am Law Econ Rev 5(1):32–60
Shepherd WG (1972) The elements of market structure. Rev Econ Stat 54(1):25–37
State Planning Committee (2001). Guidelines on encouraging and guiding nongovernment investment. No 2653, Beijing
The Tenth National People's Congress (2004) Constitution of the People's Republic of China. The Second Session of the Tenth National People's Congress, Beijing
Villalonga B (2000) Privatization and efficiency: differentiating ownership effects from political, organizational, and dynamic effects. J Econ Behav Organizat 42:43–74

Wang H, Wu W, Zheng S (2011) An econometric analysis of private sector participation in China's urban water supply. Utilit Policy 19(3):134–141

Williamson OE (1963) Managerial discretion and business behavior. Am Econ Rev 53(5):1032–1057

Zhang L (2006) Mode selection and comparison for urban water affairs reform. China Water Resources. (in Chinese)

Zhong L, Mol A, Fu T (2008) Public-private partnerships in China's urban water sector. Environ Manage 41(6):863–877

Chapter 5
Increasing Block Tariffs and Household Water Savings

Abstract In 2015, Hangzhou, a major Chinese city, introduced a water pricing reform. This reform established an unconventional Increasing Block Tariff (IBT) featuring prices set according to annual cumulative consumption and a bimonthly billing cycle. Analyzing data from a household survey and administrative water bills, we detect a small effect on low-use households but find large water savings among high-use households. Moreover, we find strong evidence that high-use households respond to future price while current price remains fixed, and that the small share of households who appear myopic do not respond to dynamic incentives. These findings may inform future efforts to design price interventions in regions facing water scarcity.

5.1 The 2015 Water Pricing Reform in Hangzhou

As the capital city of Zhejiang Province in southeast China and one of the most economically vibrant cities in China, Hangzhou is an important test case for water pricing reform. The city is at the economic and geographic center of the Yangtze River Delta. It has a humid subtropical climate with four distinctive seasons. It consists of nine districts and four counties, and has a total area of 16,596 km^2 (China City Statistical Yearbook, 2015). In 2014, the GDP of Hangzhou ranked fourth among provincial capitals, behind that of Guangzhou, Wuhan, and Chengdu, and ranked tenth among large and medium-sized cities (China City Statistical Yearbook, 2015). The disposable income per urban resident in Hangzhou was 44,632 yuan in 2014 (about US$ 6,796) (Zhejiang Statistical Yearbook, 2015). By the end of the year 2014, the total population in Hangzhou had reached 7.2 million, and in particular, the main urban area of Hangzhou, including five urban districts: Shangcheng, Xiacheng, Jianggan, Gongshu, and Xihu, accommodated a population of 2.2 million people (Zhejiang Statistical Yearbook, 2015).

Increasing Block Tariffs (IBTs) are commonly used nonlinear pricing schedules for goods such as electricity, water, or phone services, as well as in progressive tax schemes. In recent years, IBTs have been widely implemented across cities in China, to support the government's goal of encouraging water use efficiency while ensuring

© The Author(s), under exclusive license to Springer Nature Singapore Pte Ltd. 2025
L. Li, *The Impacts of Water Reforms in Rural and Urban China*,
https://doi.org/10.1007/978-981-96-6902-8_5

fair access to water. The central government first recommended IBTs for domestic water pricing in the *Circular on Improving the Regulation Work of City Water Price* (NDRC and MHURD 2009). In the *Guidance on Promoting Complete IBT Structure for Urban Domestic Water Use* (NDRC and MHURD 2013), the central government further set a timetable requiring all cities (and towns with adequate conditions) to implement IBTs by the end of 2015. Although Hangzhou has historically drawn from abundant water resources, the high cost of water supply, in part due to increasing electricity, material and labor prices, has been testing the ability of Hangzhou Water, the utility in charge of the water supply for residential and non-residential users in the main urban area of Hangzhou, to recover costs.[1] In response to these challenges, as well as in alignment with the nationwide shift toward IBTs, Hangzhou restructured and raised its water tariffs in 2015.

At the time of the Hangzhou Bureau of Commodity Price's announcement of the water pricing reform on November 26, 2014 (effective on January 1, 2015), the tariff for residential users in the main urban area of Hangzhou had not been revised for ten years. All consumers had previously faced a flat rate of 1.85 yuan/m^3 (about US$ 0.30/m^3 in 2015). The reform introduced two types of new tariffs: a new flat rate and an IBT. The flat tariff rate was increased from 1.85 yuan/m^3 to 2.95 yuan/m^3 (a 59% increase). With the IBT, in contrast, the water price in the first, lowest-consumption tier was set just slightly lower than the new flat rate, at 2.90 yuan/m^3, but a threshold of 216 m^3 was specified for cumulative annual water consumption, above which the marginal cost of consumption in the same budget period would increase. The second tier covers water consumption between 216 m^3 and 300 m^3 within that year, with a marginal price for units set to 3.85 yuan/m^3 (33% higher than the rate in the first tier). The water price for the third tier exceeding 300 m^3 was set to 6.7 yuan/m^3, or 2.3 times the water price in the first tier. At the end of each budget period (year), the tariff would revert back to that for the lowest tier, until the household again exceeded the second-tier threshold. Figure 5.1 shows these water tariffs changes over time and by household cumulative annual water consumption before and after the pricing reform.

IBT households

After the 2015 pricing reform, the IBT was applied only to households living in buildings with fewer than eight floors and having water utility-administered meters. According to Hangzhou Water, in 2015, around 620 thousand households with individual meters under the administration of Hangzhou Water could have had the IBT applied. A small group of newly assigned-IBT households (around 50 thousand) were allowed to opt out of the IBT if their houses were located in an "urban village" and were rentals. In the end, then, a total of 570 thousand households were covered by the IBT at the time, accounting for 57.6% of all residential water consumers (who total 990 thousand). We refer to these households as IBT households and their communities as IBT communities.

---

[1] For more details of Hangzhou Water, please refer to its website, http://www.hzwgc.com (in Chinese).

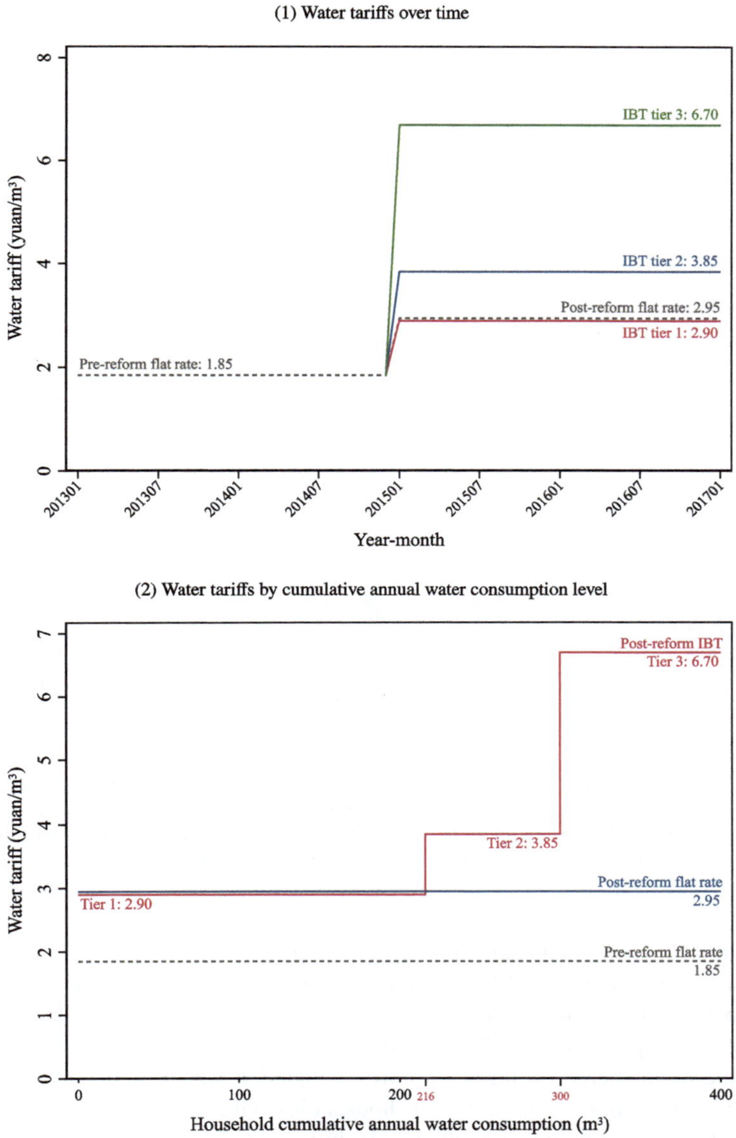

Fig. 5.1 Water tariff structures in Hangzhou. *Notes* Fig. 5.1-(1) shows the water tariff structures for residential households in Hangzhou over time. Before January 1, 2015, all households were charged a low flat rate. Starting from January 1, 2015, IBT households were charged according to a three-tier IBT, and non-IBT households were charged a new flat rate at a level slightly exceeding that of the first tier of the IBT. Figure 5.1-(2) plots these water tariffs as a function of household cumulative annual water consumption. The flat rates do not change with household cumulative annual water consumption, while the three-tier IBT has price increases beyond the thresholds of 216 m^3 and 300 m^3

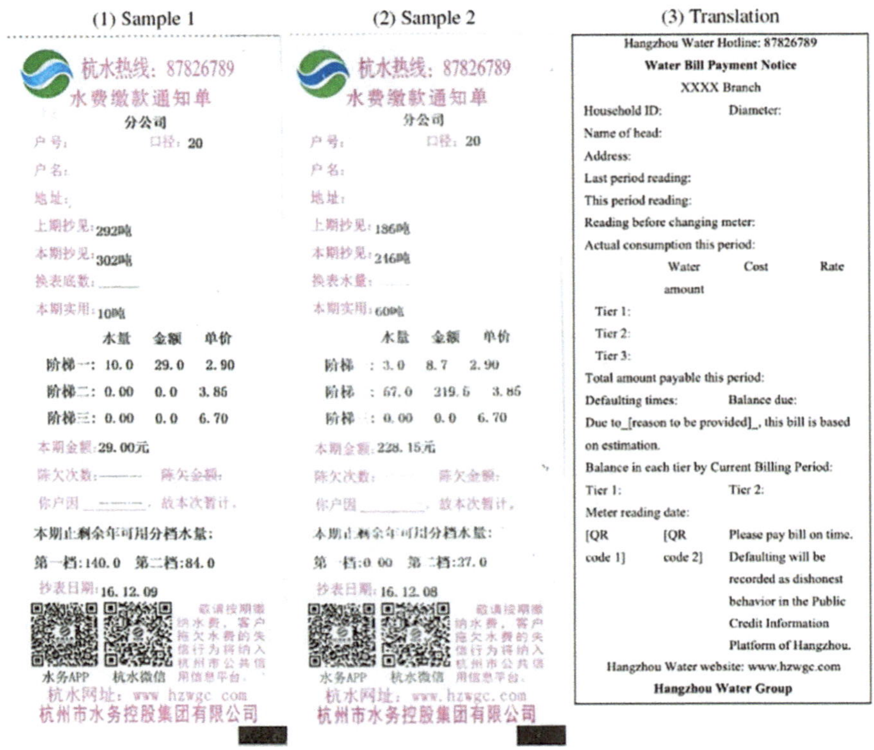

(1) Sample 1

杭水热线：87826789
水费缴款通知单
分公司
户号： 口径：20
户名：
地址：
上期抄见：292吨
本期抄见：302吨
换表底数：
本期实用：10吨

	水量	金额	单价
阶梯一：	10.0	29.0	2.90
阶梯二：	0.00	0.0	3.85
阶梯三：	0.00	0.0	6.70

本期金额：29.00元
陈欠次数： 陈欠金额：
你户因＿＿，故本次暂计。
本期止剩余年可用分档水量：
第一档：140.0 第二档：84.0
抄表日期：16.12.09
水务APP 杭水微信
敬请按期缴纳水费，客户拖欠水费的失信行为将纳入杭州市公共信用信息平台。
杭水网址：www.hzwgc.com
杭州市水务控股集团有限公司
[redacted]

(2) Sample 2

杭水热线：87826789
水费缴款通知单
分公司
户号： 口径：20
户名：
地址：
上期抄见：186吨
本期抄见：246吨
换表水量：
本期实用：60吨

	水量	金额	单价
阶梯 ：	3.0	8.7	2.90
阶梯 ：	67.0	219.5	3.85
阶梯 ：	0.00	0.0	6.70

本期金额：228.15元
陈欠次数： 陈欠金额：
你户因＿＿，故本次暂计。
本期止剩余年可用分档水量：
第 档：0.00 第二档：27.0
抄表日期：16.12.08
水务APP 杭水微信
敬请按期缴纳水费，客户拖欠水费的失信行为将纳入杭州市公共信用信息平台。
杭水网址：www.hzwgc.com
杭州市水务控股集团有限公司
[redacted]

(3) Translation

Hangzhou Water Hotline: 87826789
Water Bill Payment Notice
XXXX Branch
Household ID: Diameter:
Name of head:
Address:
Last period reading:
This period reading:
Reading before changing meter:
Actual consumption this period:

	Water amount	Cost	Rate
Tier 1:			
Tier 2:			
Tier 3:			

Total amount payable this period:
Defaulting times: Balance due:
Due to_[reason to be provided]_, this bill is based on estimation.
Balance in each tier by Current Billing Period:
Tier 1: Tier 2:
Meter reading date:
[QR code 1] [QR code 2] Please pay bill on time. Defaulting will be recorded as dishonest behavior in the Public Credit Information Platform of Hangzhou.
Hangzhou Water website: www.hzwgc.com
Hangzhou Water Group

Fig. 5.2 Samples of water bills for IBT households in Hangzhou. *Notes* (1) shows the water bill of an IBT household whose cumulative water consumption of the year falls in the first tier. (2) shows the water bill of an IBT household whose cumulative water consumption of the year falls in the second tier. (3) provides the translation of the content in a water bill

To spread the workload of meter reading among utility personnel, Hangzhou Water reads the water meters of IBT households every two months, with some households' meters being read in even months and some being read in odd months. The schedule for meter reading remained stable and consistent before and after the reform, except that an additional meter reading session was included in January 2015 for households with meters read in even months. For households with meters read in odd (even) months, the IBT was then first applied to the bill received in March (February) 2015, for water consumed after the first meter reading date in January. The annual budget of water consumption is then reset after the meter reading date in November (December) every year. Therefore, the budget period in 2015 is shorter than that in 2016, though the cumulative annual consumption thresholds for the IBT price hikes remain the same across years.

For IBT households, the water bills prior to IBT adoption included information on recent meter readings, water use in the current period, and the flat rate. Information on the amount left in the current tier and the pricing structure was added to bills after

IBT adoption. Examples of these new bills are shown in Fig. 5.2, for (1) a household consuming in the first tier, and (2) a household consuming in the first two tiers.

Non-IBT households

After the 2015 pricing reform, the new flat rate was imposed on 370 thousand households living in buildings with at least eight floors and having water meters under administration of community offices.[2] These households could not opt out of the flat rate. We refer to these households as non-IBT households and their communities as non-IBT communities. In addition, another 50 thousand newly assigned-IBT households opted into the flat rate, as discussed above. Therefore, in 2015 around 420 thousand households (42.4%) were covered by the new flat rate.

Hangzhou Water does not read meters in the non-IBT communities; instead, the building administrative office takes responsibility for the meter reading and fee collection. Meters for such non-IBT households are read on a monthly basis. The new flat rate was applied for the first time to water consumption beginning in January 2015. The meter readings and water billing data for non-IBT households are maintained by the administrative offices. A sample of the records is shown in Fig. 5.3.

5.2 Results Preview

In this study, we investigate the effect of an unconventional Increasing Block Tariff (IBT) on household water consumption and household response to the dynamic incentives it created. We exploit the natural experiment arising from the water pricing reform beginning in January 2015 in Hangzhou, the capital city of Zhejiang Province in southeast China and one of the most economically vibrant cities in China. Prior to the reform, all households in Hangzhou had faced a low and flat rate that had been unchanged for ten years. The reform involved a transition from a flat rate to a three-tier IBT for a subgroup of households whose meters were directly administered by the water utility at the time of the reform. The other households were subject to a new flat rate that was 50% higher than the prior flat rate, which was nonetheless also nearly equivalent to the lowest tier rate in the new IBT. Using a difference-in-differences (DID) approach, we are able to isolate the effect of the IBT price structure on household water consumption, relative to the simple flat rate.

An ideal experiment for whether dynamic incentives matter in influencing households' response to nonlinear prices would keep the current price fixed while generating variation in the future price (Aron-Dine et al. 2015). Three unique features of the pricing reform in Hangzhou come close to approximating such an ideal experiment. First, the budget period for the IBT is annual, while the billing cycle is bimonthly.

[2] In Hangzhou, water supply to buildings with at least eight floors needs to be re-pressurized, which has historically required this type of decentralized management system. To apply the IBT to the water consumption of non-IBT households, therefore, their water meters and this system would need to be changed, which would require substantial retrofitting. As such, it seems unlikely that such households would adjust their behavior in 2015, anticipating an imminent switch to an IBT.

(1) Sample of bill table

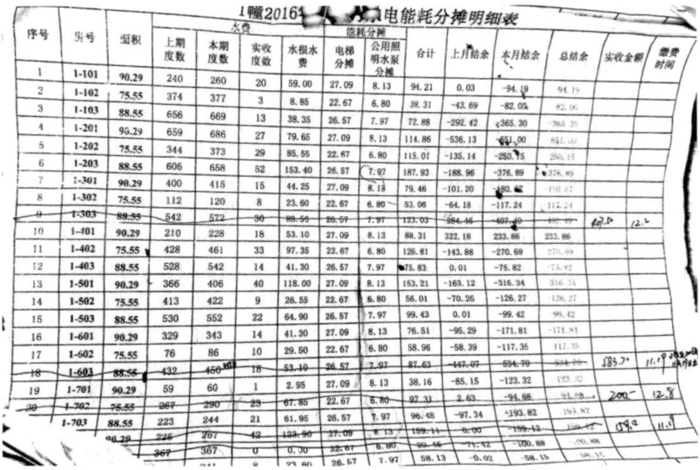

1幢2016[redacted]电能耗分摊明细表

序号	房号	面积	水费				能耗分摊		合计	上月结余	本月结余	总结余	实收金额	缴费时间
			上期度数	本期度数	实收度数	水损水费	电梯分摊	公用照明水泵分摊						
1	1-101	90.29	240	260	20	59.00	27.09	8.13	94.21	0.03	-94.19	94.19		
2	1-102	75.55	374	377	3	8.85	22.67	6.80	38.31	-43.69	-82.00	82.00		
3	1-103	88.55	656	669	13	38.35	26.57	7.97	72.88	-292.42	-365.30	365.30		
4	1-201	90.29	659	686	27	79.65	27.09	8.13	114.86	-536.13	-651.00	651.00		
5	1-202	75.55	344	373	29	85.55	22.67	6.80	115.01	-135.14	-250.15	250.15		
6	1-203	88.55	606	658	52	153.40	26.57	7.97	187.93	-188.96	-376.89	376.89		
7	1-301	90.29	400	415	15	44.25	27.09	8.13	79.46	-101.20	-180.67	180.67		
8	1-302	75.55	112	120	8	23.60	22.67	6.80	53.06	-64.18	-117.24	117.24		
9	1-303	88.55	542	572	30	88.50	26.57	7.97	123.03	-284.46	-407.49	407.49	407.5	12.2
10	1-401	90.29	210	228	18	53.10	27.09	8.13	88.31	322.18	233.86	233.86		
11	1-402	75.55	428	461	33	97.35	22.67	6.80	126.81	-143.88	-270.69	270.69		
12	1-403	88.55	528	542	14	41.30	26.57	7.97	75.83	0.01	-75.82	75.82		
13	1-501	90.29	366	406	40	118.00	27.09	8.13	153.21	-163.12	-316.34	316.34		
14	1-502	75.55	413	422	9	26.55	22.67	6.80	56.01	-70.26	-126.27	126.27		
15	1-503	88.55	530	552	22	64.90	26.57	7.97	99.43	0.01	-99.42	99.42		
16	1-601	90.29	329	343	14	41.30	27.09	8.13	76.51	-95.29	-171.81	171.81		
17	1-602	75.55	76	86	10	29.50	22.67	6.80	58.96	-58.39	-117.35	117.35		
18	1-603	88.55	432	450	18	53.10	26.57	7.97	87.63	-447.07	-534.70	534.70	583.7	11.1
19	1-701	90.29	59	60	1	2.95	27.09	8.13	38.16	-85.15	-123.32	123.32		
20	1-702	75.55	267	290	23	67.85	22.67	6.80	97.31	2.63	-94.68	94.68	200	12.8
	1-703	88.55	223	244	21	61.95	26.57	7.97	96.48	-97.34	-193.82	193.82		
		90.29	225	267	42	123.90	27.09	8.13	159.11	0.00	-159.12	159.12	[illegible]	11.9
			367	367	0	0.00	22.67	6.80	[illegible]	-71.42	-100.88	100.88		
					[illegible]	23.80	26.57	7.97	58.13	-0.02	-58.15	58.15		

(2) Translation of the table head in (1)

Details of water and electricity sharing in Block 1 in 2016														
No	Room number	Area	Water bill				Shared energy bill		Final bill	Balance last month	Balance this month	Total balance	Paid amount	Payment date
			Last reading	This reading	Billed consumption	Water bill	Elevator	Lighting and water pump						

Fig. 5.3 Sample of water bill for non-IBT households in Hangzhou. *Notes* (1) shows a sample of water bills for households in one block in one sampled non-IBT community in Hangzhou. The format of the water bill did not change during the sample period. (2) provides the translation of the table head in (1)

Specifically, households subject to the IBT face a marginal price for water consumption that is based on their cumulative consumption up to that point in the year. That is, once their cumulative consumption up to that point in the year passes the threshold for the second tier (set at 216 m^3 in the study setting), the higher price of the second tier is triggered, and they then face that new marginal price, until they cross the next threshold (which is set at 300 m^3). At the end of the year, the marginal price then reverts back to the first-tier price, and again remains there as long as the household remains below the second-tier threshold in the second year. This feature introduces variation over time in the expected future price that high users face under the IBT. Second, the threshold for the second tier of the IBT is set high. Thus for most households facing the IBT - all but the highest users, the current price remains constant at the level of the first tier. Third, for households facing the flat rate, the current and expected future prices remain the same and fixed throughout the year, regardless of household consumption level. Therefore, we are able to use a DID approach to examine the extent to which households respond to the dynamic incentives created by this type of IBT.

We construct a balanced panel data set of household water consumption from 2014 to 2016 by combining data from a household survey and administrative water billing records. The main results suggest that on average, the IBT leads to a mild and insignificant drop in household water consumption. Next, we examine household response in two subsamples, divided by household baseline annual water consumption level: low-use households (baseline below the median), and high-use households (baseline above the median). To test whether results are sensitive to outliers in the distribution of pre-reform consumption, we also consider a third subsample of moderately high-use households (baseline above the median and less than the second-tier threshold of the annual IBT), that excludes the highest users. Parsing the sample in this way, we detect a small and insignificant effect of the IBT on the water consumption of low-use households, while we find significant water savings among high-use and moderately high-use households. On average, the IBT lowers household water consumption by 0.047 m^3 a day for a high-use household. When we focus on the moderately high-use households, the water savings effect is smaller but remains statistically significant. Moreover, in all three subsamples, the effect of the IBT increases in the second year of implementation, suggesting a greater long-term effect than the short-term effect observed in 2015.

Further analysis reveals other interesting patterns in the data. For high-use households facing the IBT, the water savings effect of the IBT starts early in the year when they are still far from the second-tier threshold and the budget renewal date. Importantly, we also find that for moderately high-use households facing the IBT, water saving is especially high in the middle of the year, despite these households' high likelihood of remaining at a constant current price throughout the budget period. We take this as strong evidence that such households incorporate even a small risk of future price increases into their current water consumption decisions. In contrast, for low-use households, in the initial period of the budget period, the IBT does not result in any difference in water consumption between those facing the IBT and those facing the flat rate. This is in line with expectations because the expected future price will always be the same as the current price for such households. In addition, at year's end when the water budget is about to be renewed, the IBT leads to a significant increase in water consumption. Though the mechanism for this apparent behavioral response is unclear, it may indicate that a high remaining "balance" at year's end drives low-use households toward over-consuming water later in the year.

Additional heterogeneity analysis reveals substantial differences in the IBT effect across subgroups of high-use households. We detect little water savings among IBT households who appear highly present-minded, suggesting that future-oriented time preferences play a role in response to the dynamic incentives of this IBT design. We also find that the water conservation effect of the IBT among high-use households is greater when households have less-educated members, fewer members, or larger housing area per capita. Dropping extremely high-use households does not alter these patterns. Moreover, our results survive a series of robustness checks, including imposing alternative sample restrictions, using alternative thresholds for defining high-use households, using alternative specifications, using a data set constructed at the monthly level, accounting for measurement error in meter reading dates, and dealing with the possible truncation of non-IBT households. Finally, an alternative identification strategy that investigates consumption only among IBT households suggests that this price change significantly narrows the gap in water consumption between high- and low-use households.

5.3 Literature Review

The welfare implications of many important economic policies are determined by consumers' response to nonlinear prices. A vast literature concerns whether consumers respond at all to nonlinearities in their budget set, and which prices consumers respond to - marginal, average, or other. While standard economic theory predicts that consumers respond to marginal price, evidence from many studies reveals responses to expected marginal price (Saez 2010; Borenstein 2009) and average price (de Bartolome 1995; Liebman and Zeckhauser 2004; Feldman and Katuščák 2010; Ito 2014). In our study, we define the whole period within which the nonlinear budget set is applied as a budget period. This budget period usually coincides with the billing cycle of utilities (such as electricity, water, and gas) or the tax cycle. As consumption information is usually only available over a single budget period, the analysis of demand in the presence of nonlinear prices is typically static (Aron-Dine et al. 2015). Evidence on the extent to which consumers respond to dynamic incentives created by nonlinear prices that fluctuate within a single budget period is limited.

Analyzing the dynamic aspect of this response would be possible if information about intermediate consumption levels were available within a single budget period or by using the approach of dynamic modeling (Aron-Dine et al. 2015). Thus far, the discussion has been mostly limited to health insurance in the literature, and has not yielded a consensus. For example, Aron-Dine et al. (2015) show that individuals respond to the future price of medical care when making utilization decisions regarding choices in Medicare Part D and in the context of employer-provided health insurance. Einav et al. (2015) document significant "bunching" of annual spending on drugs around the kink in individuals' budget sets in Medicare Part D, which indicates a behavioral response to the sharp increase in out-of-pocket price beyond the kink. Also in the Medicare Part D context, however, Dalton et al. (2020) find flat spending in a period before the kink and a large spending drop after the kink, and show that a model where enrolls do not incorporate future prices into their decision-making actually fits the data best. Furthermore, using high-frequency data from residential broadband subscribers facing a three-part tariff, Nevo et al. (2016) provide descriptive evidence that consumers respond to variation in the shadow price of usage. An ideal experiment for whether dynamic incentives matter in influencing households' response to nonlinear prices would keep the current price fixed while generating variation in the future price (Aron-Dine et al. 2015). The water pricing reform in Hangzhou comes close to approximating such an ideal experiment. This reform introduced an unconventional IBT, where the budget period is annual, while the billing cycle is bimonthly. Our study investigates the effect of this unconventional IBT in Hangzhou on household water consumption and household response to the dynamic incentives it created.

Besides extending the literature on consumers' response to nonlinear budget sets, our study fits in the vast empirical literature that investigates the effect of price or non-price interventions on resource conservation. Nonlinear pricing (Olmstead 2009; Szabó 2015) and individualized rates (Smith 2022) are employed as price interventions. Recently, a growing body of literature explores the impact of non-price interventions, and the interactions of price and non-price interventions.[3] In this study, we evaluate a pure water price intervention. As there is no change in the format and frequency of water bill before and after the reform, we are able to rule out the possible confounding effect of non-price factors. We show that even in a context where water spending amounts to a small fraction of household income, the change in water pricing structure can induce significant water conservation among high-use households.

More specifically, our study also relates to empirical tests of the effects of IBTs on water consumption. To our knowledge, only two studies have isolated the causal link between IBTs and residential water consumption. Exploiting the introduction of a third price tier in an IBT for water in Santa Cruz, California, Nataraj and Hanemann (2011) find that doubling marginal price leads to a 12% decrease in water use among high-use households. Examining the conversion from a flat tariff to an IBT in North Carolina, Wichman (2014) provides heterogeneous price elasticity estimates and finds that the transition to an IBT may increase water consumption due to price decreases in the lower tiers. Due to the distinct design of each IBT and differences in the contexts in which they are applied, additional studies are worthwhile. In addition, our study is the first to consider an unconventional IBT for water pricing in which the budget is renewed only annually. This type of IBT is prevalent in China but rare elsewhere. In recent years, IBTs have been widely implemented across cities in China, to support the government's goal of encouraging water use efficiency while ensuring fair access to water. By 2019, 34 of the 36 major cities had transitioned to some form of an IBT. Among them, 21 major cities including Hangzhou (with a collective population of 145.7 million) were using an IBT with a water budget that is renewed annually. The effects of such an annual IBT design have not yet been discussed. Understanding whether and how this particular IBT design supports the Chinese government's water conservation goals is critically important for policy makers there, and for those in other counties facing similar water scarcity problems.

5.4 Identification Strategy

5.4.1 Estimating the Effect of the IBT on Water Consumption

We examine the effect of the IBT on household water consumption by exploiting the change in water tariffs occurring on January 1, 2015 in Hangzhou. Figure 5.1-(1) shows the water tariffs over time. Before the tariff change, all households faced a flat

[3] The non-price interventions include providing information (Jessoe and Rapson 2014; Delmas and Lessem 2014; Asensio and Delmas 2016; Allcott and Kessler 2019; Bollinger and Hartmann 2020; Stojanovski et al. 2020); changing billing method (Jack and Smith 2020); and rationing (Mansur and Olmstead 2012). For the interactions of price and non-price interventions, see e.g., Jessoe et al. (2014); Sudarshan (2017); Ito et al. (2018).

rate of 1.85 yuan/m^3. The pricing reform introduced two treatments: an increase in the tariff for all households and a change in the tariff structure among IBT households.

Non-IBT households did not experience a change in the tariff structure but experienced an increase in the flat rate, from 1.85 yuan/m^3 to 2.95 yuan/m^3 by 59%. For IBT households, a three-tier IBT structure replaced the flat rate, and the tariff in the first, lowest-consumption tier was set to 2.90 yuan/m^3, slightly lower than the new flat rate, for annual water consumption below 216 m^3.

The difference between the marginal price of the first tier of IBT and the new flat rate, merely 0.05 yuan/m^3, is expected to have a negligible effect on household water consumption. Considering the average household daily water consumption of 0.34 m^3 and assuming that there are 30 days in a month, the price difference would lead to an additional 0.51 yuan (around US$ 0.083) charge on a monthly water bill for a non-IBT household, compared to an IBT household. This amounts to 2.7% of the average monthly water bill before the reform (18.87 yuan) and 1.6% of the new bill after the reform (32.65 yuan), for a non-IBT household. Furthermore, the water bill accounts for a small share of household income. The average annual water bill following the reform was less than 0.3% of the average household annual disposable income in Hangzhou in 2014.[4] Therefore, the relative change across household types following the pricing reform can basically be treated as a shift in tariff structure in the IBT group, from a flat tariff rate to an IBT. In this setting, a standard DID model is appropriate and feasible for the estimation of IBT effect on household water consumption under the common trends assumption: In the absence of the pricing reform, the water consumption of the two (IBT and non-IBT) groups should follow common trends.

Besides this identification strategy, in Sect. 5.9 we apply an alternative identification approach and estimate the IBT effect on the gap between high- and low-use households in water consumption, focusing only on IBT households.

5.4.2 *Testing Household Response to the Dynamic Incentives*

We test the null hypothesis that households' water consumption does not respond to the dynamic incentives created by this nonlinear water pricing scheme. When making consumption choices today, a fully rational, forwarding-looking household facing the nonlinear price on water consumption implied by the Hangzhou-type IBT should only take account of the future price and should recognize that the current price applied to a particular water bill is not relevant. However, there are at least three reasons that households may not respond to these dynamic incentives. First, the future price may not be salient to households. They may not be completely aware of, attentive to, or understand the nonlinear budget constraint. Second, households may be myopic, discounting the future heavily and responding only to the current

[4] The average household annual water bill after the reform was about 400 yuan. The average household annual disposable income in 2014 was about 159.4 thousand yuan (48.3 thousand yuan per capita × 3.3 members per household) (Zhejiang Statistical Yearbook, 2015).

price of water. Third, household water demand may be price inelastic. If that is the case, even a considerable hike in the water tariff would not lead to much of a change in water consumption.

Following Aron-Dine et al. (2015), an ideal experiment for testing whether dynamic incentives matter in affecting households' water consumption would randomly assign individuals to settings in which the current price of water is held fixed, while dynamic incentives vary. If water consumption behaviors are well approximated by assuming that households respond only to current prices, then water consumption behaviors would not change across settings. The novelty of this study is that three unique features of the pricing reform in Hangzhou come close to approximating such an ideal experiment. First, the budget of the IBT is renewed annually, while the billing cycle is bimonthly. This feature generates dynamic incentives for certain IBT households in our setting. Second, aiming to discourage extreme consumption, the thresholds for higher tiers of IBT were set high in Hangzhou. According to Hangzhou Water, 92.6% of the residential households had annual water consumption below 216 m^3 in 2013.[5] This feature holds constant the current price of water for most IBT households throughout the budget period in our setting. Third, households under the flat rate face constant current and expected future prices throughout the year, regardless of household consumption. Below, we elaborate the approach we use to test the null hypothesis.

Let t be a specific month or bimonth in an IBT budget period after the reform, and T be the last month or bimonth before the IBT budget set renewal, which occurs on an annual basis, then $t \in (1, ..., T)$. For a household under a flat tariff rate, the current price, p_t^c, and the expected future price, $\tilde{p}_t^f$, remain constant and equal all the time, i.e., $p_t^c = \tilde{p}_t^f = p$, where p denotes the new flat rate in effect after January 2015. Here we suppress the household subscript i for simplicity.

The IBT with an annually renewed budget set introduces several complications. Let q_t be the cumulative annual water consumption in period t. $\bar{Q}^2$ and $\bar{Q}^3$ are the thresholds for the second tier and the third tier. p^n refers to the tier-n price of the IBT, $n \in (1, 2, 3)$. The current price, p_t^c, faced by a household depends on q_t:

$$p_t^c = \begin{cases} p^1 \text{ if } q_t \leq \bar{Q}^2, \\ p^2 \text{ if } \bar{Q}^2 < q_t \leq \bar{Q}^3, \\ p^3 \text{ if } q_t > \bar{Q}^3. \end{cases} \tag{5.1}$$

We use the expected future price (the price right before the budget set renewal date), $\tilde{p}_t^f$, to summarize the dynamic incentive facing a household at a given time t. It is defined as:

[5] Still, the risk of exceeding 216 m^3 is non-negligible. Among high-use households in our sample, 9.3% (14.2%) of them have their annual water consumption in 2015 (2016) exceeds the threshold and 12.1% (24.5%) have their consumption in 2015 (2016) exceeds 200 m^3, which leaves less than a month of typical consumption as a buffer.

$$\tilde{p}_t^f = \tilde{Pr}(in_t^1) \times p^1 + \tilde{Pr}(in_t^2) \times p^2 + \tilde{Pr}(in_t^3) \times p^3,$$
$$s.t. \sum_{n=1}^{3} \tilde{Pr}(in_t^n) = 1, \tag{5.2}$$

where $\tilde{Pr}(in_t^n), n \in (1, 2, 3)$, is a household's expected probability at time t of falling in tier n before the next budget set renewal date. These expected probabilities reflect the household's uncertainty about future water consumption.

Let Q^B denote a household's baseline annual water consumption and Q^m denote a threshold for a low level of annual water consumption. In this study, we use the median of household baseline annual water consumption for Q^m. Note that $Q^m < \bar{Q}^2$, as $\bar{Q}^2$ is set high.

For low water users ($Q^B \leq Q^m$), their expected probabilities of falling in the second and third tiers are zero, so we have $\tilde{Pr}(in_t^2) = \tilde{Pr}(in_t^3) = 0$. Then the future price faced by these IBT households is always the same as the current price, i.e. $p_t^c = \tilde{p}_t^f = p^1$ for every $t \in (1, ..., T)$. In the case that p^1 is close to p, we expect little effect of IBT on these low water users.

For relatively higher-use households ($Q^B > Q^m$), $\tilde{Pr}(in_t^2)$ and $\tilde{Pr}(in_t^3)$ are determined by the household's baseline annual water consumption, the balance remaining in the first tier and the second tier, respectively, and the time remaining until the next budget set renewal date. In the initial period after the budget set renewal date, i.e., when t is small and $q_t \leq \bar{Q}^2$, we could have $p_t^c = p^1$. However, these households face uncertainty about whether their consumption will result in higher future prices, so $\tilde{Pr}(in_t^2) \geq 0$ and $\tilde{Pr}(in_t^3) \geq 0$, then $\tilde{p}_t^f \geq p^1$. However, as t gets larger, q_t may exceed $\bar{Q}^2$, so that p_t^c and $\tilde{p}_t^f$ evolve in tandem. For example, if $\bar{Q}^2 < q_t \leq \bar{Q}^3$, we could have $p_t^c = p^2$, and due to $\tilde{Pr}(in_t^1) = 0$, $\tilde{Pr}(in_t^2) \geq 0$, and $\tilde{Pr}(in_t^3) \geq 0$, then $\tilde{p}_t^f \geq p^2$. Consequently, for high-use households, if the IBT affects water consumption, we will only be able to distinguish the effects of current and future prices during the initial period.

Next, we focus on moderately high-use households, whose Q^B satisfies $Q^m < Q^B < \bar{Q}^2$, among the high-use households. Considering their baseline water consumption level, these households are unlikely to enter the second tier of the IBT, so that $q_t \leq \bar{Q}^2$ and $p_t^c = p^1$ holds for every $t \in (1, ..., T)$. Meanwhile, these households may still face uncertainty about whether their consumption will result in higher future prices, so $\tilde{Pr}(in_t^2) \geq 0$ and $\tilde{Pr}(in_t^3) \geq 0$, and consequently, $\tilde{p}_t^f \geq p^1$. Moreover, as households update $\tilde{Pr}(in_t^2)$ and $\tilde{Pr}(in_t^3)$ over time, right before the budget set renewal date, both $\tilde{Pr}(in_t^2)$ and $\tilde{Pr}(in_t^3)$ tend towards zero, and $\tilde{p}_t^f$ eventually returns to p^1. To sum up, for these households, the IBT results in there being a constant current price and a likely perceived deviation of the future price from the current price between the two budget set renewal dates. Therefore, we are able to examine whether households respond to the dynamic incentives created by the IBT among the group of moderately high-use households.

5.5 Data

5.5.1 Household Survey and Water Billing Data

We construct a balanced panel data set of household water consumption that combines data from a household survey and administrative water bills.

The household survey was conducted between December 2016 and January 2017, which allowed us to collect information on water bill identifiers, households' demographic and socioeconomic characteristics, such as the number of household members, the age composition of household members, and years of schooling.[6] A multi-stage and stratified sampling was used to select households. In the first stage, three of five main urban districts in Hangzhou were retained, and two sub-districts in each urban district were randomly selected. Each sub-district consists of a group of communities. We further selected one IBT community and one non-IBT community from each sub-district. Figure 5.4 shows the location of these 12 communities within urban Hangzhou. From each community, we then randomly enrolled roughly 50 households.[7] Regarding this eligibility, following Ito (2014), we included only households who had settled in their premises before January 2014, to be conservative about potential sorting that could have occurred because of the pricing reform, and focused on households that were on the standard tariff. In each surveyed household, either the household head or the head's spouse answered the survey questions. In the end, the survey covered 602 households, 302 in IBT communities and 300 in non-IBT communities.

Next, for the surveyed IBT households, we were able to obtain water meter readings, dates, and billing data from 2013 to early 2017, by linking account numbers obtained from the household survey to the billing database of Hangzhou Water. As of early 2017, all surveyed IBT households remained covered by the IBT imposed in January, 2015. In our sample, two thirds of the meters were read in even months, and the remainder in odd months. We find that the schedule of meter reading was strictly followed.[8] The schedule remained the same before and after the reform, except for the aforementioned additional meter reading session in January 2015 for households with meters read in even months.[9]

---

[6] The water bill identifiers are water bill account numbers for the IBT households and apartment addresses for the non-IBT households.

[7] A counting method for household selection was applied: (1) Enumerators started from the first floor and steadily moved upwards; (2) Every n^{th} household on the right hand side was invited to participate in the survey; (3) Finally, if the household was not qualified to participate, enumerators skipped to the next household on the right hand side.

[8] In our sample, we only detect four cases of deviation in the month of bill reading, out of 5,429 water meter readings spanning 2014–2016. These cases are due to meter replacement.

[9] As shown in Sect. 5.1, the IBT households with meters read in odd months and in even months have somewhat different budget periods, and the number of meter readings in the 2015 budget period differs. In Sect. 5.8, we explore whether the IBT effect is sensitive to these differences in the billing schedule. We first exclude from the analysis IBT households with meters read in odd

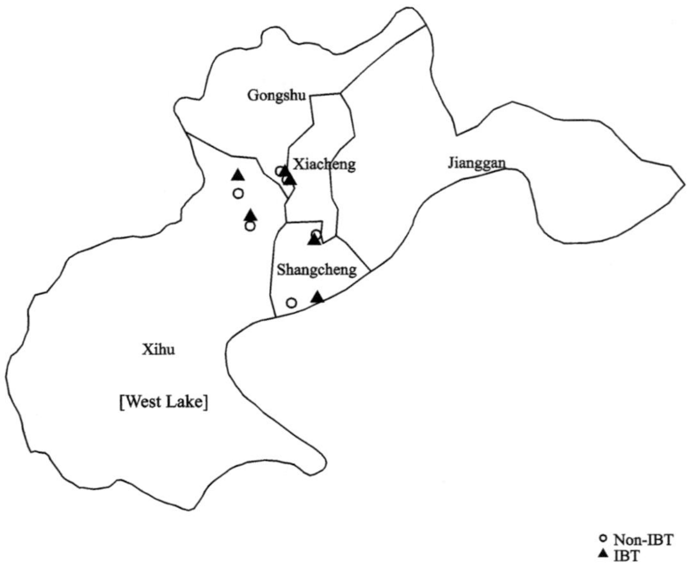

Fig. 5.4 Location of sampled communities. *Notes* This figure shows the map of the five main urban districts in Hangzhou and the locations of the 12 sampled communities. The map is produced using the data from the County-Level Assembly of the 2010 China Population Census. The locations of the 12 communities are shown with open circles for non-IBT groups and black triangles for IBT groups

For the surveyed non-IBT households, we were able to extract water meter readings and billing data from 2014 to early 2017, by linking household address information obtained from the household survey to water billing records obtained from the community administrative offices. As of early 2017, all surveyed non-IBT households remained under the new flat rate imposed in January, 2015. Their water meters were read monthly with no exception, and the schedule of meter reading and the format of water bills remained the same before and after the reform.

To obtain water consumption data that was comparable across households with different IBT and non-IBT billing cycles, we calculate household daily water consumption by calendar month using the water billing data and the water meter reading dates.

The water meters of IBT households are managed by Hangzhou Water and are read every other month. Considering an IBT household with the meter read on January 6, March 6, and May 6 in 2015, the March 6 bill (bill A) reflects water consumed between January 6 and March 6 (60 days), while the bill from May 6 (bill B) reflects consumption between March 6 and May 6 (61 days). Since water consumption in February is fully inclusive in bill A, daily water consumption in February is estimated as $28 \times \frac{Volume\ in\ bill\ A}{60\ days}$. For March, 6 days are covered by bill A, and 25 are covered by bill B, so the daily water consumption in March is calculated as follows:

months, and then exclude IBT households with meters read in even months. Imposing the sample restrictions does not alter our results.

$$Household\ daily\ water\ consumption = \frac{6 \times \frac{Volume\ in\ bill\ A}{60\ days} + 25 \times \frac{Volume\ in\ bill\ B}{61\ days}}{31}. \quad (5.3)$$

As the water meter readings from Hangzhou Water are available from January/February 2013 to January/February 2017, we are able to use this method to calculate household daily water consumption for each calendar month from March 2013 to December 2016 for the IBT households.

The water meters of non-IBT households are read on the monthly basis by the administrative office of each community. Considering a household with the meter read on January 6, February 6, and March 6 in 2015, the February 6 bill (bill C) reflects water consumed between January 6 and February 6 (31 days), while the March 6 bill (bill D) reflects consumption between February 6 and March 6 (28 days). Hence, the daily water consumption in February is calculated as follows:

$$Household\ daily\ water\ consumption = \frac{6 \times \frac{Volume\ in\ bill\ C}{31\ days} + 22 \times \frac{Volume\ in\ bill\ D}{28\ days}}{28}. \quad (5.4)$$

As the water billing data for non-IBT households are available from January 2014 to January 2017, we are able to use this method to calculate household daily water consumption for each calendar month from January 2014 to December 2016 for the non-IBT households.

Due to the nature of record-keeping in the non-IBT communities, we only have imprecise ranges of monthly meter reading dates.[10] In the main analysis, we assume that the meters for all non-IBT households are read on the midpoint date for a particular community. This procedure introduces measurement error in the household water consumption for non-IBT households. Yet, given that the meter reading is organized by community administrative offices, the error is unlikely to be systematically related to any determinants of household water consumption. Nevertheless, in Sect. 5.8, we conduct simulations by varying the meter reading date within the given range for each meter reading in a given community, and show the robustness of our results to accounting for the measurement error.

5.5.2 Sample

To ensure that we obtain precise measures of household water consumption, we apply a set of specific sample restrictions. First, we include meter readings that were regularly scheduled or less than four months from the last reading.[11] Second, we exclude

[10] Meter reading for non-IBT households is organized at the community level. A team is trained by community administrators to conduct readings within a time period that typically spans 3–7 days. Each community has a specific format for recording. Considering the standard meter reading format and protocols as described by key informants, we expect that readers generally follow the same routes each month.

[11] We consider a meter reading that is more than two months from the last reading to be abnormal. In the main analysis, we include abnormal meter readings that were more than two months but less than four months from the last reading, i.e., we allow the incidence of missed meter readings as

extreme outliers, specifically households who had annual water consumption in 2015 or 2016 that was less than 20% or more than 500% of their own annual water consumption in 2014. To construct household annual water consumption, we first use the above-mentioned billing data to construct household daily water consumption in each calendar month during the sample period, taking into account of the variation in the billing cycle over time and across households in the IBT and non-IBT communities. Next, we obtain household annual water consumption by aggregating household daily water consumption in each calendar month to the yearly level. The collective set of sample restrictions exclude 20 households out of the 602 households. The final sample thus consists of 582 households, of which 282 are IBT households and 300 are non-IBT households.[12]

In Fig. 5.5, we plot the water tariffs and the distributions of household annual water consumption by year and household group. We find that for all years, the distribution of non-IBT households' consumption is more compact than (and is possibly truncated from the bottom relative to) that of the IBT households, while the median consumption of non-IBT households is greater than that of IBT households.[13]

For both groups of households, most observations fall below 216 m^3, the threshold for the second tier in the IBT. Very few observations, all from IBT households, exceed 300 m^3, the threshold for the third tier in the IBT. Thus, it is not surprising that we do not observe any bunching around 216 m^3 or 300 m^3 in either group of households, before and after the pricing reform.

As elaborated in Sect. 5.4, low and high water users would be differently affected by the IBT, so we investigate the effect of IBT for low and high water users separately. We take household annual water consumption in 2014 as the baseline household annual water consumption level, and then calculate the median of this baseline level among the 582 households, which is 120.78 m^3.[14] Next, we divide the sample of households into two subsamples according to whether the baseline water con-

---

long as the next scheduled reading was normal. Excluding all the abnormal meter readings does not alter our results. See Sect. 5.8 for details.

[12] We cannot be certain why the IBT households are more likely to experience abnormal readings or extreme outliers. It may have to do with the higher meter reading load for the utility relative to the community-administered system, or other constraints facing utility personnel. It may also have to do with some specific characteristics associated with IBT households. Since our empirical models control for household fixed effects, any time-invariant household or community characteristics should not affect our estimates. Nevertheless, we show in Sect. 5.8 that imposing alternative sample restrictions does not alter our results.

[13] We cannot be certain of the reason(s) for this truncation, which may stem from differences arising from meter reading practices in the two groups, or represent real differences in consumption patterns within the groups. Our identification strategy does not rely on these distributions being equivalent. Moreover, as shown in Sect. 5.8, our results are robust to sample restrictions that exclude low-use households with baseline annual water consumption level below the minimum levels observed in the non-IBT group.

[14] We show in Figs. 5.6 and 5.10 that for IBT households, the trend and patterns of water consumption in 2014 are very similar to the trend and patterns in 2013, suggesting that 2014 is a typical year.

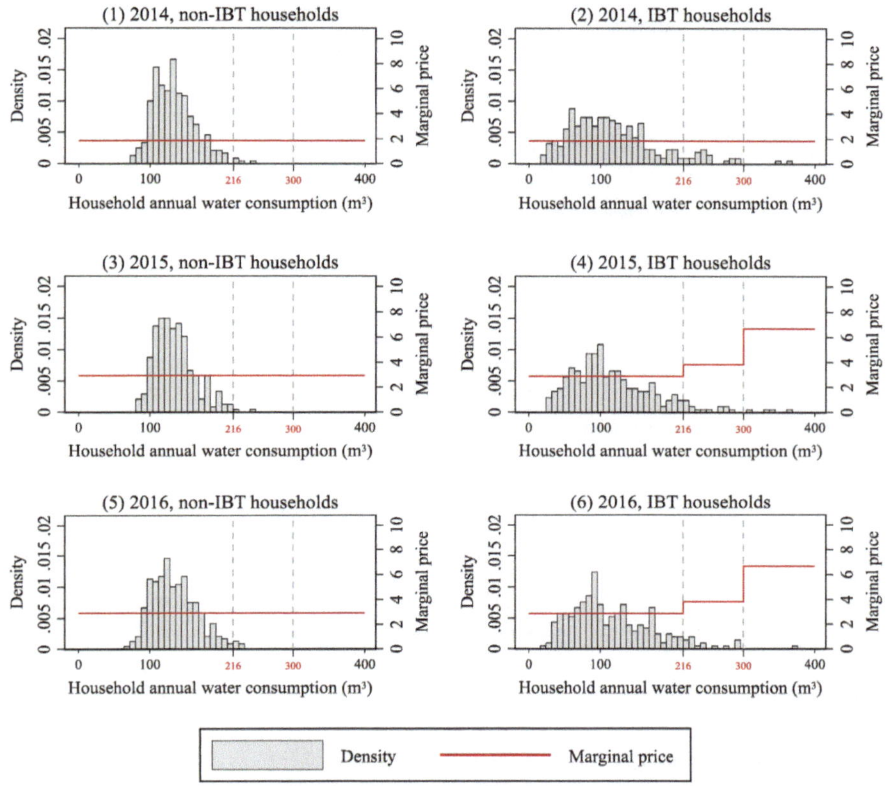

Fig. 5.5 Distribution of household annual water consumption and the corresponding water tariffs. *Notes* The histograms show the distribution of household annual water consumption across different years, for the IBT and non-IBT households. The red line in each graph plots the marginal price of water as a function of consumption. The thresholds for the second tier and the third tier of the IBT structure are 216 m^3/yr and 300 m^3/yr, respectively

sumption level was below or above the median.[15] In what follows, we refer to these two subsamples as low-use households and high-use households, respectively.[16] Furthermore, we obtain the subsample of moderately high-use households by excluding

[15] We show in Sect. 5.8 that using alternative thresholds for defining high-use households, including the 25th percentile and the 75th percentile of the household annual water consumption in 2014, and the median of the household annual water consumption in 2013 for IBT households, generates comparable estimates. As expected, using the higher threshold leads to larger estimates, since that particular subsample is comparatively higher use. The latter approach, using the 2013 year of consumption also largely addresses concerns that our results might be driven by reversion to the mean among exceptionally high users within the IBT group in 2014. High users in 2013 respond very similarly to high users in 2014.

[16] In Sect. 5.5.4, we explore the determinants of being a high-use household, and find that lower housing area per capita, more household members, fewer children, and more years of schooling are associated with a higher probability of being a high-use household in 2014.

Table 5.1 Summary statistics

	All	By household annual water consumption in 2014		
		Low	High	Moderately high
	(1)	(2)	(3)	(4)
IBT group	0.485	0.593	0.373	0.323
	(0.500)	(0.492)	(0.484)	(0.469)
Household annual water consumption (m^3)				
in 2014	124.6	88.95	161.3	151.7
	(48.99)	(26.90)	(38.34)	(22.22)
in 2015	125.5	94.45	156.9	149.1
	(47.72)	(32.02)	(39.82)	(27.42)
in 2016	124.0	94.40	153.7	149.0
	(47.96)	(34.20)	(40.90)	(33.57)
Household daily water consumption (m^3)				
in 2014	0.341	0.244	0.442	0.416
	(0.134)	(0.074)	(0.105)	(0.061)
in 2015	0.344	0.259	0.430	0.408
	(0.131)	(0.088)	(0.109)	(0.075)
in 2016	0.339	0.258	0.420	0.407
	(0.131)	(0.093)	(0.112)	(0.092)
Floor number	5.290	5.224	5.359	5.477
	(3.778)	(3.526)	(4.025)	(4.168)
Number of household members	3.132	2.892	3.380	3.346
	(0.818)	(0.753)	(0.810)	(0.803)
Number of children under age 18	0.711	0.685	0.739	0.727
	(0.524)	(0.534)	(0.513)	(0.526)
Number of members aged above 55	0.357	0.264	0.453	0.427
	(0.669)	(0.626)	(0.697)	(0.680)
Highest years of schooling	14.21	13.81	14.62	14.61
	(3.326)	(3.766)	(2.749)	(2.838)
Housing area per capita (m^2)	22.68	26.40	18.86	18.86
	(9.908)	(11.18)	(6.476)	(6.531)
Observations	582	295	287	260

Notes This table reports the sample means and standard deviations (in parentheses) for all 582 households and by subsample. "Low" refers to households with annual water consumption in 2014 below the median level in 2014. "High" refers to households with annual water consumption in 2014 above the median level in 2014. "Moderately high" refers to households with annual water consumption in 2014 above the median level and below the second-tier threshold of the IBT, 216 m^3

extremely high-use households from the high-use households (those with baseline annual water consumption above 216 m^3).

In Table 5.1, we provide the summary statistics for the full sample and by household baseline water consumption level.

5.5.3 Outcome Variable

The outcome variable in the main analysis is household daily water consumption as measured on a bimonthly basis. Due to the billing cycle being bimonthly for IBT households and monthly for non-IBT households, daily water consumption for a non-IBT household in a calendar month is more variable than that for an IBT household.[17] To smooth out this differential fluctuation in measured water consumption, we aggregate water consumption over every two adjacent calendar months and then compute average household daily water consumption corresponding to each two month period in the data set.[18] Therefore, we construct a balanced panel data set of household daily water consumption on a bimonthly basis from 2013 to 2016 for IBT households and from 2014 to 2016 for non-IBT households. In the main analysis, we focus on the sample period from 2014 to 2016, the common time period for the two groups of households. Our results are robust to using the period from 2013 to 2016. Note that aggregating household water consumption to the bimonthly level may lead to attenuated seasonality. We show in Sect. 5.8 that using consumption measured at the monthly level does not alter our main findings, however.

In Fig. 5.6, we present these bimonthly trends in household daily water consumption by household baseline water consumption level and household tariff type.[19] For all four groups, the household water consumption has a clear seasonal pattern. Winter is associated with relatively lower water consumption. As the temperature rises, water consumption increases to a peak in summer. For the IBT households, whether annual consumption in 2014 was above or below the median, the bimonthly pattern of household daily water consumption in 2014 is similar to that in 2013, suggesting that the consumption in 2014, the year preceding the tariff change, was not unusual. We do notice a clear declining pattern of water consumption after January 2015, however, among high-use IBT households, while the other three groups have largely similar levels before and after the tariff change. This provides suggestive evidence that IBT may reduce the water consumption of high-use households, which we explore formally below using a DID framework. Moreover, we are aware of one systematic difference in the seasonal pattern of water consumption between the IBT and non-IBT households. For the non-IBT households, there is a spike in consumption in the bimonthly period spanning July and August, while for the IBT

[17] The monthly trends of household daily water consumption for both IBT and non-IBT households are similar to the bimonthly trends, except that there is a spike in water consumption in February for non-IBT households. See the bimonthly trends in Fig. 5.6 and the monthly trends in Fig. 5.10.

[18] By aggregating water consumption over every two adjacent calendar months, we obtain the average household daily water consumption on a bimonthly basis (i.e., January-February, March-April, May-June, July-August, September-October, and November-December) for both IBT and non-IBT households.

[19] We do not present the time trends for moderately high-use households in Fig. 5.6, as their pattern of water consumption is very similar to that of all high-use households.

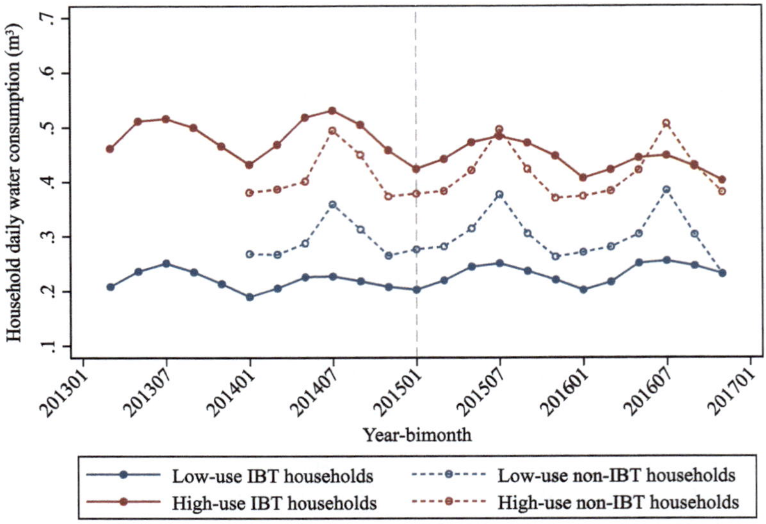

Fig. 5.6 Trends in household daily water consumption over time on a bimonthly basis. *Notes* This figure plots the time trends of household daily water consumption among IBT and non-IBT households, differentiated based on baseline water consumption. Each circle or open circle represents the average daily water consumption of the sampled households in the corresponding year-bimonth period. For example, the red open circle in the year-bimonth of "201401" indicates the average daily water consumption level of high-use non-IBT households between January and February, 2014. The vertical dashed line represents the timing of the water pricing reform

households, the spike in the same bimonthly period is present but less distinct. As the validity of the DID framework relies on the common trends assumption, we address the issue by allowing different seasonal patterns of water consumption for these two groups of households in the empirical model (see details in Sect. 5.6.1).

5.5.4 *The Determinants of Being an Above-Median Household*

In the main analysis, we divide the sample into two subsamples according to whether the household annual water consumption in 2014 is below or above the median among the surveyed households. Here we explore the determinants of being an above-median household. We use a probit model that includes a series of predetermined household characteristics and community fixed effects, and report the results in Table 5.2. All household characteristics in this model are measured for the year 2014, before the 2015 water pricing reform. We find that lower housing area per capita, more household members, fewer children, and higher years of schooling are associated with a higher probability of being an above-median household in 2014. Floor number and

Table 5.2 Determinants of being an above-median household

	Dep. var.: being a high-use household
	Probit
Floor number	0.013
	(0.017)
Housing area per capita (m^2)	–0.030***
	(0.011)
Number of household members	0.574***
	(0.138)
Number of children under age 18	–0.247**
	(0.117)
Number of members aged above 55	–0.065
	(0.098)
Highest years of schooling	0.048**
	(0.024)
Observations	588
Pseudo R^2	0.247
$\overline{Y}$	0.499
Community FE	Y

Notes *, **, and *** indicate significance at 10%, 5%, and 1%, respectively. The sample consists of 588 households whose annual water consumption in 2014 can be calculated. A probit model is applied for estimation with community fixed-effects controlled for. Coefficients from the probit regression are reported. Standard errors in parentheses are clustered at the community level

number of members aged above 55 are not significantly associated with the probability of being a high-use household. To account for the possibility of different trends in water consumption across households with different characteristics, we control for the interactions of the household characteristics in 2014 and the year-bimonth dummies in the equations for main analysis (Eqs. (5.5) and (5.6)).

5.6 Main Results

In this section, we first present the model for estimating the average effect of the IBT on household water consumption and associated regression results. Then, we discuss the model for testing household response to dynamic incentives under the IBT, and those estimation results.

5.6.1 The Average Effect of IBT on Water Consumption

Our main analysis employs a Difference-in-Differences (DID) framework to identify the effect of the shift from the flat rate tariff to IBT pricing on household water consumption. For a household i, the daily water consumption in year y bimonth b, Y_{iyb}, can be written as:

$$Y_{iyb} = \beta IBThh_i \times Post_{yb} + \delta_i + \gamma_{yb} + IBThh_i \times \theta_b + X_i \times \rho_{yb} + \epsilon_{iyb}, \quad (5.5)$$

where $IBThh_i$ is an indicator for assignment of household i to the IBT, which equals one for IBT households and zero otherwise. $Post_{yb}$ is an indicator for the period following implementation of the new tariffs. It equals one for the periods from January 2015 onward, and zero otherwise. The parameter of interest is β, which can be interpreted as the causal effect of the IBT structure on household daily water consumption. Household fixed effects δ_i are included to control for time-invariant household characteristics that may be associated with the probability of being an IBT household and with household water consumption. We further include year-bimonth fixed effects γ_{yb} to control for time trends (including seasonality) in consumption that are common to all households in the absence of the IBT.

In this DID framework, we identify the impact of the IBT from variation in daily household water consumption across time within households. The key assumption for obtaining unbiased estimates of β is the common trends in water consumption for IBT and non-IBT households in the absence of the IBT. In Fig. 5.6, we show that pre-treatment trends of household water consumption in 2014 have a similar pattern, declining in winter and increasing in summer, regardless of consumption and tariff group status. However, as noted previously, Fig. 5.6 reveals a systematic difference in the seasonal pattern of water consumption between the IBT and non-IBT households. To allow for the difference, we therefore control for the interaction of the indicator for IBT households and a set of bimonthly dummies, $IBThh_i \times \theta_b$.

Moreover, to account for the possibility of different trends in water consumption across households with different characteristics, we follow Hoynes et al. (2016) and include the interaction terms of a set of predetermined household characteristics X_i and year-bimonth dummies ρ_{yb}.[20] ϵ_{iyb} is a random error term. The standard errors are clustered at two levels: household and community-bimonth period. Clustering at the household level accounts for any serial correlation over time within the same household, and clustering at the community-bimonth level allows for any correlation

[20] The household characteristics include housing area per capita, number of household members, number of children under age 18, and highest years of schooling among members, which are shown to be associated with the probability of being a high-use household in Sect. 5.5.4. Floor number and number of members aged above 55 are not significantly associated with the probability of being a high-use household. We do not include weather here, as the 12 surveyed communities are close in distance. The longest distance between two communities is less than 10 km. Neither do we consider outdoor water use, as all the surveyed households live in apartment buildings.

across households within a community in a given bimonthly period (e.g., the bimonth of January-February in any year).[21]

Table 5.3 reports the average effect of the IBT on household water consumption. We control for household fixed effects in all columns. In column (1), we control for year-bimonth dummies, assuming common trends for all households. We estimate that on average, the IBT lowers household daily water consumption by 0.009 m^3. In column (2), we additionally control for the difference in the seasonality of water consumption between IBT and non-IBT households by adding interactions of the indicator for IBT households and the bimonthly period indicators. The point estimate does not change, suggesting that the estimated effect is not sensitive to controlling for the seasonal difference between the treatment and control groups. In column (3), we further allow the time trends to vary across households with different characteristics. The point estimate again barely changes, suggesting that differential latent trends in water consumption across households with different characteristics do not affect the estimate for the IBT treatment effect. We conclude that the introduction of the IBT may have a small conservation effect overall, but note that the estimate is not statistically significant at conventionally-reported levels (p-value = 0.155).

We hypothesize that the IBT may have distinct effects on the water consumption of high- and low-use households, however. In columns (4) and (5), we apply the same flexible specification as in column (3), but this time consider the subsamples of low and high-use households separately. We find that for the low-use households, the IBT has a positive, but small and statistically imprecise effect on household daily water consumption (column (4)). For high-use households, in contrast, the effect is negative and statistically significant at the 1% level (column (5)). On average, the IBT lowers household daily water consumption by 0.047 m^3 among high-use households, which is equivalent to about 11% of the average daily consumption. This suggests that high-use households are price sensitive.[22]

The magnitude of the effect is comparable to that in Nataraj and Hanemann (2011), who exploit the introduction of a third price tier in an IBT for water in Santa Cruz, California and found that doubling marginal price led to a 12% decrease in water use among high-use households in that setting. Moreover, this estimated effect amounts to a reduction of 17.2 m^3 in household annual water consumption and to annual

[21] In the main analysis, the number of clusters for the community-bimonth level is 72 (= 12 × 6).

[22] In prior work, high-use households have been found to be more price sensitive than other households (El-Khattabi et al. 2021). In our context, high-use households are not necessarily more price sensitive than low-use households. Rather, they are the only ones for whom higher prices in the second- and third-tiers of the IBT are truly relevant. As elaborated in Sect. 5.4, the usage uncertainty that high-use IBT households face may lead to them perceiving much higher future prices. It should be noted that we do not observe households' expected probabilities of exceeding this threshold, which makes it difficult to estimate the price elasticity of demand for these households. Nonetheless, we describe the assumptions behind two versions for such a calculation in detail in Sect. 5.11. The calculation yields implied demand elasticities of −2 and −2.9 in 2015, and −4.3 and −4.9 in 2016, respectively. It is worth mentioning that low-use households' small quantity responses to future prices does not show the absence of price sensitivity. A reasonable interpretation is that their sensitivity is nearly unmeasurable in this study; as such, we do not attempt to calculate a price elasticity of demand for this group.

Table 5.3 The effect of IBT pricing on household daily water consumption

	Dep.var.: Household daily water consumption (m^3)					
	All			By household annual water consumption in 2014		
				Low	High	Moderately high
	(1)	(2)	(3)	(4)	(5)	(6)
IBThh × Post	–0.009	–0.009	–0.010	0.006	–0.047***	–0.022**
	(0.007)	(0.007)	(0.007)	(0.008)	(0.013)	(0.010)
Observations	10,341	10,341	10,341	5,179	5,162	4,676
R^2	0.768	0.777	0.782	0.672	0.669	0.592
Num of clusters (household)	582	582	582	295	287	260
Num of clusters (community-bimonth)	72	72	72	72	72	72
$\overline{Y}_{1,2014}$	0.318	0.318	0.318	0.213	0.486	0.425
$\overline{Y}_{0,2014}$	0.366	0.366	0.366	0.294	0.415	0.410
Household FE	Y	Y	Y	Y	Y	Y
Year-bimonth FE	Y	Y	Y	Y	Y	Y
IBThh × bimonth dummies	N	Y	Y	Y	Y	Y
Household controls × year-bimonth dummies	N	N	Y	Y	Y	Y

Notes *, **, and *** indicate significance at 10%, 5%, and 1%, respectively. Columns (1)–(3) show the estimates from the regressions using the full sample of households. The specification in column (3) is in line with Eq. (5.5). Columns (4) and (6) report the results for the subsamples of low-use, high-use, and moderately high-use households, respectively. Household controls that are interacted with year-bimonth dummies include the number of household members, number of children under age 18, highest years of schooling among members, and housing area per capita (all in the year of 2014). The standard errors in parentheses are clustered at two levels: household and community-bimonth. $\overline{Y}_{1,2014}$ and $\overline{Y}_{0,2014}$ denote the sample mean of household daily water consumption in 2014 for IBT and non-IBT households, respectively

water savings of 8.5 million m^3 when extrapolated to the whole of Hangzhou city. If the first tier price of the IBT, 2.90 yuan/m^3, is charged for the water saved, then the annual monetary savings amount to 24.6 million yuan (equivalent to US$ 3.7 million) for the whole of Hangzhou city. Meanwhile, for Hangzhou Water, the pricing reform would increase annual total revenue by at least 121.6 million yuan (around US$ 19.8 million).

One might be concerned that our identification strategy does not fully address systematic differences in the seasonal pattern of water consumption between the IBT and non-IBT households, shown in Fig. 5.6. As a validity test, we plot the residuals of the regressions in columns (4) and (5) for the period before the pricing reform in Fig. 5.7. The basic motivation is to investigate whether the regression residuals among IBT and non-IBT households, for household daily water consumption, follow similar pre-treatment trends over time after accounting for household fixed effects, time fixed effects, the difference in the seasonal trends between IBT and non-IBT households, and the difference in the time trends across households with different characteristics. Figure 5.7 shows that for low-use households, the means of the residuals in both groups generally center around 0 before the pricing reform, providing strong evidence for common trends in water consumption, conditional on these fixed effects and seasonal trend controls. A similar pattern is detected for high-use households. In addition, the standard deviations of the residuals for IBT households are consistently larger than those for non-IBT households, indicating the presence of heteroskedasticity across communities. Clustering the standard errors at the household and community-bimonth levels addresses this heteroskedasticity across different community types.

It is possible that the water conservation effect of IBT for high-use households is driven by outliers, that is, high-use households whose baseline annual water consumption in 2014 was greater than 216 m^3. To see whether it is the case, in column (6), we drop these 27 highest use households from the analysis and focus on moderately high-use households whose baseline annual water consumption in 2014 is below 216 m^3. We find that on average IBT lowers daily water consumption of these households by 0.022 m^3 (equivalent to 5.3% of the average daily consumption), and this effect is statistically significant at the 5% level. This indicates that even high-use households with a relatively low probability of entering the second tier of the IBT respond to the nonlinear pricing scheme by reducing water consumption. In Sect. 5.8, we consider the robustness of our findings to more sample restrictions.

The persistence of a water saving effect is relevant for assessing the long-term value of the IBT instrument as a water conservation tool. By the end of 2016, the new tariffs had been implemented in Hangzhou for two full calendar years. To examine the persistence of the effects of the IBT structure, we generate an indicator for each of the two calendar years post the reform, and interact each of these with the indicator for IBT households. Next, we replace the key variables of interest in Eq. (5.5), $IBThh_i \times Post_{yb}$, with these separate interactions and run the regressions using the three subsamples. We find that among low-use households, the estimated IBT effects are small and statistically insignificant for both 2015 and 2016. For high-use households, we find a significant water conservation effect of the IBT in both 2015

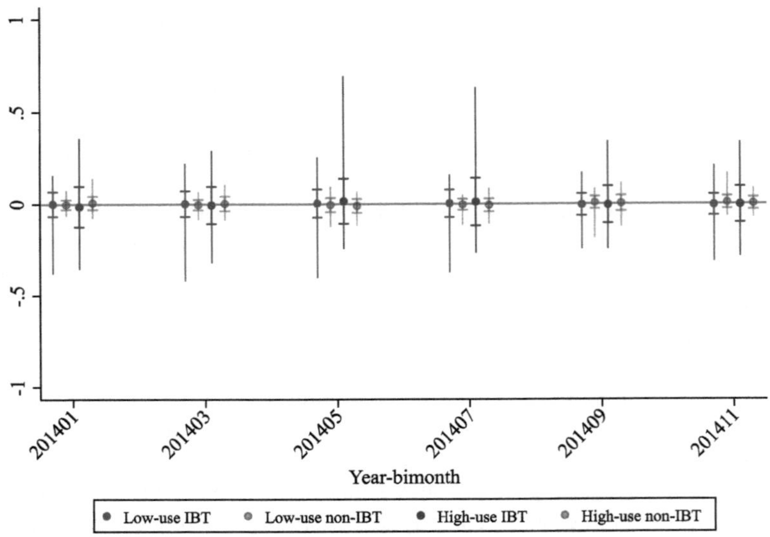

Fig. 5.7 Pre-treatment trends of regression residuals in household daily water consumption over time on a bimonthly basis. *Notes* We use the residuals from the regressions presented in Table 5.3 to plot the pre-treatment trends. The residuals for low-use IBT and non-IBT households are from the regression in column (4), and the residuals for high-use IBT and non-IBT households are from the regression in column (5). Each circle represents the mean of residuals for each type of households in the given bimonth, each range plot with capped spikes provides mean-SD and mean+SD, and each range plot with spikes provides the minimum and the maximum

and 2016, and the effect is larger in the second year of implementation than in the first year, indicating a larger long-term effect than a short-term effect, consistent with the finding in Deryugina et al. (2020) on electricity demand. Excluding the extremely high-use households from the regression yields similar results. As this larger long-term effect could be attributed to learning or to the longer budget period in 2016 (see Sect. 5.1 for details), these differences across years may not represent a substantive increase in conservation behavior. See Sect. 5.10 for a detailed discussion of the long-term effect of the IBT.

5.6.2 Household Response to Dynamic Incentives Under IBT

As elaborated in Sect. 5.4, in a given budget period, the Hangzhou IBT generates dynamic incentives for high-use IBT households. However, lack of price salience, myopia, and inelastic water demand would deter households from responding. In the following, we empirically examine whether households in fact take dynamic incentives into account in their water consumption decisions.

We first interact the indicator for IBT households, $IBThh_i$, with dummy variables for every year-bimonth period between January 2015 and December 2016, μ_{jd}. Next, we replace the key variable of interest in Eq. (5.5), $IBThh_i \times Post_{yb}$, with these separate IBT-year-bimonth interactions. Thus, Eq. (5.5) becomes:

$$Y_{iyb} = \left(\sum_{\substack{j=2015,\\2016}} \sum_{\substack{1 \leq d \leq 11,\\odd}} (IBThh_i \times \mu_{jd})\beta_{jd} \right) + \delta_i + \gamma_{yb} + IBThh_i \times \theta_b + X_i \times \rho_{yb} + \epsilon_{iyb}. \quad (5.6)$$

As γ_{yb} reflects the year-bimonth trends of household water consumption in the absence of the IBT, β_{jd} captures the effect of the IBT on household water consumption, relative to that of non-IBT households in the corresponding year-bimonth after January 2015. Again, the standard errors are clustered at the household and community-bimonth levels. We report the regression results in Table 5.4 and plot the estimates for β_{jd} and their 95% confidence intervals in Fig. 5.8.

Among low-use households, the IBT has a small and insignificant effect on water consumption before September in both 2015 and 2016. Thus, there is no significant difference between IBT and non-IBT households in water consumption during the specific period in the two years following the reform. Interestingly, we find that the IBT causes increased water consumption from September onward for low-use households. It is possible that once households realize, relatively late in the budget period, that the chance of triggering the second-tier rate of the IBT is low, they increase water consumption. This finding is consistent with Brent and Ward (2019) who observe that low-use households increase water consumption in response to improved price information, though in this case the drivers for this response cannot be clearly identified.

For high-use households, in contrast, the water savings effect of the IBT begins early in the budget period, during the month of March in both years. We confirm that in both 2015 and 2016, none of the IBT households had accumulated a water consumption amount greater than 216 m^3, the second-tier threshold, by the month of June. This suggests that these households incorporate the potential future price increase into their water consumption decision in the initial period when water consumption is still far away from the second-tier threshold and the budget set renewal date. Specifically, the IBT appears to discourage water consumption, especially in spring and summer, in both years. Moreover, the IBT lowers water consumption in the winter at the end of 2016 but not 2015.

To rule out the possibility that the extremely high-use households drive these results and to understand households' response to dynamic incentives in a cleaner setting, we focus on the moderately high-use households whose annual water consumption in 2014 was below 216 m^3. As elaborated in Sect. 5.4, for these households, the current price of water is most likely to remain at the first-tier rate during the whole budget period, but the expected probability of entering the second tier could be positive and varies over time, which leads to a deviation of the expected future price from the current price. If the households only respond to the current price, we should not detect any IBT effect on water consumption over time, regardless of the variation in

Table 5.4 Household response to dynamic incentives under the IBT

	Dep.var.: Household daily water consumption (m^3)		
	Low	High	Moderately high
	(1)	(2)	(3)
IBThh × YB201501	0.002	–0.007	–0.008
	(0.009)	(0.011)	(0.011)
IBThh × YB201503	0.001	–0.026**	–0.015
	(0.013)	(0.011)	(0.011)
IBThh × YB201505	–0.013	–0.073***	–0.065***
	(0.011)	(0.027)	(0.019)
IBThh × YB201507	–0.000	–0.049	–0.030
	(0.008)	(0.030)	(0.019)
IBThh × YB201509	0.025**	–0.004	0.014
	(0.010)	(0.025)	(0.013)
IBThh × YB201511	0.009	–0.009	0.015
	(0.008)	(0.014)	(0.015)
IBThh × YB201601	–0.003	–0.022	0.003
	(0.009)	(0.019)	(0.016)
IBThh × YB201603	–0.010	–0.043***	–0.011
	(0.013)	(0.016)	(0.018)
IBThh × YB201605	–0.006	–0.104***	–0.073***
	(0.015)	(0.029)	(0.025)
IBThh × YB201607	–0.009	–0.103***	–0.059***
	(0.016)	(0.029)	(0.016)
IBThh × YB201609	0.029	–0.063**	–0.016
	(0.018)	(0.026)	(0.019)
IBThh × YB201611	0.049***	–0.068***	–0.019
	(0.017)	(0.024)	(0.018)
Observations	5,179	5,162	4,676
R^2	0.674	0.675	0.597
Num of clusters (household)	295	287	260
Num of clusters (community-bimonth)	72	72	72
$\overline{Y}_{1,2014}$	0.213	0.486	0.425
$\overline{Y}_{0,2014}$	0.294	0.415	0.410
Household FE	Y	Y	Y
Year-bimonth FE	Y	Y	Y
IBThh × bimonth dummies	Y	Y	Y
Household controls × year-bimonth dummies	Y	Y	Y

Notes *, **, and *** indicate significance at 10%, 5%, and 1%, respectively. Equation (5.6) is applied for the estimation in each subsample. The standard errors in parentheses are clustered at two levels: household and community-bimonth. "YB[yyyymm]" denotes a year-bimonth dummy for one of the year-bimonth periods between January 2015 and December 2016. For example, "YB201501" equals one for the period between January and February, 2015, and zero otherwise. $\overline{Y}_{1,2014}$ and $\overline{Y}_{0,2014}$ denote the sample mean of household daily water consumption in 2014 for IBT and non-IBT households, respectively. The coefficients on the interactions between the indicator for IBT households and the year-bimonth dummies and the 95% confidence intervals are plotted in Fig. 5.8

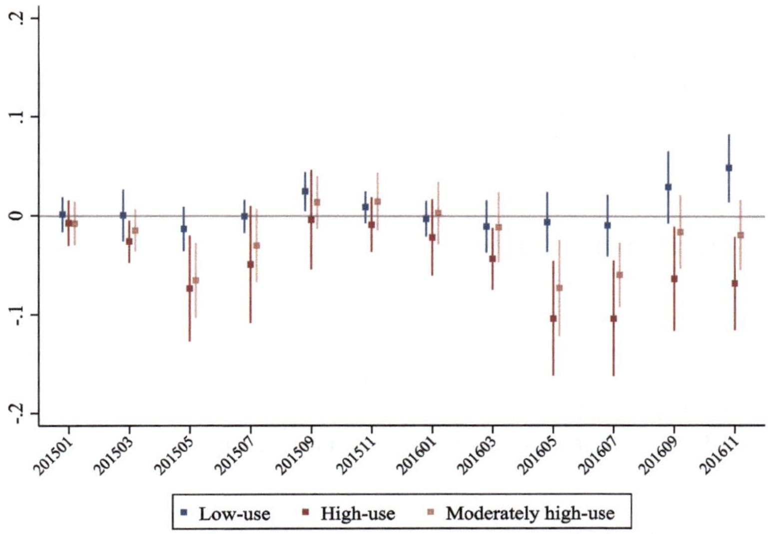

Fig. 5.8 The effect of the IBT on household daily water consumption across year-bimonth periods. *Notes* The figure plots the impact of the IBT on household daily water consumption in each year-bimonth period, separately for low-use, high-use, and moderately high-use households. The squares indicate the point estimates for the interactions of the indicator for IBT households and the year-bimonth dummies in Table 5.4, and the vertical segments indicate the 95% confidence intervals

the price elasticity of water demand over time. However, in column (3) of Table 5.4 and in Fig. 5.8, we find statistically significant water conservation effects due to the IBT in May–June 2015 and in May–June and July–August in 2016.[23] This finding from the moderately high-use households provides strong evidence that households incorporate the possibility of higher future prices into their water consumption decisions.

Moreover, in both 2015 and 2016, the water savings effect of the IBT among moderately high-use households disappears at years' end, when the budget set is about to be renewed. It seems likely that households thus update their expected probability of crossing the threshold by referring to the balance in the first tier and concluding that this probability is very low at the end of the year, which results in a decision to relax water saving behavior. Another possibility is that moderately high-use households have a low price elasticity of water demand in winter.

Note that compared to high-use households, the estimated water savings effect among these moderately high-use households is smaller in almost all year-bimonths. This pattern could be attributed to extremely high-use households facing a higher expected future price or a higher current price than those faced by moderately high-

[23] We confirm from the data that no moderately high-use IBT household had cumulative annual water consumption exceeding 216 m^3 by August in both 2015 and 2016.

use households.[24] It is also possible that extremely high-use households may have a greater price elasticity of water demand than moderately high-use households.

In addition, we employ an alternative identification strategy to examine the causal effect of the shift to an IBT on the gap in water consumption between high- and low-use households.

5.7 Heterogeneity Analysis

In the main analysis, we found evidence of a substantial and statistically meaningful water conservation effect of the IBT on household water consumption among high-use households. In this subsection, we examine whether this effect varies across households with different characteristics: time preferences, housing condition, household demographics, and socioeconomic variables.

5.7.1 Time Preferences

Following Werthschulte and Löschel (2021), we explore the role of present bias in influencing the water savings effect. At the end of the household survey, we conducted a time preference game to derive time preferences of the survey respondent (household head or the head's spouse). We presented the respondent with two decision situations, and each decision situation was presented using Multiple Price Lists (MPLs) (Holt and Laury 2002).

The first MPL consisted of 12 decisions. In each decision, the respondent was asked to indicate whether he/she would prefer receiving 15 yuan today (option A), or some varying larger amount in six months (option B). We presented option B in an ascending order (increasing it from 16 yuan to 30 yuan across the 12 choices) and for each decision, we also provided the implied interest rate. The second MPL also consisted of 12 decisions. In each decision, the respondent indicates whether he/she would prefer receiving 15 yuan one month later (option A), or receiving a larger amount in seven months (option B). For detailed instructions concerning the time preference game, please refer to the supplementary material in Sect. 5.13.

We expect that in the first MPL a respondent would prefer 15 yuan today at the beginning but that they might switch to option B as the amount gets larger. A switching point in a MPL indicates interval information on discounting.[25] We find

[24] Extremely high-use households may face a higher expected future price during the whole budget period. However, they should only face a higher current price late in the period, as none of the IBT households had accumulated a water consumption amount greater than 216 m^3 by the month of June in both 2015 and 2016.

[25] For example, in the first MPL, if a respondent chose option A when option B is less than 25.5 yuan (No. 1–7 in Set 1) and chose option B when option B is equal to or greater than 25.5 yuan (No. 8–12 in Set 1), the respondent's switching point is No. 8, and his/her discount rate is in the range of 60–70%.

Table 5.5 Heterogeneity analysis

	Dep. var.: Household daily water consumption (m^3)		
	Low	High	Moderately high
	(1)	(2)	(3)
Panel A. Present bias			
IBThh × Post ($\hat{\beta}$)	0.008	–0.063***	–0.038***
	(0.009)	(0.015)	(0.014)
IBThh × Post × Present bias ($\hat{\beta}_p$)	–0.018	0.084***	0.053***
	(0.017)	(0.021)	(0.016)
IBThh × Post × Future bias ($\hat{\beta}_f$)	–0.004	0.005	0.027
	(0.013)	(0.027)	(0.020)
Observations	5,179	5,162	4,676
R^2	0.672	0.674	0.596
p-value of F-test for present bias ($H_0 : \beta + \beta_p = 0$)	0.452	0.188	0.141
p-value of F-test for future bias ($H_0 : \beta + \beta_f = 0$)	0.740	0.029	0.449
Panel B. Education level			
IBThh × Post	–0.001	–0.158***	–0.083
	(0.035)	(0.059)	(0.051)
IBThh × Post × Highest years of schooling	0.001	0.007**	0.004
	(0.002)	(0.004)	(0.003)
Observations	5,179	5,162	4,676
R^2	0.672	0.670	0.593
Panel C. Number of household members			
IBThh × Post	–0.027	–0.184***	–0.129***
	(0.034)	(0.048)	(0.038)
IBThh × Post × Number of household members	0.011	0.039***	0.031***
	(0.012)	(0.012)	(0.011)
Observations	5,179	5,162	4,676
R^2	0.672	0.672	0.595
Panel D. Housing area			
IBThh × Post	–0.006	–0.019	0.039
	(0.016)	(0.033)	(0.029)
IBThh × Post × Housing area per capita/10	0.005	–0.014	–0.031**
	(0.006)	(0.014)	(0.012)
Observations	5,179	5,162	4,676
R^2	0.672	0.669	0.594
Household FE	Y	Y	Y
Year-bimonth FE	Y	Y	Y
IBThh × bimonth dummies	Y	Y	Y
Household controls × year-bimonth dummies	Y	Y	Y

Notes *, **, and *** indicate significance at 10%, 5%, and 1%, respectively. Each column in each panel indicates a separate regression. Equation (5.5) with the interaction of the responding household control and $IBThh_i \times Post_{yb}$ added in is applied for estimation. The standard errors in parentheses are clustered at two levels: household and community-bimonth

that among the 602 surveyed households, the median switching point was the 9th decision, that is, half of participants prefer 27 yuan in six months over 15 yuan today. Again, we expect that in the second MPL a respondent would choose option A at the beginning and may switch to option B when the amount gets larger. We find that the median switching point is the 9th decision, that is, the respondent prefers 27 yuan in seven months over 15 yuan in one month.

Using a quasi-hyperbolic discounting utility model (Laibson 1997), we determine a respondent's present/future bias by observing the change in the respondent's switching point between the first and second multiple price lists (MPLs). Assume a respondent makes decisions to maximize utility:

$$U_t = u_t + \beta \sum_{k=t+1}^{T} \delta^{k-t} u_k, \tag{5.7}$$

with $u_t = m_t^{\alpha}$ from the experimental payment m_t at time t, $\alpha > 0$ measures risk preference, $\delta > 0$ is a discount factor, and $\beta > 0$ captures present bias. We assume that the respondent is risk neutral, so that $\alpha = 1$. We use two MPLs (Set 1 and Set 2) to estimate β and δ, and one month indicates one period. For Set j, $j \in 1, 2$, we assume indifference between the underlying payment options at the midpoint $\bar{m}^j$ at the switching point. For example, in the first MPL, if the participant prefers 15 yuan today over 24 yuan (No. 7 in Set 1) in six months and 25.5 yuan in six months (No. 8 in Set 1) over 15 yuan today, we assume indifference between payment today and in six months at $\bar{m}^1 = 24.75$. Formally, the difference is given by:

$$\begin{aligned} 15 &= \beta\delta^6 \cdot \bar{m}^1, \\ \beta\delta \cdot 15 &= \beta\delta^7 \cdot \bar{m}^2. \end{aligned} \tag{5.8}$$

Then we have

$$\beta = \frac{\bar{m}^2}{\bar{m}^1}. \tag{5.9}$$

Therefore, we can estimate β by comparing $\bar{m}^j$ or the switching points in two MPLs.

If $\bar{m}^1 = \bar{m}^2$, i.e., the respondent switches in the first and second MPLs in the same decision, we have $\beta = 1$. We consider that the respondent makes time-consistent choices (no bias). If $\bar{m}^1 > \bar{m}^2$, i.e., the respondent's switching point decreases from the first MPL to the second MPL, we have $\beta < 1$. It suggests that a declining amount of money is needed to compensate for future utility as time passes compared to the present. We consider this respondent to be present-biased. If $\bar{m}^1 < \bar{m}^2$, i.e., the respondent's switching point increases from the first MPL to the second MPL we have $\beta > 1$. We consider the respondent to be future-biased, as an increasing amount of money is needed to compensate for the individual's future utility as time passes compared to the present. Among the 602 households, 64 (10.6%) are present-biased and 145 (24.1%) are future-biased. We construct two dummy variables $Present\ bias$

and $Future\ bias$, and augment Eq. (5.5) with the interactions of the dummy variables with $IBThh_i \times Post_{yb}$.

Panel A of Table 5.5 reports the estimation results. Column (1) shows no relationship between present bias and the water savings effect of the IBT among low-use households. Column (2) reveals that the IBT does not induce water savings among high-use households with present bias, and this pattern remains in column (3) when we focus on moderately high-use households. On average, a moderately high-use IBT household without present bias would save 0.038 m^3 per day after the pricing reform (equivalent to 9.1% of the average daily consumption). A user with present bias would use 0.015 m^3 more per day ($= -0.038 + 0.053$, equivalent to 3.6% of the average daily consumption), although we cannot reject the null hypothesis of zero effect at the conventional levels. The results are in line with our prediction in Sect. 5.4 that myopia would impair households' response to dynamic incentives.

5.7.2 Other Heterogeneity Analysis

We further explore whether the IBT effect differs by household socioeconomic status, household demographic structure, and housing condition. We measure household socioeconomic status by highest years of schooling among members, household demographic structure by the number of household members, and housing condition by housing area per capita. For estimation, we add an interaction of $IBThh_i \times Post_{yb}$ and each of the household controls to Eq. (5.5).

Panel B of Table 5.5 reports effects by household education. Column (2) shows that increasing the highest schooling level of household members by one year reduces the conservation effect by 0.007 m^3 a day for high-use households (equivalent to 1.6% of the average daily consumption). Thus, though high-use households tend to have higher education on average (Table 5.1), within this group, households with higher socioeconomic status appear less likely to conserve water. This is in line with existing literature that higher status households are less sensitive to water prices (Mansur and Olmstead 2012; Wichman et al. 2016; Wichman 2017). For both low-use households (column (1)) and moderately high-use households (column (3)), the estimated coefficient on the interaction is small and statistically insignificant, suggesting that heterogeneity by education level is driven by extremely high-use households.

In Panel C, we report the heterogeneity analysis by household size. We show in column (1) that the IBT effect on low-use households does not differ by the number of household members. Column (2) shows that having one additional household member reduces the water conservation effect of the IBT in the high-use households by 0.039 m^3 per day (equivalent to 8.8% of the average daily consumption), and this per-member decrease is statistically significant at the 1% level. The effect does not disappear if we exclude extremely high-use households (column (3)). It may be harder for households with more members to conserve water given the multiple people involved.

Lastly, Panel D presents the results for housing condition. Again, we do not detect any effect among low-use households (column (1)). Column (2) reveals, however, that the larger the housing area per capita, the greater the water conservation effect for high-use households, and the estimate for the interaction is statistically significant for moderately high-use households (column (3)). A 10 m^2 increase in housing area per capita increases the water savings effect of the IBT by 0.031 m^3 (equivalent to 7.5% of the average daily consumption). It appears that households with large housing area per capita are more responsive to dynamic incentives, as additional water uses (e.g., cleaning or tending indoor plants) that come with larger living spaces may be easier to adjust.

5.8 Robustness Checks

As discussed here, our findings hold up across a battery of robustness checks, including imposing alternative sample restrictions, using alternative thresholds for defining high-use households, using alternative specifications, using the data set constructed at the household-monthly level, accounting for recording error in the meter reading dates for non-IBT households, and dealing with the possible truncation of non-IBT households.

5.8.1 Imposing Alternative Sample Restrictions

We conduct five tests to show that our main estimates are robust to imposing alternative sample restrictions. We apply Eq. (5.5) for estimation and report the estimates in columns (1)–(5) of Table 5.6.

As shown in Sect. 5.1, IBT households with meters read in odd months and in even months have different budget periods and in 2015 in particular, have different numbers of meter readings. To see whether the effect of IBT is sensitive to the billing schedule, we repeat the estimation by first excluding the IBT households billed in odd months, and then excluding the IBT households billed in even months. Columns (1) and (2) show that the estimates are highly robust to the billing schedules. Although the estimate for moderately high-use households is not statistically significant at conventional levels (p-value=0.151), the magnitude of the estimate is very close to the estimate in the main results.

In the main analysis, we allow the incidence of missed meter readings as long as the next scheduled reading was normal and include households who had annual water consumption in 2015 and 2016 between 20% and 500% of the annual water consumption in 2014. We show in column (3) that excluding all the abnormal meter readings does not alter our results. Secondly, we show in column (4) that tightening the sample restriction to the range of 25% and 400% yields an estimate that is smaller than the main estimate for above-median households but remains statistically significant at the 1% level. Thirdly, we exclude households whose annual water consumption in 2014 is below the level of "basic" needs and those whose annual water consumption in 2014 goes beyond 300 m^3. The World Health Organization (WHO) considers 20 liters per person per day as the level at which "basic" needs are met.[26] With the information of 20 liters per person per day, 365 days in a year, and the number of household members in 2014, we are able to calculate this lower bound for household annual water consumption for each household. For the upper bound, we then take the threshold for the highest tier of the Hangzhou IBT implemented in January 2015, 300 m^3. Column (5) shows that the results still remain close to the main estimates.

To see whether households' response to dynamic incentives under the IBT is robust to imposing alternative sample restrictions, we further apply Eq. (5.6) for estimation and plot the estimates for the interactions. Figure 5.9 (1)–(5) presents patterns very similar to Fig. 5.8. Therefore, we conclude that our main results are robust to billing schedules and are unlikely to be driven by abnormal values in water consumption.

5.8.2 Using Alternative Thresholds for Defining High-Use Households

We conduct three tests to show that our main estimates are robust to using alternative thresholds for high-use households. We apply Eq. (5.5) for estimation and report the estimates in columns (6)–(8) of Table 5.6.

In the main analysis, we define households whose annual water consumption in 2014 is above the median as high-use households. We show in columns (6) and (7) that changing the threshold to the 25th percentile or the 75th percentile of the annual water consumption in 2014 yields similar estimates to those of our main analysis. Next, to address potential concerns over reversion to the mean for high use households in 2014, we use the median of the annual water consumption in 2013 as the threshold for identifying high-use IBT households. As elaborated in Sect. 5.5, we calculate the household daily water consumption for each calendar month from March to December in 2013 for the IBT households. Then we take the 10-month water consumption in 2013 as a proxy for the annual water consumption of IBT households. We find that 85% of the 288 IBT households retain their high- or low-use type when we change the threshold from the median of the 2014 consumption to that of the 2013 consumption. Moreover, we show in column (8) that using the median of the annual water consumption in 2013 does not alter our findings.

To see whether households' response to dynamic incentives under the IBT is robust to the thresholds for defining high-use households, we further apply Eq. (5.6) for estimation and plot the estimates for the interactions. Figure 5.9 (6)–(8) presents

---

[26] See the *Domestic Water Quantity, Service Level and Health* (https://www.who.int/water_sanitation_health/diseases/WSH0302.pdf, accessed on September 19, 2021).

Table 5.6 Robustness tests

	Dep. var.: Household daily water consumption (m^3)											
	Alternative sample restrictions					Alternative thresholds			Alternative specifications			Alternative data structure
	No IBT hhs billed in odd months	No IBT hhs billed in even months	No abnormal meter reading	Annual consump-tion 1/4 to 4 times of the level in 2014	Excluding possible outliers	25th percentile	75th percentile	2013 median for IBT hhs	Using frequency weights	Log of outcome as dep. var.	Per capita consump-tion as dep. var.	At monthly level
	(1)	(2)	(3)	(4)	(5)	(6)	(7)	(8)	(9)	(10)	(11)	(12)
Panel A. Low-use households												
IBThh × Post	0.001	0.019	0.009	0.004	0.009	0.010	0.008	0.009	0.006	0.017	0.002	0.006
	(0.008)	(0.012)	(0.008)	(0.007)	(0.008)	(0.013)	(0.006)	(0.008)	(0.008)	(0.033)	(0.003)	(0.007)
Observations	4,215	3,124	5,040	5,161	5,076	2,541	7,789	4,666	315,320	5,179	5,179	10,383
R^2	0.709	0.647	0.673	0.677	0.657	0.598	0.708	0.686	0.672	0.701	0.848	0.636
$\overline{Y}_{1,2014}$	0.204	0.232	0.217	0.213	0.214	0.178	0.242	0.203	0.213	0.213	0.0739	0.213
$\overline{Y}_{0,2014}$	0.294	0.294	0.294	0.294	0.294	0.244	0.330	0.294	0.294	0.294	0.119	0.294
Panel B. High-use households												
IBThh × Post	−0.029**	−0.073***	−0.044***	−0.039***	−0.049***	−0.043***	−0.067***	−0.037***	−0.048***	−0.130***	−0.017***	−0.047***
	(0.012)	(0.024)	(0.013)	(0.012)	(0.013)	(0.009)	(0.018)	(0.011)	(0.013)	(0.032)	(0.004)	(0.013)
Observations	4,424	3,978	5,140	5,108	5,076	7,800	2,552	5,675	314,278	5,162	5,162	10,324
R^2	0.719	0.677	0.677	0.679	0.622	0.733	0.651	0.703	0.669	0.600	0.724	0.637
$\overline{Y}_{1,2014}$	0.484	0.490	0.487	0.485	0.472	0.430	0.556	0.439	0.486	0.486	0.145	0.486
$\overline{Y}_{0,2014}$	0.415	0.415	0.415	0.415	0.415	0.375	0.475	0.415	0.415	0.415	0.132	0.415

(continued)

Table 5.6 (continued)

	Dep. var.: Household daily water consumption (m^3)											
	Alternative sample restrictions					Alternative thresholds			Alternative specifications			Alternative data structure
	No IBT hhs billed in odd months	No IBT hhs billed in even months	No abnormal meter reading	Annual consump-tion 1/4 to 4 times of the level in 2014	Excluding possible outliers	25th percentile	75th percentile	2013 median for IBT hhs	Using frequency weights	Log of outcome as dep. var.	Per capita consump-tion as dep. var.	At monthly level
	(1)	(2)	(3)	(4)	(5)	(6)	(7)	(8)	(9)	(10)	(11)	(12)
Panel C. Moderately high-use households												
IBThh × Post	–0.020*	–0.023	–0.019*	–0.017*	–0.022**	–0.026***	–0.032**	–0.014*	–0.022**	–0.082***	–0.009***	–0.022**
	(0.012)	(0.016)	(0.010)	(0.009)	(0.010)	(0.007)	(0.012)	(0.008)	(0.010)	(0.029)	(0.003)	(0.010)
Observations	4,100	3,744	4,660	4,640	4,662	7,314	2,066	5,189	284,686	4,676	4,676	9,352
R^2	0.642	0.663	0.600	0.597	0.591	0.689	0.567	0.648	0.593	0.550	0.733	0.554
$\overline{Y}_{1,2014}$	0.427	0.422	0.426	0.424	0.425	0.382	0.476	0.384	0.425	0.425	0.130	0.425
$\overline{Y}_{0,2014}$	0.410	0.410	0.410	0.410	0.410	0.372	0.467	0.410	0.410	0.410	0.132	0.411
Household FE	Y	Y	Y	Y	Y	Y	Y	Y	Y	Y	Y	Y
Year-T FE	Y	Y	Y	Y	Y	Y	Y	Y	Y	Y	Y	Y
IBThh × T dummies	Y	Y	Y	Y	Y	Y	Y	Y	Y	Y	Y	Y
Household controls × year-T dummies	Y	Y	Y	Y	Y	Y	Y	Y	Y	Y	Y	Y

Notes *, **, and *** indicate significance at 10%, 5%, and 1%, respectively. Each column in each panel represents one regression. Equation (5.5) is applied for estimation. Column (1)/(2) excludes IBT households billed in odd/even months. Column (3) excludes observations that involve any missed meter readings. Column (4) only includes households with annual water consumption level in the range of 25% and 400% of the baseline level in 2014. Column (5) only includes households with annual water consumption in 2014 above the "basic" needs and below 300 m^3. In columns (6)–(8), alternative thresholds are used to define high-use households: annual water consumption in 2014 above the 25th or the 75th percentile, and for IBT households annual water consumption in 2013 above the median. In column (9), the number of days in the corresponding year-bimonth period is used as the frequency weights. The dependent variable is logged household daily water consumption in column (10) and household daily water consumption per capita in column (11). In column (12), the data constructed at the monthly level are used for regressions. $\overline{Y}_{1,2014}$ and $\overline{Y}_{0,2014}$ denote the sample mean of household daily water consumption in 2014 for IBT and non-IBT households, respectively. "T" indicates bimonth in columns (1)–(12) and month in column (12). The standard errors in parentheses are clustered at the levels of household and community-T

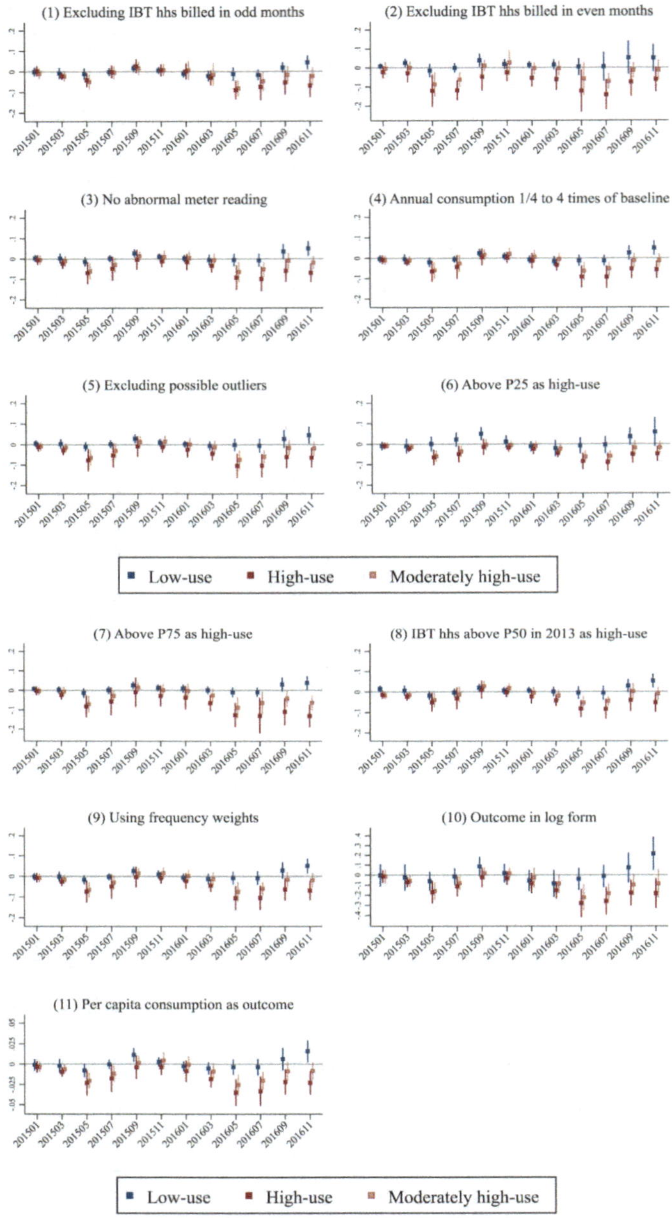

Fig. 5.9 Robustness checks for households' response to dynamic incentives under the IBT. *Notes* For each robustness check elaborated in Sect. 5.8, we apply Eq. (5.6) to three subsamples: low-use, high-use, and moderately high-use households for estimation. The squares indicate the point estimates for the interactions of the indicator for IBT households and the year-bimonth dummies, and the vertical segments indicate the 95% confidence intervals

patterns consistent with Fig. 5.8. Therefore, we conclude that our main results are robust to using alternative thresholds for defining high-use households.

5.8.3 *Using Alternative Specifications*

We show the robustness of our estimates to alternative specifications, including using frequency weights, using logarithm form of outcome, and using per capita outcome.

In the main analysis, a single observation corresponds to a two-month period, with equal weights placed on all observations. However, the number of billing days actually varies from period to period. We show in column (9) of Table 5.6 that using the actual number of days in the corresponding year-bimonth period as frequency weights in the regressions yields results that are very similar to the main estimates.

We use the level of consumption as the dependent variable in the main analysis. As a robustness check, we show in column (10) that using the logarithm form of water consumption yields similar results. We detect a 13% decrease and a 8.2% decrease in daily water consumption for high-use households and moderately high-use households, respectively, which translate into 0.063 m^3 and 0.035 m^3 a day, slightly larger than the main estimates in columns (5)–(6) in Table 5.3. For low-use households, we detect no effect of the IBT.

To see whether our estimates are robust to explicitly accounting for the number of household members, we replace the dependent variable with household daily water consumption per capita. We show in column (11) that the IBT lowers household daily water consumption per capita by 0.017 m^3 for high-use households, and by 0.009 m^3 for moderately high-use households. As the average number of household members is around 3.4 in both subsamples (see Table 5.1), using per capita consumption as the dependent variable generates estimates greater than the main results in the magnitude. Again, we detect little effect of the IBT on the per capita water consumption of low-use households.

Figure 5.9 (9)–(11) plots the estimates for the interactions from applying Eq. (5.6) for estimation. The patterns are very similar to Fig. 5.8. Thus we show that our main results are robust to alternative specifications.

5.8.4 *Using a Monthly Level Data Set*

Due to the billing cycle being bimonthly for IBT households and monthly for non-IBT households, daily water consumption for a non-IBT household in a calendar month is more variable than that for an IBT household (see Fig. 5.10). As elaborated in Sect. 5.5, we aggregate water consumption over every two adjacent calendar months in the main analysis, to smooth out this differential fluctuation in measured water consumption, and obtain the bimonthly trends in Fig. 5.6. We then use the bimonthly-level data set for analysis.

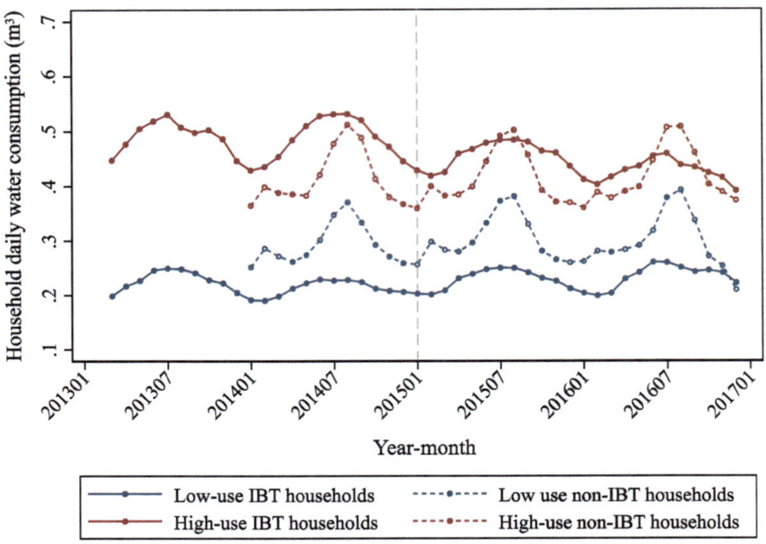

Fig. 5.10 Trends in household daily water consumption over time on a monthly basis. *Notes* This figure plots the time trends of household daily water consumption among IBT and non-IBT households, differentiated based on baseline water consumption level. Each circle or open circle represents the average daily water consumption of the sampled households in the corresponding year-month period. For example, the red open circle in the year-month of "201401" indicates the average daily water consumption level of high-use non-IBT households in January, 2014. The vertical dashed line represents the timing of the water pricing reform

As a robustness check, we use the monthly-level data set and apply a model analogous to Eq. (5.5) for estimation. For a household i, the daily water consumption in year y month m, Y_{iym}, can be written as:

$$Y_{iym} = \beta IBThh_i \times Post_{ym} + \delta_i + \gamma_{ym} + IBThh_i \times \theta_m + X_i \times \rho_{ym} + \epsilon_{iym}. \quad (5.10)$$

All the variables are defined in the same way as those in Eq. (5.5), except that the subscript b for bimonthly is replaced with m for monthly. Here β indicates the average effect of IBT on household daily water consumption. The standard errors are clustered at two levels: household and community-month. The estimates are reported in column (12) in Table 5.6.

To examine household response to dynamic incentives in the IBT, we generate a series of dummy variables for every month from January 2015 to December 2016, and interact these year-month indicators with the indicator for IBT households. Next, we replace $IBThh_i \times Post_{ym}$ in Eq. (5.10) with these separate IBT-year-month interactions. We report the estimates for the IBT-year-month interactions in Table 5.7 and plot the estimated coefficients and the 95% confidence intervals in Fig. 5.11. Overall, we find that using the data set at the the monthly level produces results in line with the results from the bimonthly-level data set.

Table 5.7 Households' response to dynamic incentives: Using the monthly-level data set

	Dep.var.: Household daily water consumption (m^3)		
	Low	High	Moderately high
	(1)	(2)	(3)
IBThh × YM201501	0.004 (0.009)	0.006 (0.014)	0.001 (0.012)
IBThh × YM201502	–0.004 (0.011)	–0.021** (0.011)	–0.017 (0.011)
IBThh × YM201503	0.002 (0.013)	–0.025*** (0.009)	–0.011 (0.011)
IBThh × YM201504	–0.001 (0.014)	–0.027* (0.014)	–0.018 (0.012)
IBThh × YM201505	–0.010 (0.010)	–0.065*** (0.023)	–0.061*** (0.018)
IBThh × YM201506	–0.019 (0.014)	–0.081** (0.031)	–0.069*** (0.023)
IBThh × YM201507	–0.009 (0.012)	–0.065** (0.030)	–0.044** (0.021)
IBThh × YM201508	0.008 (0.008)	–0.033 (0.031)	–0.015 (0.021)
IBThh × YM201509	0.024** (0.010)	–0.001 (0.029)	0.014 (0.019)
IBThh × YM201510	0.026** (0.011)	–0.006 (0.023)	0.014 (0.010)
IBThh × YM201511	0.019 (0.012)	–0.004 (0.016)	0.016 (0.014)
IBThh × YM201512	–0.003 (0.007)	–0.012 (0.018)	0.015 (0.021)
IBThh × YM201601	–0.009 (0.010)	–0.016 (0.018)	0.006 (0.014)
IBThh × YM201602	0.002 (0.012)	–0.027 (0.022)	0.001 (0.022)
IBThh × YM201603	–0.007 (0.014)	–0.025 (0.019)	0.010 (0.022)
IBThh × YM201604	–0.014 (0.014)	–0.062*** (0.017)	–0.032 (0.021)
IBThh × YM201605	–0.011 (0.014)	–0.098*** (0.026)	–0.072*** (0.025)
IBThh × YM201606	0.000 (0.018)	–0.109*** (0.034)	–0.073*** (0.027)
IBThh × YM201607	–0.011 (0.018)	–0.110*** (0.033)	–0.072*** (0.022)
IBThh × YM201608	–0.007 (0.015)	–0.097*** (0.028)	–0.047** (0.020)
IBThh × YM201609	0.011 (0.021)	–0.065** (0.028)	–0.016 (0.019)

(continued)

Table 5.7 (continued)

	FE	RE	
	(1)	(2)	
IBThh × YM201610	0.043**	–0.062**	–0.015
	(0.019)	(0.025)	(0.019)
IBThh × YM201611	0.041**	–0.071***	–0.023
	(0.018)	(0.023)	(0.018)
IBThh × YM201612	0.056***	–0.065**	–0.015
	(0.017)	(0.026)	(0.020)
Observations	10,383	10,324	9,352
R^2	0.639	0.643	0.558
Number of clusters (household)	295	287	260
Number of clusters (community-month)	144	144	144
$\overline{Y}_{1,2014}$	0.213	0.486	0.425
$\overline{Y}_{0,2014}$	0.294	0.415	0.411
Household FE	Y	Y	Y
Year-month FE	Y	Y	Y
IBThh × month dummies	Y	Y	Y
Household controls × year-month dummies	Y	Y	Y

Notes *, **, and *** indicate significance at 10%, 5%, and 1%, respectively. The monthly-level household water consumption data are used for analysis. Equation (5.10) with $IBThh_i \times Post_{yb}$ replaced with the IBT-year-month interactions is applied for estimation in each subsample. "YM[yyyymm]" denotes a year-month dummy for one of the year-month periods between January 2015 and December 2016. For example, "YM201501" equals one for the period of January, 2015, and zero otherwise. The standard errors in parentheses are clustered at two levels: household and community-month. $\overline{Y}_{1,2014}$ and $\overline{Y}_{0,2014}$ denote the sample mean of household daily water consumption in 2014 for IBT and non-IBT households, respectively. The estimated coefficients on the IBT-year-month interactions and the 95% confidence intervals are plotted in Fig. 5.11

5.8.5 *Dealing with the Measurement Error in Meter Reading Dates for Non-IBT Households*

The water meters of non-IBT households are read every month by the administrative office of each community. However, these offices only record a range of meter reading dates in a given year. When we construct daily water consumption for the non-IBT households in the main analysis, we assume that the meter reading date falls on the midpoint of the corresponding range. Here, we conduct simulations in which the meter reading can take place on any date in the range and show that our main estimates still hold.

With the information on the range of meter reading dates for each community in a given year, we first randomly draw a meter reading date from the range for each community in each year-month period. We then use the randomly drawn meter reading dates to calculate household daily water consumption in each calendar month, which is used to construct household daily water consumption on the bimonthly basis.

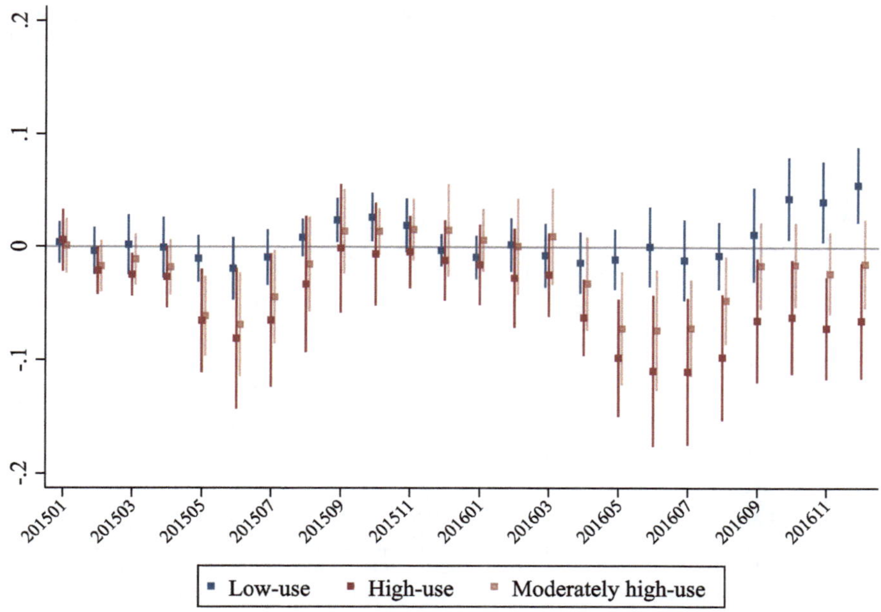

Fig. 5.11 The effect of the IBT on household daily water consumption on a monthly basis. *Notes* The figure plots the impact of the IBT on household daily water consumption in each year-month period, separately for low-use, high-use and moderately high-use households. The squares indicate the point estimates for the interactions of the indicator for IBT households and the year-month dummies in Table 5.7, and the vertical segments indicate the 95% confidence intervals

We next estimate the effect of the IBT in the subsamples of low-use households, high-use households, and moderately high-use households, separately. We run 1,000 trials of this simulation, and plot the distributions of the simulated estimates for each subsample in Fig. 5.12. We find that in all subsamples the simulation estimates are generally concentrated around the main estimates (columns (4)–(6) of Table 5.3). We take this finding as strong evidence that the measurement error in the meter reading dates for the non-IBT households does not appear to challenge our findings.

5.8.6 *Dealing with the Possible Truncation of Non-IBT Households*

In the baseline analysis, we define low-use households as the subset with annual water consumption level below median (120.78 m^3). As shown in Fig. 5.5, for all years, the distribution of non-IBT households' consumption is possibly truncated from the bottom relative to that of the IBT households. The minimum annual water consumption of non-IBT households was 77.9 m^3 in 2014, 80.4 m^3 in 2015, and

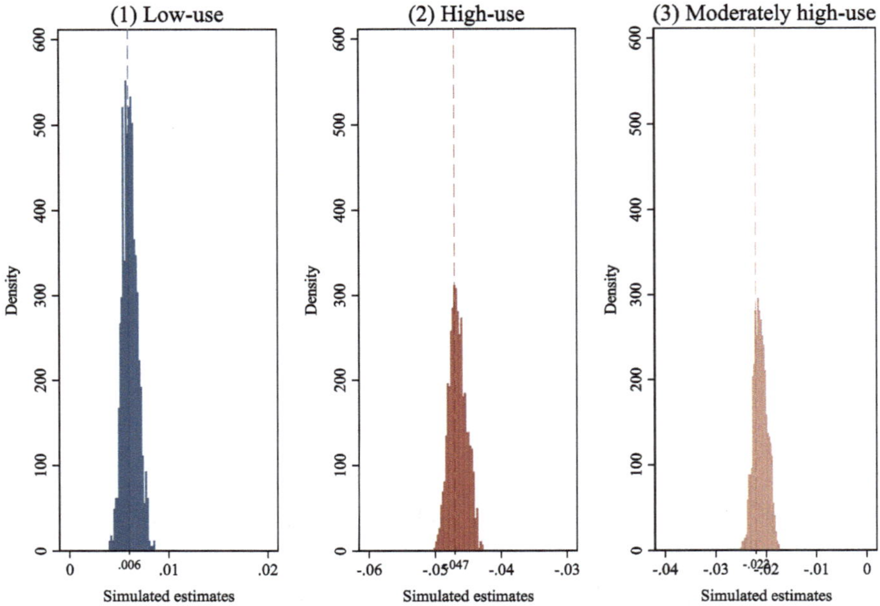

Fig. 5.12 Distribution of estimates from simulations. *Notes* This figure shows the distribution of estimates for the impact of the IBT on household daily water consumption from simulations, separately for low-use, high-use, and moderately high-use households. With the information on the range of meter reading dates for each non-IBT community in a given year, we randomly draw a meter reading date from the range for each community in each year-month. We use the randomly drawn meter reading dates to calculate household daily water consumption in each calendar month, which is then used to construct household daily water consumption on the bimonthly basis. Next, we run separate regressions in the subsamples of low-use households, high-use households, and moderately high-use households. We do the simulation for 1,000 times and plot the distribution of the simulated estimates for each subsample. The vertical lines indicate the main estimates from columns (4)–(6) in Table 5.3

68.0 m^3 in 2016. We show that excluding low-use households with baseline annual water consumption level below 77.9 (or 80.4 or 68.0) m^3 yields similar null effects of the IBT on low-use households' consumption (Table 5.8). Therefore, truncation of non-IBT households, if exists, is unlikely to alter our findings.

5.9 The IBT Effect on the Gap Between High- and Low-Use Households

In the main analysis, we employed a DID framework to identify the causal link between IBT pricing and household water consumption. In this subsection, we focus on IBT households and use an alternative identification strategy to investigate the

Table 5.8 More robustness tests about the possible truncation of non-IBT households

	Dep.var.: Household daily water consumption (m^3)		
Range of baseline water consumption level	77.9–120.78 m^3	80.4–120.78 m^3	68.0–120.78 m^3
	(1)	(2)	(3)
IBThh × Post	–0.012	–0.014	–0.008
	(0.011)	(0.011)	(0.009)
Observations	3,655	3,570	4,098
R^2	0.541	0.537	0.566
Number of clusters (household)	205	200	230
Number of clusters (community-bimonth)	72	72	72
$\overline{Y}_{1,2014}$	0.275	0.278	0.260
$\overline{Y}_{0,2014}$	0.295	0.296	0.294
Household FE	Y	Y	Y
Year-bimonth FE	Y	Y	Y
IBThh × bimonth dummies	Y	Y	Y
Household controls × year-bimonth dummies	Y	Y	Y

Notes *, **, and *** indicate significance at 10%, 5%, and 1%, respectively. The minimum annual water consumption of non-IBT households was 77.9 m^3 in 2014, 80.4 m^3 in 2015, and 68.0 m^3 in 2016. In columns (1)–(3), we exclude low-use households with baseline annual water consumption level below 77.9, 80.4, and 68.0 m^3, respectively. Equation (5.5) is applied for estimation. The standard errors in parentheses are clustered at two levels: household and community-bimonth. $\overline{Y}_{1,2014}$ and $\overline{Y}_{0,2014}$ denote the sample mean of household daily water consumption in 2014 for IBT and non-IBT households, respectively

causal effect of IBT on the gap in water consumption between high- and low-use households. Among the IBT households, both high- and low-use households experienced the same pricing change; however, as elaborated in Sect. 5.4, the effects of the pricing change could be different, because high-use households face the possibility of price increases with consumption, while low-use households never approach the threshold for the second tier, and thus both current and expected future prices stay at the first tier of the IBT.

We apply the following model for this estimation, which is also a DID specification:

$$Y_{iyb} = \phi Highusehh_i \times Post_{yb} + \sigma_i + \nu_{yb} + Highusehh_i \times \theta_b + X_i \times \rho_{yb} + \xi_{iyb}, \quad (5.11)$$

where Y_{iyb} and $Post_{yb}$ are defined in the same way as in Eq. (5.5), $Highusehh_i$ is an indicator for high-use households, which equals one for households with baseline water consumption above the median, σ_i represents a household fixed effect, and ν_{yb} indicates year-bimonth period fixed effects. By controlling for the interaction of the indicator for high-use households and the set of bimonthly dummies, $Highusehh_i \times \theta_b$, we allow for different seasonal trends of high- and low-use households. The interactions of a set of household characteristics X_i and year-bimonth dummies ρ_{yb} indicate different trends in water consumption across households with different characteristics. If the common trends assumption for high- and low-use IBT households holds, ϕ can be interpreted as the causal effect of the IBT on the gap in water consumption between high- and low-use households. The standard errors are clustered at two levels: household and community-year-bimonth.

Panel A column (1) of Table 5.9 reports the results from the regression using the bimonthly water consumption data for all IBT households between 2014 to 2016. On average, the IBT lowers the gap between high- and low-use households in daily water consumption by 0.078 m^3, and the estimate is statistically significant at the 1% level. Since the gap was around 0.273 m^3 in 2014, our estimate amounts to a 28.6% reduction in the gap. As the water meter readings for IBT households are available from January/February 2013 onward, we also run a regression using the data from 2013 to 2016 and report the results in column (2).[27] The estimated effect gets slightly smaller, at 0.073 m^3, but remains statistically significant at the 1% level.

In Panel B, we show that excluding extremely high-use households from the regressions generates smaller estimates for the IBT effect on this water consumption gap. On average, the IBT lowers the gap in daily water consumption between moderately high- and low-use households by 0.054 m^3 (a 25.5% cut in the gap). The choice of the sample time span does not alter this result.

Overall, the results from using the alternative identification strategy reveal that the pricing reform does narrow the gap in water consumption between high- and low-use households.

5.10 The Long-Term Effect of the IBT

By the end of 2016, the new tariffs had been implemented in Hangzhou for two full calendar years. To examine the persistence of the effects of the IBT structure, we generate two dummy variables, one for the calendar year of 2015 and the other for the calendar year of 2016, and interact each of these with the indicator for IBT households. Then, we replace the key variables of interest in Eq. (5.5), $IBThh_i \times Post_{yb}$, with these separate interactions and run the regressions using the three subsamples. Results are reported in Table 5.10.

We show in column (1) that among low-use households, the estimated IBT effects are small and positive for both 2015 and 2016. Neither estimate is statistically significant at conventional levels, and we cannot reject the null hypothesis that the IBT effect in 2015 and that in 2016 are the same (p-value = 0.579).

In column (2), we show that for high-use households, the IBT lowered daily water consumption by 0.028 m^3 in 2015 and by 0.067 m^3 in 2016 (equivalent to 6.3% and

[27] Due to the nature of the household daily water consumption (see details in Sect. 5.5), March-April 2013 is the earliest year-bimonth period for which household daily water consumption can be consistently constructed.

Table 5.9 The IBT effect on the water consumption gap between high- and low-use households

	Dep. var.: Household daily water consumption	
	IBT households 2014–2016	IBT households 2013–2016
	(1)	(2)
Panel A: All IBT households		
High-use hh × Post	–0.078***	–0.073***
	(0.014)	(0.015)
Observations	4,941	6,307
R^2	0.763	0.706
Number of clusters (household)	282	282
Number of clusters (community-year-bimonth)	108	138
$\overline{Y}$ of high-use households in 2014	0.486	0.486
$\overline{Y}$ of low-use households in 2014	0.213	0.213
Panel B: IBT households with extremely high-use households excluded		
High-use hh × Post	–0.054***	–0.054***
	(0.012)	(0.014)
Observations	4,527	5,778
R^2	0.701	0.632
Number of clusters (household)	259	259
Number of clusters (community-year-bimonth)	108	138
$\overline{Y}$ of high-use households in 2014	0.425	0.425
$\overline{Y}$ of low-use households in 2014	0.213	0.213
Household FE	Y	Y
Year-bimonth FE	Y	Y
IBThh × bimonth dummies, high-use × bimonth dummies	Y	Y
Household controls × year-bimonth dummies	Y	Y

Notes *, **, and *** indicate significance at 10%, 5%, and 1%, respectively. Each column in each panel represents one regression. Equation (5.11) is applied for estimation. "High-use hh" equals one if a household's annual water consumption in 2014 is above the median, and zero otherwise. Household controls that are interacted with year-bimonth dummies include number of household members, number of children under age 18, highest years of schooling among members, and housing area per capita. The standard errors in parentheses are clustered at two levels: household and community-year-bimonth

15% of the average daily consumption). Both estimates are statistically significant at the 1% level. Moreover, we reject the hypothesis that the water conservation effect of the IBT in 2015 is equal to that in 2016 (p-value=0.006). This analysis reveals that the water conservation effect of the IBT is in fact larger in the second year of implementation than in the first year, indicating a larger long-term effect than a

Table 5.10 The long-term effect of the IBT

	Dep.var.: Household daily water consumption (m^3)		
	Low	High	Moderately high
	(1)	(2)	(3)
IBThh × Year 2015	0.004	–0.028**	–0.015
	(0.007)	(0.012)	(0.010)
IBThh × Year2016	0.008	–0.067***	–0.029**
	(0.010)	(0.017)	(0.013)
Observations	5,179	5,162	4,676
R^2	0.672	0.672	0.593
Num of clusters (household)	295	287	260
Num of clusters (community-bimonth)	72	72	72
$\overline{Y}_{1,2014}$	0.213	0.486	0.425
$\overline{Y}_{0,2014}$	0.294	0.415	0.410
p-value	0.579	0.006	0.237
Household FE	Y	Y	Y
Year-bimonth FE	Y	Y	Y
IBThh × bimonth dummies	Y	Y	Y
Household controls × year-bimonth dummies	Y	Y	Y

Notes *, **, and *** indicate significance at 10%, 5%, and 1%, respectively. For estimation, we replace *IBThh* × *Post* in Eq. (5.5) with the interactions of the indicator for IBT households and year dummies for 2015 and 2016. The standard errors in parentheses are clustered at two levels: household and community-bimonth. $\overline{Y}_{1,2014}$ and $\overline{Y}_{0,2014}$ denote the sample mean of household daily water consumption in 2014 for IBT and non-IBT households, respectively. The p-value is for the test on the equality of the coefficients on *IBThh* × *Year2015* and *IBThh* × *Year2016*

short-term effect, consistent with the finding in Deryugina et al. (2020) on electricity demand. Column (3) shows that excluding the extremely high-use households from the regression yields similar results.

Several factors may contribute to this larger long-term effect. First, it is possible that as the households accumulate knowledge on this pricing schedule and the effectiveness of different household water conservation strategies, they make more effective long-term behaviour changes and/or install water-efficient devices. Another possible reason is that the budget period in 2015 was shorter than it was in 2016 (see Sect. 5.1 for details). Therefore, for high-use households, the IBT effect might logically increase in the calendar year of 2016, as more households deemed it possible they would reach the second-tier threshold. Hence, we should not necessarily conclude that these differences across years represent a substantive increase in conservation behavior.

5.11 The Implied Price Elasticity of Water Demand for High-Use Households

Our study finds strong evidence that high-use households respond to unobserved expected future prices. In order to calculate meaningful price elasticities that incorporate such expectations as in Sect. 5.4, we must make assumptions about the beliefs that households have about their probabilities of exceeding the higher-tier thresholds in any given year-bimonth. Here, we make several such assumptions and explain what they imply about price elasticities of water demand for the high-use households in our sample.[28] However, it is important to mention that the results are only suggestive and should be interpreted with caution.

First, we compute an assumed expected probability that a household's annual water consumption will exceed the second-tier threshold (216 m^3) in each year-bimonth following the pricing reform, $\tilde{Pr}(in^2_{yb})$, for all high-use IBT households in our sample, and obtain the sample average in each year-bimonth.[29] We assume that $\bar{\tilde{Pr}}(in^2_{yb})$ begins at the average rate of exceedence of the threshold in a given budget period, so we have $\tilde{Pr}(in^2_{201501}) = 0.093$ and $\tilde{Pr}(in^2_{201601}) = 0.142$.[30] Next, we assume that in the following bimonths within each budget period, the household adjusts its expected probability of exceeding the second-tier threshold according to a linear function of the cumulative deviation from the threshold, that is implied by a household's current rate of consumption. Let $CumAmount_{yb}$ denote the household's cumulative annual water consumption in a year-bimonth. Then, in a given year-bimonth, the household's expected annual water consumption in the corresponding budget period can be calculated as $\widetilde{AnnuAmount}_{yb} = CumAmount_{yb}/(b+1) \times 12$, and the cumulative deviation is $\widetilde{CumDeviation}_{yb} = (\widetilde{AnnuAmount}_{yb} - \bar{Q}^2)/\bar{Q}^2$, where $\bar{Q}^2$ is 216 m^3. Then $\forall b \in (3, 5, ..., 11)$, we have:

$$\tilde{Pr}(in^2_{yb}) = \min\left[\max\left(\tilde{Pr}(in^2_{y,b-2}) + \widetilde{CumDeviation}_{yb},\ 0\right),\ 1\right]. \quad (5.12)$$

By averaging the probabilities across households in each year-bimonth, we obtain $\bar{\tilde{Pr}}(in^2_{yb})$.

[28] For low-use households, the IBT effect on consumption is close to null and not precisely measured, so we do not feel comfortable reporting elasticities.

[29] Since the third-tier threshold (300 m^3) is high enough to be practically irrelevant in our sample, we ignore the probability of exceeding that threshold.

[30] Among the households with a high level of baseline water consumption, 9.3% had annual water consumption in 2015 exceeding 216 m^3 and 14.2% had annual consumption in 2016 exceeding 216 m^3.

Table 5.11 Implied price elasticities of high-use households based on assumptions

Year-bimonth	Average price elasticities	
	Version 1	Version 2
	$\tilde{Pr}(in^2_{201501}) = 0.093$, $\tilde{Pr}(in^2_{201601}) = 0.142$	$\tilde{Pr}(in^2_{201501}) = 0.2$, $\tilde{Pr}(in^2_{201601}) = 0.2$
	(1)	(2)
201501	–0.53	–0.25
201503	–4.60	–2.49
201505	–7.40	–5.51
201507	–3.96	–3.14
201509	–0.29	–0.25
201511	–0.66	–0.59
Avg in 2015	–2.91	–2.04
201601	–1.09	–0.78
201603	–5.12	–4.09
201605	–7.89	–6.98
201607	–6.67	–6.08
201609	–4.00	–3.72
201611	–4.68	–4.39
Avg in 2016	–4.91	–4.34

Notes This table reports the average price elasticities of high-use IBT households in each year-bimonth and in each year post the pricing reform, which are calculated based on assumptions about these households' expected probabilities of exceeding the second-tier threshold of the IBT. The only difference between the two versions is the assumptions about $\tilde{Pr}(in^2_{201501})$ and $\tilde{Pr}(in^2_{201601})$. See Sect. 5.11 for the details of the calculation

Second, we use the average probability in each year-bimonth to determine the average expected future price in the corresponding year-bimonth:

$$\overline{\tilde{p}}^f_{yb} = (1 - \overline{\tilde{Pr}}(in^2_{yb})) \times p^1 + \overline{\tilde{Pr}}(in^2_{yb}) \times p^2, \tag{5.13}$$

where p^1 is the first-tier rate of the IBT, 2.90 yuan/m^3, and p^2 is the second-tier rate, 3.85 yuan/m^3.

Last, we use the following formula to calculate the price elasticity in year y and bimonth b:

$$e_{yb} = \frac{\%\Delta Demand_{yb}}{\%\Delta Price_{yb}} = \frac{\dfrac{\hat{\beta}_{yb}}{\overline{Y}_{\text{high-useIBT},2014,b}}}{\dfrac{\overline{\tilde{p}}^f_{yb} - p^1}{p^1}}, \tag{5.14}$$

where $\hat{\beta}_{yb}$ indicates the estimate for the IBT effect on high-use households' water consumption in the corresponding year-bimonth (see Eq. (5.6) and column (2) of

Table 5.4 in Sect. 5.6.2), and $\overline{Y}_{\text{high-useIBT},2014,b}$ indicates the average household daily water consumption of high-use IBT households in 2014 in bimonth *b*.

The above procedure yields average elasticities in the two years of −2.9 to −4.9 for high-use households (see column (1) of Table 5.11).

We also do a similar calculation where the only difference is that we assume that the probability of exceeding the second-tier threshold begins at 0.20 in a given budget period, which is policy-makers' target maximum rate of exceedence of the second-tier threshold in the population.[31] The probability then changes in similar (linear) fashion to the first approach. This yields average elasticities in the two years of −2.0 to −4.3 for high-use households (see column (2) of Table 5.11).

For high-use households, these elasticities appear somewhat large, but this could be because households overestimate their risk of exceeding the price thresholds, which could be very salient for those in the IBT group given the messaging these households received around the rationale for the IBT and the need to conserve.

5.12 Conclusion

In this study, we investigated the causal effect of shifting to a form of nonlinear pricing - specifically, a unique type of IBT that is increasingly being implemented in China with tier thresholds set according to annual household water consumption. We exploited a natural experiment arising from the 2015 water pricing reform as implemented in Hangzhou, China. Using a DID approach, we found substantial water savings among high-use households exposed to the IBT, whereas low-use households' consumption behavior was unaffected. On average, shifting to an IBT reduced the daily water consumption of a high-use household by 0.047 m^3, which amounts to an annual water savings of 17.2 m^3 for such households, and to 8.5 million m^3 when extrapolated over the whole of Hangzhou City.

Our analytical approach explored household response to dynamic incentives based on the insight that this particular reform only exposed some households to changing current or expected future prices, specifically, high-use households. We found that high-use households save water even when they are far away from the second-tier threshold of the IBT and the budget set renewal date. We also found evidence of water savings for moderately high-use households who are likely to face a constant current price at the first tier of the IBT and a varying expected future price throughout the budget period. The findings suggest that these households incorporate potential future price increases under the IBT into their water consumption decisions. Further supporting this idea, heterogeneity analysis reveals that among high-use households, those with present bias do not save water under the IBT, consistent with a prediction

[31] The *Guidance on Promoting Complete IBT Structure for Urban Domestic Water Use* issued in 2013 jointly by the National Development and Reform Commission and the Ministry of Housing and Urban-Rural Development, China, suggests that the second-tier threshold of the IBT should be determined based on the average water consumption of 80% of the households, in order to meet the basic water needs.

that myopic households would not respond to such dynamic incentives. We believe that this study is among the first to provide evidence of household response to dynamic incentives generated by nonlinear pricing in the context of water consumption.

In effect, the policy case for IBTs, and details of their design, is usually complicated by other objectives such as equity and efficiency (Whittington et al. 2015). The unconventional IBT for water pricing that is discussed in this study (and now common in China) reveals a persistent water savings effect for high-use households but no substantive effect on the water consumption of low-use households. In addition, the gap in water consumption between high- and low-users narrows after the implementation of the IBT. Such high-users tend to have more educated households members, higher income, and more assets. These results may therefore help inform future efforts to induce more equitable water conservation in similar locations facing water scarcity problems.

In addition, it is worth mentioning that in the particular application that we studied, the twin policy targets of increased revenue and improved water conservation were achieved at a relatively low cost. However, certain qualifications are in order to avoid misinterpreting this apparent double dividend. First, the increased revenue largely depends on the tariff increase that affected all households in Hangzhou. A price-neutral change to this type of annual IBT structure would, on its own, reduce revenue. Second, extending the reform to cover the non-IBT households in this case would reduce net revenues further, owing to the additional costs of converting the metering system in the buildings that were not covered by the change to an IBT. Thus, an IBT reform of this nature, without a corresponding price hike, may only generate conservation benefits. Understanding the relative welfare effects, and their distribution across the population, of alternative designs such as a shift to annual IBTs alone, a shift to annual IBTs paired with tariff increases, and tariff increases alone, is a potentially interesting objective for future research. Future research could also consider the conditions under which such welfare impacts might vary, given their implications for longer term utility service quality and capital investment needs.

5.13 Supplementary Material

The Instructions of the Time Preference Game

Now, I invite you to play a game of 24 decisions. There is real money involved, as I will explain.

First, you will decide whether you want to receive a set amount of money recently, or a larger amount in the future in each decision.

Second, as you will see, each decision is numbered, and the computer will select the decision to be actually played, at the end of the game.

Before we start, please provide your Alipay account information, so that we can make the payment later: ________________

In each of the first 12 decisions, shown below, I want you to decide whether you would prefer the set amount today (15 yuan), or a larger amount in 6 months. To make the game easier for you, we have also shown you the interest rate that corresponds to the gain over 6 months, if you choose to take the money later.

Set 1—Please indicate whether you prefer option A or B in each pair of options

No.	Option A	Option B	Interest	Decision
	(pay today, unit: yuan)	(pay in 6 months, unit: yuan)	rate	(A or B)
1	15	16	7%	
2	15	16.5	10%	
3	15	18	20%	
4	15	19.5	30%	
5	15	21	40%	
6	15	22.5	50%	
7	15	24	60%	
8	15	25.5	70%	
9	15	27	80%	
10	15	28.5	90%	
11	15	29.25	95%	
12	15	30	100%	

Next, we will move to the second set. In this set of 12 decisions, option A is paid in 1 month, and option B is paid in 7 months. The time difference between the two payments is the same as in set 1, but each amount is delayed by 1 month. We have again shown you the interest rate that corresponds to the gain over 6 months, which is the same as before. Please decide whether you would prefer the set amount in 1 month (15 yuan), or the larger amount in 7 months.

Set 2—Please indicate whether you prefer option A or B in each pair of options

No.	Option A	Option B	Interest	Decision
	(pay in 1 month, unit: yuan)	(pay in 7 months, unit: yuan)	rate	(A or B)
13	15	16	7%	
14	15	16.5	10%	
15	15	18	20%	
16	15	19.5	30%	
17	15	21	40%	
18	15	22.5	50%	
19	15	24	60%	
20	15	25.5	70%	
21	15	27	80%	
22	15	28.5	90%	
23	15	29.25	95%	
24	15	30	100%	

* Instructions for the enumerators: Use the random number generator to select one number between 1 and 24. The respondent will be paid according to his/her choice in the decision with the corresponding number.

Now, one of the 24 decisions will be randomly selected to play. Your random number is [#].

You will be paid according to your choice in the decision No.[#].

References

The National Development and Reform Commission and the Ministry of Housing and Urban–Rural Development (2009) Circular on improving the regulation work of city water price. Beijing

The National Development and Reform Commission and the Ministry of Housing and Urban–Rural Development (2013) Guidance on promoting complete IBT structure for urban domestic water use. Beijing

Allcott H, Kessler JB (2019) The welfare effects of nudges: a case study of energy use social comparisons. Am Econ J Appl Econ 11(1):236–276

Aron-Dine A, Einav L, Finkelstein A, Cullen M (2015) Moral hazard in health insurance: do dynamic incentives matter? Rev Econ Stat 97(4):725–741

Asensio OI, Delmas MA (2016) The dynamics of behavior change: evidence from energy conservation. J Econ Behav Organ 126:196–212

Bollinger BK, Hartmann WR (2020) Information versus automation and implications for dynamic pricing. Manage Sci 66(1):290–314

Borenstein S (2009) To what electricity price do consumers respond? Residential demand elasticity under increasing-block pricing. Preliminary draft April, 1–37

Brent DA, Ward MB (2019) Price perceptions in water demand. J Environ Econ Manag 98:1–21

Dalton CM, Gowrisankaran G, Town RJ (2020) Salience, myopia, and complex dynamic incentives: evidence from medicare part D. Rev Econ Stud 87(2):822–869

de Bartolome CA (1995) Which tax rate do people use: average or marginal? J Public Econ 56(1):79–96

Delmas MA, Lessem N (2014) Saving power to conserve your reputation? The effectiveness of private versus public information. J Environ Econ Manag 67(3):353–370

Deryugina T, MacKay A, Reif J (2020) The long-run dynamics of electricity demand: evidence from municipal aggregation. Am Econ J Appl Econ 12(1):86–114

Einav L, Finkelstein A, Schrimpf P (2015) The response of drug expenditure to nonlinear contract design: evidence from Meicare Part D. Quart J Econ 130(2):841–899

El-Khattabi AR, Eskaf S, Isnard JP, Lin L, McManus B, Yates AJ (2021) Heterogeneous responses to price: evidence from residential water consumers. J Environ Econ Manage 107:102430

Feldman NE, Katuščák P (2010) Effects of predictable tax liability variation on household labor income. Working paper, https://www.cerge-ei.cz/pdf/gdn/rrc/RRCIX_04_paper_01.pdf

Holt CA, Laury SK (2002) Risk aversion and incentive effects. Am Econ Rev 92(5):1644–1655

Hoynes H, Schanzenbach DW, Almond D (2016) Long-run impacts of childhood access to the safety net. Am Econ Rev 106(4):903–934

Ito K (2014) Do consumers respond to marginal or average price? evidence from nonlinear electricity pricing. Am Econ Rev 104(2):537–563

Ito K, Ida T, Tanaka M (2018) Moral suasion and economic incentives: field experimental evidence from energy demand. Am Econ J Econ Pol 10(1):240–267

Jack K, Smith G (2020) Charging ahead: prepaid metering, electricity use, and utility revenue. Am Econ J Appl Econ 12(2):134–168

Jessoe K, Rapson D (2014) Knowledge is (less) power: experimental evidence from residential energy use. Am Econ Rev 104(4):1417–1438

Jessoe K, Rapson D, Smith JB (2014) Towards understanding the role of price in residential electricity choices: evidence from a natural experiment. J Econ Behav Organ 107:191–208

Laibson D (1997) Golden eggs and hyperbolic discounting. Quart J Econ 112(2):443–477

Liebman JB, Zeckhauser RJ (2004) Schmeduling. Working paper, http://www.econ.yale.edu/~shiller/behmacro/2004-11/schmeduling-zeckhauser.pdf

Mansur ET, Olmstead SM (2012) The value of scarce water: measuring the inefficiency of municipal regulations. J Urban Econ 71(3):332–346

Nataraj S, Hanemann WM (2011) Does marginal price matter? a regression discontinuity approach to estimating water demand. J Environ Econ Manag 61(2):198–212

Nevo A, Turner JL, Williams JW (2016) Usage-based pricing and demand for residential broadband. Econometrica 84(2):411–443

Olmstead SM (2009) Reduced-form versus structural models of water demand under nonlinear prices. J Business Econ Stat 27(1):84–94

Saez E (2010) Do taxpayers bunch at kink points? Am Econ J Econ Pol 2(3):180–212

Smith SM (2022) The effects of individualized water rates on use and equity. J Environ Econ Manag 114(July):102673

Stojanovski O, Leslie GW, Wolak FA, Huerta Wong JE, Thurber MC (2020) Increasing the energy cognizance of electricity consumers in mexico: results from a field experiment. J Environ Econ Manag 102:102323

Sudarshan A (2017) Nudges in the marketplace: the response of household electricity consumption to information and monetary incentives. J Econ Behav Organ 134:320–335

Szabó A (2015) The value of free water: analyzing South Africa's free basic water policy. Econometrica 83(5):1913–1961

Werthschulte M, Löschel A (2021) On the role of present bias and biased price beliefs in household energy consumption. J Environ Econ Manag 109:102500

Whittington D, Nauges C, Fuente D, Wu X (2015) A diagnostic tool for estimating the incidence of subsidies delivered by water utilities in low- and medium-income countries, with illustrative simulations. Utilit Policy 34:70–81

Wichman CJ (2014) Perceived price in residential water demand: evidence from a natural experiment. J Econ Behav Organ 107:308–323

Wichman CJ (2017) Information provision and consumer behavior: a natural experiment in billing frequency. J Public Econ 152:13–33

Wichman CJ, Taylor LO, von Haefen RH (2016) Conservation policies: who responds to price and who responds to prescription? J Environ Econ Manag 79:114–134

Part III
Conclusion

Chapter 6
Conclusion

Over the past four decades, China's unprecedented economic boom and rapid urbanization have transformed the nation, but at a significant cost. Water quality deterioration, water scarcity, and chronic under-investment in water infrastructure have posed serious challenges, particularly in rural areas with poor access to safe drinking water and in cities facing escalating water demand. Recognizing the urgency of these issues, the Chinese government has introduced a series of water sector reforms aimed at addressing these critical concerns. This book has examined three key water reforms that have significantly shaped domestic water consumption in China. Through rigorous econometric analysis using large-scale micro-level survey data, we have established causal relationships between these policy interventions and their outcomes.

First, the Chinese government launched the rural drinking water program in the 1980s, aiming to improve rural residents' access to safe drinking water. Our findings indicate that exposure to this program had profound long-term impacts on human capital development. Specifically, *in utero* exposure to treated tap water increased childhood height and improved cognitive test scores in adolescence.

Second, China opened the urban water sector to private investors in the early 1990s. Our analysis reveals that private sector participation (PSP) was associated with increased output, improved financial performance, and enhanced efficiency, while service quality remained largely unchanged.

Third, the Increasing Block Tariff (IBT) policy was adopted as a demand-side management tool to curb excessive water consumption in urban areas. Unlike the conventional IBT model, which resets budget monthly, many Chinese cities implemented a novel approach where pricing tiers were determined based on annual cumulative consumption. Leveraging a water pricing reform in Hangzhou, our analysis shows that while the IBT with an annually renewed budget had a limited effect on low-use households, it resulted in substantial water savings among high-use households.

© The Author(s), under exclusive license to Springer Nature Singapore Pte Ltd. 2025
L. Li, *The Impacts of Water Reforms in Rural and Urban China*,
https://doi.org/10.1007/978-981-96-6902-8_6

Key Insights for Policy and Research

Our findings highlight three critical insights that are relevant for policymakers and researchers alike:

1. Heterogeneous Effects Across Groups

    - The benefits of in utero exposure to treated tap water were significantly greater for children born to less-educated mothers. This suggests that expanding water infrastructure in rural areas not only improves immediate health outcomes but also contributes to reducing socioeconomic disparities and enhancing long-term social mobility.
    - Compared with large water utilities serving urban population in prefectural level cities, PSP had a more pronounced and comprehensive effect on county-level water utilities. It suggests that the effects of PSP depend on the scale of the utility.
    - The water savings effect of IBT was strongest among high-use households with future-oriented time preferences, lower education levels, fewer household members, or larger per capita housing areas. These findings can help identify households that are less responsive to IBT or other price-based interventions, allowing for more targeted policy adjustments.

2. The Importance of Program Design and Implementation

    - Examining childhood disease patterns, we find that tap water exposure reduced non-waterborne digestive diseases but had no significant effect on waterborne diseases. This suggests that the primary health benefit of improved water infrastructure comes from removing chemical pollutants rather than eliminating microbial contamination, likely because boiling water is already a common practice in China.
    - PSP-driven performance improvements did not significantly vary by the extent of private participation, but collective capital investment outperformed other private capital sources in reducing managerial expenses. These findings highlight the importance of selecting the type of PSP model that aligns with a government's objectives and operational priorities.
    - While IBT is widely recognized as a progressive pricing mechanism, its effectiveness depends on how it is structured. Our study underscores the importance of designing IBT to maximize conservation effects.

3. The Timing of Safe Drinking Water Access Matters

    - The critical window for health improvements from tap water exposure is the *in utero* period, while the cognitive benefits of safe drinking water exposure, however, are most pronounced in early childhood. This finding emphasizes the need to prioritize maternal and early-life access to safe drinking water.

Looking Ahead: The Future of Water Reforms in China

These three water reforms are still evolving. In 2016, the rural drinking water program was upgraded to the rural drinking water safety consolidation and enhancement program, reflecting the government's continued commitment to improving rural residents' access to safe drinking water. PSP adoption progresses slowly but steadily among county-level water utilities, which served approximately 195 million urban residents in 2012. In urban areas, IBT adoption has become widespread. By the end of 2023, over 98% of Chinese cities had implemented IBT policies, and more than 50% of these cities had adopted the annual cumulative consumption model. These trends underscore the growing recognition of IBT's role in water conservation and the need for further refinements in its design.

The water reforms examined in this book have had profound and lasting impacts on human capital, economic efficiency, and resource sustainability. As China continues to face water scarcity challenges, the lessons from these policy interventions will be invaluable for future water governance. Policymakers could continue refining these programs, ensuring equitable access to safe drinking water while balancing economic efficiency and environmental sustainability.

Glossary

Average Treatment Effect A treatment, or policy, effect averaged across the population.

Behavioral Response Changes in individual or household behavior in reaction to external stimuli, such as price changes, policy interventions, or information campaigns.

Bias The difference between the expected value of an estimator and the population value that the estimator is supposed to be estimating.

Boiling Water A common practice in China where water is boiled before consumption to inactivate disease-causing microorganisms, reducing the risk of waterborne diseases.

Build-Operate-Transfer (BOT) A contractual arrangement in which a private entity builds and operates a facility for a set period before transferring ownership back to the government.

Build-Own-Operate (BOO) A private sector participation model where a private entity builds, owns, and operates a facility indefinitely without transferring ownership back to the government.

Build-Transfer (BT) A contractual arrangement in which a private entity finances and constructs a facility and then immediately transfers ownership to the government upon completion.

Catch-Up Growth The process in which a child's growth accelerates to compensate for previous stunting or underdevelopment.

Causal Effect A ceteris paribus change in one variable that has an effect on another variable.

Chemical Pollutants Harmful substances in water such as heavy metals (e.g., lead, arsenic) or industrial chemicals that can adversely affect health.

Cognitive Abilities/Skills Mental abilities such as word recognition, quantitative reasoning, and problem-solving. These skills are critical for educational attainment, labor market outcomes, and overall well-being.

© The Editor(s) (if applicable) and The Author(s), under exclusive license to Springer Nature Singapore Pte Ltd. 2025

L. Li, *The Impacts of Water Reforms in Rural and Urban China*,
https://doi.org/10.1007/978-981-96-6902-8

Common Trends Assumption A key assumption in DID analysis, which posits that, in the absence of treatment, the treatment and control groups would have followed similar trends over time.

Concession A legal agreement granting a private firm the right to operate a public service for a defined period under government supervision.

Confounders External variables that influence both the independent and dependent variables, confounding the estimation of the causal link between them and potentially leading to biased results.

Confounding Effect An effect caused by an external variable confounding the estimation of the causal link between independent and dependent variables, leading to biased results.

Cost-Benefit Analysis A method used to evaluate the economic efficiency of a policy or intervention by comparing its costs and benefits.

Difference-in-Differences (DID) An econometric method used to estimate causal effects by comparing the changes in outcomes over time between a treatment group and a control group.

Domestic Water Sector The segment of an economy that involves households and residential water consumption, including water usage for drinking, cooking, sanitation, and other daily needs.

Dynamic Incentives Variations in future price, created by a nonlinear pricing schedule.

Early Childhood The developmental stage from birth to approximately five years of age.

Early Life The period from conception through early childhood.

Early-Life Exposure The environmental and social conditions experienced by individuals during the prenatal period and early childhood.

Empirical Model A mathematical or statistical representation of the relationship between variables, constructed to test hypotheses or estimate causal effects using observed data.

Empirical Specification The specific functional form and set of variables included in a regression or econometric model, chosen to test a hypothesis or estimate a relationship of interest while addressing potential biases.

Empirical Strategy A systematic plan or approach for analyzing data to answer a research question.

Endogeneity A term used to describe the presence of an endogenous explanatory variable.

Endogenous Variables In simultaneous equations models, variables that are determined by the equations in the system.

Event Study An econometric analysis of the effects of an event, such as a change in government regulation or economic policy, on an outcome variable.

False Discovery Rate (FDR) The expected proportion of false positives among all rejected hypotheses in multiple testing.

Fixed-Effects Model An unobserved effects panel data model where the unobserved effects are allowed to be arbitrarily correlated with the explanatory variables in each time period.

Foreign Investors Individuals or entities from outside a country who invest in domestic projects or businesses.

Franchise Agreement A legal arrangement granting a private entity the right to operate a public service within a defined area for a specified period.

F**-test** A statistical test used to compare the fits of different models or to test the joint significance of multiple coefficients in a regression model.

Health Investments Efforts made by parents or guardians to improve or maintain the health of their children, such as seeking medical care or ensuring proper nutrition.

Height-for-Age Z-Score A measure used to assess whether a child's height is within the normal range for their age and gender.

Heterogeneity Analysis The examination of how treatment effects or relationships of interest vary across different subgroups or individuals within a population.

Heterogeneity Variations in characteristics, behaviors, or outcomes across different groups or individuals.

Heterogeneous Effects Differences in the causal impact of a treatment or intervention across individuals or groups.

Hukou A household registration system in China that officially registers individuals as permanent residents of a specific area and classifies them as either agricultural or non-agricultural, determining their access to social services and benefits.

Human Capital The collective skills, knowledge, abilities, experience, health, and other attributes embodied in individuals that contribute to their ability to perform labor and produce economic value.

Human Capital The skills, knowledge, and health that individuals accumulate over their lifetimes, which contribute to their productivity and economic potential.

Identification Strategy A methodological approach used to isolate the causal effect of a treatment or variable of interest.

Increasing Block Tariff (IBT) A nonlinear pricing structure where the price per unit of a resource (e.g., water or electricity) increases as consumption exceeds predefined thresholds.

Intention-to-Treat (ITT) Estimate A statistical estimate that evaluates the impact of a treatment or intervention based on initial group assignment, regardless of whether individuals fully adhered to the intervention.

In Utero **Exposure** The exposure to certain environmental factors that occur during pregnancy, particularly impacting fetal health and development.

In Utero Prenatal period.

Joint Venture A business arrangement in which two or more parties agree to pool their resources to accomplish a specific task, such as managing a water utility.

Local Average Treatment Effect (LATE) An econometric concept that estimates the causal effect of a treatment on a specific subgroup of individuals who comply with an instrumental variable.

Marginal Effect The effect on the dependent variable that results from changing an independent variable by a small amount.

Marginal Price The cost of consuming one additional unit of a good or service.

Measurement Error The difference between an observed variable and the variable that belongs in a multiple regression equation.

Measurement Error The difference between the observed value of a variable and its true value.

Mechanism Analysis The investigation of the channels through which a treatment or intervention produces its effects, aiming to uncover the underlying processes that link the treatment to the outcome.

Monopoly A market structure where a single firm dominates the supply of a particular good or service, often leading to higher prices and reduced competition.

Natural Experiment A situation where the economic environment—sometimes summarized by an explanatory variable—exogenously changes, perhaps inadvertently, due to a policy or institutional change.

New Cooperative Medical Scheme (NCMS) A public health insurance program in rural China designed to provide affordable healthcare for rural residents.

Nonlinear Pricing Pricing structures where the cost per unit of a good or service varies based on the quantity consumed.

Operation & Maintenance Contract An agreement in which a private company is responsible for operating and maintaining a public utility but does not own it.

Operation Outsourcing A contractual arrangement in which a government or public utility contracts a private entity to manage and operate a facility or service without transferring ownership.

Panel Data A data set constructed from repeated cross sections over time. With a *balanced* panel, the same units appear in each time period. With an *unbalanced* panel, some units do not appear in each time period, often due to attrition.

Patriotic Public Health Campaign *Aiguo Weisheng Yundong* in Chinese. An initiative by the central government of China in 1951 aimed at improving public health.

Per Capita Water Availability The average amount of water available per person in a given region, often used to assess water scarcity.

Potential Channels The mechanisms through which a treatment, policy, or variable of interest may influence an outcome.

Predetermined Variable In a simultaneous equations model, either a lagged endogenous variable or a lagged exogenous variable.

Present Bias A behavioral tendency where individuals prioritize immediate rewards over future benefits, often leading to suboptimal long-term decisions.

Price Elasticity of Demand The percentage change in demand given a 1% ceteris paribus increase in price, measuring how sensitive the quantity demanded of a good or service is to changes in its price.

Private Investors Individuals or entities that invest their own capital in businesses or projects with the expectation of financial returns.

Private Sector Participation (PSP) A collaborative arrangement between the government and private sector entities to improve service delivery, in this case, in the water sector.

Program Evaluation An analysis of a particular private or public program using econometric methods to obtain the causal effect of the program.

Public Utilities Essential services provided to the public, such as water supply, electricity, and sanitation, often regulated by the government.

p-**Value** The smallest significance level at which the null hypothesis can be rejected. Equivalently, the largest significance level at which the null hypothesis cannot be rejected.

Random-Effects Model The unobserved effects panel data model where the unobserved effect is assumed to be uncorrelated with the explanatory variables in each time period.

Renovate-Operate-Transfer (ROT) A model where a private entity renovates or upgrades an existing public asset, operates it for a specified period to recover investment costs, and then transfers it back to the government.

Reporting Error Discrepancies between the true value of a variable and the value reported by respondents.

Responses to Dynamic Incentives The behavioral responses of individuals to future price changes, rather than current prices.

Robustness Checks A set of supplementary analyses conducted to verify the reliability and stability of the main results.

Rural Drinking Water Program An initiative by the central government of China in 1984 aimed at improving access to safe drinking water in rural areas by constructing water treatment plants and pipeline systems.

Safe Drinking Water Water that is free from contaminants such as microorganisms, heavy metals, and harmful chemicals, making it suitable for human consumption without adverse health effects.

Sample Selection A process of constructing sample not by random sampling but by selecting on the basis of some observed or unobserved characteristic.

Seasonality Periodic fluctuations in behavior or outcomes that occur at regular intervals, often tied to seasonal changes.

Share Transfer The process of selling a portion of a company's ownership from one party to another, commonly used in privatization efforts.

Significance Level The probability of a Type I error in hypothesis testing.

State-Owned Enterprises (SOEs) Companies that are owned and operated by the government.

Surface Water Water from natural sources such as rivers, lakes, and ponds, often used as a primary drinking water source in areas without treated water.

Tap Water Coverage The percentage of households or regions with access to treated tap water.

Tariff Adjustment The modification of utility prices to reflect changes in costs, demand, or regulatory policies.

Time Preferences How individuals value present versus future rewards.

Transfer-Operate-Transfer (TOT) A model where a private entity takes over the operation of an existing public asset for a specified period before returning it to the public sector.

Treated Tap Water Water that has been purified to remove contaminants, including chemical pollutants and disease-causing microorganisms, before being supplied to households.

Type I Error A rejection of the null hypothesis when it is true.

Urban-Rural Gap/Disparity The disparity in access to resources, services, and income between urban and rural areas.

Utility Tariffs Charges levied by utility companies for the provision of essential services like water and electricity.

Water Accessibility The ease with which individuals or communities can obtain safe and reliable water, often influenced by infrastructure and economic factors.

Water Conservation/Savings The reduction in water usage through behavioral changes, technological improvements, or policy interventions.

Water Demand Management Strategies and policies aimed at optimizing water usage through pricing, conservation efforts, and technological improvements.

Water Governance The political, social, economic, and administrative systems in place to manage water resources and services.

Water Infrastructure The physical structures and facilities, such as pipelines, treatment plants, and reservoirs, used to supply, treat, and distribute water.

Water Monitoring System A system used to assess the quality of water sources, often measuring levels of contaminants and safety for various uses.

Water Pricing The system or method used to determine the charges for water services, reflecting costs, demand, and policy objectives in the provision and management of water resources.

Water Purification Technology Technologies used to remove contaminants from water, including microorganisms and chemical pollutants, to make it safe for consumption.

Water Quality The chemical, physical, and biological characteristics of water, which determine its suitability for consumption and other uses.

Water Reforms Policy and institutional changes aimed at improving the management, efficiency, and sustainability of water resources and services.

Water Scarcity A condition where the demand for water exceeds the available supply, often exacerbated by population growth, economic development, and environmental factors.

Water Security The reliable availability of an adequate quantity and quality of water for human and environmental needs.

Water Supply System The infrastructure and processes used to deliver water from sources to consumers, including treatment plants, pipelines, and distribution networks.

Water Tariffs Charges levied by water utilities for the provision of water.

Water Treatment Plants Facilities equipped with technology to remove microorganisms and chemical impurities from water.

Water Utility An organization responsible for the provision and maintenance of water supply infrastructure and services.

Waterborne Diseases Diseases caused by microorganisms such as bacteria, viruses, or protozoa in drinking water.

Welfare Implications The effects of a policy or intervention on the well-being of individuals or society.

MIX
Papier aus verantwortungsvollen Quellen
Paper from responsible sources
FSC® C105338

If you have any concerns about our products,
you can contact us on
ProductSafety@springernature.com

In case Publisher is established outside the EU,
the EU authorized representative is:
Springer Nature Customer Service Center GmbH
Europaplatz 3, 69115 Heidelberg, Germany

Printed by Libri Plureos GmbH
in Hamburg, Germany